UPDATING
STANDARD
COST
SYSTEMS

UPDATING STANDARD COST SYSTEMS

Carole B. Cheatham
and Leo R. Cheatham

Q

Quorum Books
Westport, Connecticut • London

Library of Congress Cataloging-in-Publication Data

Cheatham, Carole.
    Updating standard cost systems / Carole B. Cheatham and Leo R.
Cheatham.
        p. cm.
        Includes bibliographical references and index.
        ISBN 0-89930-716-7 (alk. paper)
        1. Cost accounting—United States.   I. Cheatham, Leo R.   II. Title.
HF5686.C8C444 1993
657′.42—dc20   92-34376

British Library Cataloguing in Publication Data is available.

Library of Congress Catalog Card Number: 92-34376
ISBN: 0-89930-716-7

First published in 1993

Quorum Books, 88 Post Road West, Westport, CT 06881
An imprint of Greenwood Publishing Group, Inc.

Printed in the United States of America

The paper used in this book complies with the Permanent Paper Standard
issued by the National Information Standards Organization (Z39.48—1984).

10 9 8 7 6 5 4 3 2 1

Contents

Figures

Preface

This book represents an attempt to integrate many new ideas and techniques that apply to cost management in the manufacturing environment of the 1990s. In addition we have tried to present original suggestions that seemed to us to be practical and workable for improving cost systems. We expect that the next few years will bring many changes in manufacturing along with new ideas and applications, and at least some of what is presented here will become outdated or seem naive to a more sophisticated reader. Indeed our own thinking has gone through considerable evolution in the year or so it has taken to write this book. However, we believe the material provides a starting point for accountants and managers who struggle with the effect of advanced technologies on their firms' cost accounting procedures.

The academic world in which we function is less of an ivory tower than some would believe. Nevertheless it does furnish opportunities for reflection that are denied to those involved in the day-to-day operations of business. The ideas generated from our perspective obviously need to be tried and tested in the more practical world of business. What seems worthwhile should be retained, what is worthless should be rejected, and what needs changing should be adapted to the needs of the readers and their organizations.

Thanks are in order to Tony Gambino, who accepted our article, "Updating Standard Cost Systems," for the *Journal of Accountancy* as well as some earlier work in the cost management area. The ideas in the article formed the basis for what became this book.

We appreciate the people at Quorum Books who made the book a reality, especially Tom Gannon, who urged us to write it, and Eric Valentine, who encouraged us to finish it.

We are indebted to our students, colleagues, and the administration at Northeast Louisiana University for their patience and encouragement. Special thanks are due to our department heads, Jim Hood and Ernie Moser, and our dean, Art Bethke. We are deeply grateful for an academic climate that fosters practical research.

Our graduate assistants, Carolyn Dennis and Scott Thomas, made innumerable trips to the library. The NLU interlibrary loan staff was unfailingly helpful and efficient. We would like to extend our appreciation to them for expediting our research.

Last, but not least, we want to thank parents and family for their support and encouragement throughout our careers and during the writing of this book.

CHAPTER 1

Coping with the New Manufacturing Environment

Until the 1980s many companies operated with manufacturing techniques that were not vastly different from the techniques used in the early part of the century—processes that were developed during the Industrial Revolution. Likewise, their procedures for accounting for the products manufactured were essentially the same.

The 1980s brought many changes in manufacturing processes. Probably the most apparent difference is more automation—computer-integrated manufacturing (CIM), robotics, and more sophisticated equipment of every type. Other changes include an increased emphasis on quality and continuous improvement and use of just-in-time inventory systems and work-cell factory arrangements.

As the factory was altered, cost accounting procedures became outdated. Accounting is, after all, a financial model of business. When changes occur in the business, accounting should change to reflect them. Unfortunately, accounting systems have yet to catch up with the manufacturing procedures of the 1980s and 1990s.

Managers of companies that fail to make appropriate modifications in their accounting systems will find they have inaccurate product cost figures and lack data for making decisions. They may lose their competitive edge because they do not have the necessary information for operating in the new manufacturing environment.

This book tells how to update standard cost systems to make them relevant and useful for the 1990s and beyond. It discusses how to identify the causal factors in cost (the cost drivers) and measure the right variables, ways to foster continuous improvement rather than maintaining the status quo, and procedures for implementing change. It explores ways to assess the decision to purchase automation equipment and shows how to apply cost control procedures to marketing and research-and-development costs as well as manufacturing costs.

Before discussing the new accounting procedures, however, it is necessary to explain the changes in the manufacturing environment. The purpose of this chapter is to examine the impetus for change as well as the transformations that have occurred.

COMPETITION FROM ABROAD

The 1980s saw increased competition from abroad. From the end of World War II through the 1970s U.S. exports exceeded imports. In 1970 imports were $60.5 billion while exports were $68.9 billion. By 1980 imports had risen to $318.9 billion, but exports were an even higher $351 billion. However, 1983 saw a negative balance of trade when imports were $358.7 billion and exports were only $352.5 billion (McEachern 1988: frontispiece). The negative balance continued and became proportionately larger throughout the 1980s.

As the trade balance shifted in favor of foreign producers, American manufacturers blamed a variety of factors, including less expensive labor costs abroad and unfavorable exchange rates. They also found fault with government policies that failed to protect domestic industries and pointed to policies of foreign governments that assisted industry and fostered trade abroad.

American industry was slow in acknowledging that many of its problems came from within and had nothing to do with what foreign producers or their government did. Most managers had grown up in an era when the U.S. dominated world trade. World War II left much of the world's industry devastated, and demand for American goods was strong. Even if U.S. companies were not particularly cost efficient, profits remained acceptable because of the strong markets both at home and abroad.

As foreign industry regained its position, American manufacturers had to relearn to compete. Many began to realize that subtle changes in consumer tastes had occurred. While they assumed that an acceptable product at a low cost was what the customer preferred, they began to find that consumers turned to foreign producers because their products were of higher quality.

Worse still, domestic producers began to find that they could no longer compete on the basis of lower cost. Foreign manufacturers were also able to make products at low cost. Some of the lower cost was because of less expensive labor. However, other factors included more sophisticated automation and less product diversity. Foreign producers had built new factories since World War II, and their technology was newer than in U.S. factories. They also gained an edge in cost efficiency by limiting the number of different products or models they produced. American manufacturers assumed that consumers wanted variety, and their outdated cost systems failed to reveal the cost impact of providing it.

Although it would seem to be a contradiction, the emphasis on quality by producers abroad was also a factor that reduced their costs. They found that self-inspection by workers was much less expensive than having a separate inspection team. Moreover they emphasized correcting the process rather than correcting the product. Correcting the process was a one-time cost, not a continual cost of reworking defective products.

Meanwhile, American manufacturers found they had difficulty competing because their management philosophies were rigid and blocked new ideas. While U.S. managers and accountants devised sophisticated inventory systems to account for their large, diversified inventories, the Japanese eliminated the inventories. While U.S. managers used economic production lot size formulas to decide the quantity of production, the Japanese worked to reduce a significant variable in the formulas—the setup costs.

Thus American industry found itself struggling to compete with foreign producers in the 1980s and began to be open to new ideas that were successful abroad. The combination of the economic crisis and the questioning of old philosophies set the stage for the development of a new manufacturing environment.

As globalization of markets continues in the 1990s with eastern Europe and the former Soviet Union moving toward free-market economies, it is imperative that American manufacturers keep pace with their foreign competitors. The new markets offer tremendous opportunities, but domestic industries can easily be outstripped by Japan or a united Europe or another foreign competitor if they fail to adjust their management strategies and develop accounting systems that give them accurate cost information.

EMPHASIS ON PRODUCTIVITY

The development of new manufacturing techniques in the 1980s in response to foreign competition affected U.S. productivity favorably. After the 1982 recession, U.S. industry experienced productivity gains that exceeded the entire postwar period. However, growth slowed to a mere 2 percent in 1988 and 1989 in contrast to Japan and Germany's 4 to 5 percent, renewing fears that the U.S. would become deindustrialized as a result of foreign competition (Koretz 1990: 24).

In the postwar era American producers were not concerned with growth in the productivity of foreign producers because these competitors had very small bases to work with. They were able to post very large gains as they rebuilt their industries after the war. However, leaders in U.S. industry did become concerned in the 1970s when their domestic plant productivity slowed far more rapidly than that of other advanced nations (Koretz 1990: 24). The result of this concern was a new emphasis on productivity in the 1980s.

The U.S. Labor Department measures growth in productivity in terms of increases in output per labor hour. A better definition would define productivity in terms of output obtained from all inputs. Labor as an input is becoming increasingly less significant as more automation takes place. Historical and foreign country comparisons are distorted when production from workers using automated processes are compared with those processes that are labor-intensive. A more valid output measure would be the total cost of all inputs in a price-index-adjusted currency. This system would reflect the benefits of using automation and labor in the combinations that minimize costs of production. It also reflects currency exchange rate advantages of some countries if the dollar is used as the standard and other countries' outputs are converted to this measure.

When discussing productivity in a manufacturing setting, managers are likely to talk about increasing throughput or decreasing cycle times. *Increasing throughput* means increasing the amount of product produced in a given time period while *decreasing cycle times* means reducing the production time for a given output.

In their attempts to increase productivity in the 1980s, managers tried to determine what was causing their costs—in other words, they tried to determine their cost drivers. The simplistic cost systems of the day usually assumed only one cost driver, which was volume of production. The examination of costs in most firms revealed a host of cost drivers, including such factors as number of setups, number of different products, material movements, and engineering change orders.

Firms also attempted to eliminate nonvalue-adding activities. In the typical factory most products spend far more time sitting somewhere waiting to be worked on than they do in actual production. Furthermore many activities do not add value per se. Among the activities that do not add value are moving, inspecting, training, and supervising. Manufacturers began to increase productivity as they eliminated these nonvalue-adding activities.

The success of foreign competitors and the new emphasis on productivity have caused manufacturers to question some of the old management philosophies and the ways they have always done business. Some of the new ideas and challenges that characterized the 1980s were minimal inventory systems, emphasis on quality, increased automation, redesigned factory layouts, commitment to continuous improvement, the concept of removal of constraints, and shortened product life cycles.

JUST-IN-TIME AND MINIMAL INVENTORY SYSTEMS

Few people agree on what a just-in-time (JIT) system is. In the narrowest sense JIT means elimination of all unnecessary inventories. In the broadest sense JIT is an "aesthetic ideal, a natural state of simplicity" (Zipkin 1991: 42). As a middle ground JIT may be defined as "a system of production control that seeks to minimize raw material and work in process (WIP) inventories; control (eliminate) defects; stabilize production; continuously simplify the production process; and create a flexible, multi-skilled work force" (Calvasina, Calvasina, and Calvasina, 1989: 41). The discussion that follows assumes JIT in the narrow sense of eliminating all unnecessary inventories. Other facets of the JIT philosophy, such as those raised in the Calvasina definition, are addressed in separate topic areas.

The traditional view of inventories by U.S. manufacturers was that a business had to balance the cost of carrying inventory against the cost of stockouts. Because the fear of stockouts was high, most producers carried large amounts of inventory.

In the raw materials area, manufacturers worried about running out of some essential item that would mean the production line would have to be shut down. Dollar figures of how much per minute or hour it cost for a shutdown were somehow computed, and the threat loomed large in the minds of all production managers. They felt they must carry excessive safety stocks of raw materials because suppliers and transporters were unreliable, lead times might be lengthy, and usage during lead times might be higher than anticipated.

In the work in process area, manufacturers believed that stocks of semifinished product must be carried to compensate for scheduling problems and bottlenecks in production. Excess finished products were often carried because production cycle times were so long that customers would not wait for an order to be produced. Therefore they had to buy out of stock. Furthermore manufacturers believed that customers preferred variety, so it was necessary to stock many different models of a particular product.

These beliefs were shaken when American companies that had inventory turnovers of 4 or 5 times a year looked at their Japanese counterparts and saw turns of 25 to 30 times. U.S. manufacturers began to realize that holding excessive inventories was a way of masking certain operational problems that had more direct solutions. Advance delivery schedules with a few suppliers could mean frequent, dependable deliveries. Better scheduling could compensate for uneven usage. Bottlenecks in production could be identified and eliminated. Stocks of finished goods were unnecessary if cycle times were low enough that a customer's order could be processed after it was received.

Another impetus for reducing inventories in the 1980s was the increase in interest costs. Producers began to recognize that carrying inventory tied up funds that could not be used elsewhere in the business. They began to realize that there were more profitable uses for money than having it tied up in inventory.

A final reason for reducing inventories in the 1980s was that manufacturers began to simplify all production processes. Having large amounts of inventory, particularly in the work in process area, only hampered production. Some companies recognized that they needed a good housecleaning. Manufacturers began to produce only when a customer placed an order, to view production as being pulled through from the sales end rather than pushed through from the production end. With this kind of outlook, there was no need for workers to produce just to keep them busy. Indeed there was no need to produce at all unless there was an order. The result was a lean and mean approach that severely curtailed inventories of semifinished products.

EMPHASIS ON QUALITY

Another traditional management philosophy of the 1950s and 1960s was that a manufacturer should produce a product of acceptable quality at minimum cost. When foreign producers gained a marketing advantage by producing a high quality product, the old ideas were shaken. Curiously, foreign producers were also cost competitive. In electronics U.S. manufacturers' share of the world market is about 10 percent, or less than one-third of what it was in 1965. Foreign competitors can provide a product that is both higher in quality and lower in cost. In contrast, the U.S. home appliance industry is alive and well and under no threat from foreign competition. Companies like GE, Whirlpool, Maytag, and others have maintained their market shares by emphasizing high quality (Howell and Soucy 1987: 22).

Companies that have successfully upgraded the quality of their products have pushed back the emphasis on quality to the earliest possible point in the production process. The traditional approach was to inspect the product, usually in the final stages of production. Then the defects were corrected or the product was sold as scrap or factory seconds. If the product was to be reworked, it was usually shelved until enough defective units had collected to warrant a special run. In the meantime the defective products sat with all costs invested, using capital in much the same fashion as other excess inventories.

Manufacturers trying to improve quality began to emphasize employee participation. "Do it right the first time," became the order of the day. Workers were encouraged to inspect the product themselves rather than rely on a separate team of inspectors. For supervisors and workers trained in the traditional environment, the new philosophy was sometimes difficult to accept. Supervisors had tended to be punitive rather than rewarding when defects were discovered. Consequently, workers frequently hid defects rather than point them out. Both supervisors and workers tended to pass the defects on to the next process, hoping that they would not be blamed for the problem. Overcoming such attitudes required training supervisors and workers as well as a wholehearted commitment from top management to the goal of a quality product.

However, emphasizing quality in the product eventually began to be replaced by stress on quality in the process for many U.S. manufacturers. In other words, managers began to realize that if they detected the problems with the process, the product would take care of itself. Again this required a revolution in the thinking of both supervisors and workers. If it was found to be defective, the process had to be shutdown. The specter of shutting down the assembly line haunted most traditional supervisors, who were used to meeting production quotas rather than making quality products.

In some companies the supply of components and raw materials contained so many defects manufacturers thought it necessary to inspect them before putting them into production. However, as inventories were decreased through partnerships with suppliers, the defects were also reduced or eliminated. Manufacturers who were buying a substantial portion of a supplier's output could expect and demand quality components.

Probably the best time to stress quality is in the design stage of the product. If a product is designed in a manner that makes it difficult to produce, any corrective measures taken downstream will be destined to fail. Engineering changes resulting from poor designs may be ineffective as well as costly. The 1980s saw manufacturers stressing quality from design to finished product, but the most successful companies emphasized prevention of defects rather than detection and correction.

INCREASED AUTOMATION

The most visible difference in today's factories is the increased use of automation. Although development of new technology has always been a U.S. strength, adoption of that technology in factories has not been as rapid as might be expected. It took the global competition of the 1970s to alert many manufacturers of the need for automation. While Japan and Germany rebuilt their factories with new technology after World War II, U.S. companies continued with the equipment of the 1950s and 1960s. The challenges of the 1970s forced many companies to realize that they needed to automate to compete.

The reasons for not automating earlier included opposition from unions and the unwillingness of investors to undertake the necessary expenditures. However, a great deal of the blame has to be placed on methods of evaluating potential plant and equipment expenditures. Capital budgeting techniques compared the cash outflows for the investment with the cash inflows from the new equipment. Although techniques were sophisticated, given the information put into the models, cash inflows typically were underestimated. The result was that equipment purchases were often rejected even though they would have benefited the company. Cash inflows were usually stated in terms of savings in operating expenses. Other potential gains and savings from such factors as increased quality, greater flexibility, and better delivery times were ignored.

Another problem with the way capital projects were evaluated was that typically the company had no continual review process for the equipment in place. The result was that replacements were not evaluated unless the old equipment broke down or management became aware of new alternatives by attending a trade show, talking to a salesperson, or hearing that the competition had purchased new equipment. This continues to be a problem in many companies.

Still another problem with the way capital projects were weighed was that the evaluation tended to be applied to individual pieces of equipment. The trend in the 1980s was to look at the factory system as a whole and to replace entire systems when necessary rather than making piecemeal purchases of stand-alone equipment.

Making equipment replacements "by the numbers," that is by the indications shown in traditional capital budgeting models, is still a problem. Much of the automation of the 1980s occurred in spite of, rather than because of, what the numbers indicated. The impetus for replacing systems and upgrading technology frequently came from nonfinancial executives who realized the benefits were being undervalued.

As it came about in the 1980s, automation was on three levels—stand-alone pieces of equipment, work cells, and the fully integrated factory (Howell and Soucy 1987: 25). Typical of the stand-alone pieces of equipment that were purchased were numerically controlled machines, computer-aided design technology, and robots. Stand-alone pieces of equipment usually perform one function, such as a robot that does welding. In contrast the work cell includes equipment of several types and produces a product virtually from start to finish. The highest level of automation is the fully integrated factory, which uses highly automated processes in a systems approach to produce a variety of products.

REDESIGNED FACTORY LAYOUTS

As factories became more automated in the 1980s, new factory layouts became necessary or desirable. The typical factory of the 1950s and 1960s was organized along functional lines, with masses of similar equipment placed together. Large volumes of production were then pushed through the process, going from one group of machines to another.

The trend in the 1980s was to break up the large masses of similar equipment into work cells. For example, if a manufacturing process required a mixing, molding, and finishing operation, the old layout would place all the mixing machines together in one place or department, and all the molding and finishing machines would be similarly grouped. Workers usually did not move out of their department and learned how to operate only one type of equipment. The new arrangement put a mixing machine, a molding machine, and a finishing machine in a group. Workers could operate all three types of equipment and trade off tasks when it would be advantageous to do so.

A work cell is usually conceptualized as a U-shape with materials accessed through the open top of the U and the machines arranged around the bottom of the U. However, physical layout is not as important as the idea of planning the work flow to facilitate production of small batches of product. Indeed some processes are saddled with certain pieces of large, costly equipment that cannot be moved ("monuments"). In these cases work flow must be scheduled so that this equipment is used efficiently.

The work cell represents an effort to tailor plant layout to the general leaner and meaner approach of the 1980s. One advantage of the work-cell arrangement is that an order can be processed from start to finish in a short time. Better cycle times mean less work in process and finished goods inventories as well as better delivery times to the customer. Another advantage is that it facilitates job enrichment and cuts worker boredom and fatigue by allowing workers more variety in their tasks. It also builds morale as work-cell members see themselves as part of a team effort. The increased flexibility also means a wider variety of products can be produced in the same space.

Still another advantage of work cells is that they help to achieve a continuous flow of product and eliminate what has been called the *hockey stick phenomenon*. Most factories of the 1950s and 1960s operated by pushing through large masses of production. Because of bottlenecks and scheduling problems, shipments were frequently delayed. Toward the end of the month, when it became apparent that the plant would not meet its production quotas or month-end financial goals, production would be expedited by working overtime or by using whatever measures were necessary to get the product to the shipping dock. Thus most product was shipped in the last few days of the month, creating a hockey stick-shaped line when shipments were graphed against time. Fortunately, the work-cell arrangement helps prevent such a crisis environment.

COMMITMENT TO CONTINUOUS IMPROVEMENT

One feature of most of the changes in the manufacturing environment is that they came more from concepts or philosophies than from specific techniques. Of those concepts, one of the most pervasive is the idea of continuous improvement. *Continuous improvement* means that the business must always strive to be better—that it must refuse to maintain the status quo. One pair of authors described continuous improvement as "a philosophy that states that production, engineering, and marketing excellence require ongoing attention and learning" (Turney and Anderson 1989: 37).

A concept as elegantly simple as continuous improvement can be attributed to several sources. Japanese-style management techniques, which encourage refinements in quality and productivity, obviously foster continuous improvement. However, the idea has taken hold in American industry primarily through the efforts of Eli Goldratt, coauthor of *The Goal: A Process of On-going Improvement*. Rather than a manual on manufacturing or financial techniques, *The Goal* is a novel that describes how a plant manager manages to keep his plant open and save his failing marriage. His struggles evidently struck a real chord of recognition in U.S. managers, and his solutions apparently rang true. In 1987 *Management Accounting* reported that more than 5,000 corporations had purchased the book and that sales were 2,000 copies a week. It has been translated into 9 languages and is being used at 40 universities (Jayson 1987: 21).

Goldratt works closely with Robert Fox, coauthor of the follow-up to *The Goal* called *The Race*. Fox's career took him through the traditional route of vice president of manufacturing and general manager but with extensive study of manufacturing systems in Europe and Japan. Eli Goldratt was an Israeli physicist. His interest in manufacturing started when he invented a formula to help a friend schedule work flow in his chicken coop factory. Goldratt's formula has since developed into the Optimized Production Technology (OPT) software system.

Continuous improvement was accepted because it was an idea whose time had come. While foreign manufacturers rebuilt their plants and tried to become competitive with the U.S. after World War II, American manufacturers were complacent. American industry was content to accept the status quo because it was the leader. However, its position eroded as the competition made slow, steady improvements. Toyota, for example, reduced the time of a critical die-change operation from several hours to a few minutes, a change that occurred over some twenty-five years (Zipkin 1991: 41). When it became apparent that U.S. industry was falling behind, ideas like continuous improvement became acceptable.

Goldratt and Fox, however, are far from ivory tower altruists. They see goals such as customer service and quality as being only means to an end. The ultimate goal of a company, as described in *The Goal* and *The Race,* is to make money, both now and in the future. As a means to that end they advocate use of their OPT concepts or what is better called the *theory of constraints*.

THEORY OF CONSTRAINTS

Theory of constraints as it applies to manufacturing is the idea that factors that limit production should be systematically eliminated. The most obvious constraints are capacity bottlenecks or physical constraints. However, the theory permits a much broader definition of constraints, and Goldratt acknowledges that the main limits are policy constraints (Umble and Srikanth 1990: x). As constraints are removed, the product can flow through the factory in a synchronized fashion.

Some confusion has arisen as to the relationship of OPT, synchronous manufacturing, and the theory of constraints. These are actually the same concepts as originally espoused in *The Goal*. The different terms represent the evolving nature of the ideas. In his foreword to Umble and Srikanth's *Synchronous Manufacturing,* Goldratt explains that Blair Thompson, then head of the Saginaw Steering Gear division of General Motors, suggested *synchronous manufacturing* was a better name than *optimized production technology* (OPT). Thompson claimed that "the software was the least important component of this effort and that the principles, or 'thoughtware,' as they were called, were the most important part" (Umble and Srikanth 1990: ix). Although Goldratt supported the use of the term *synchronous manufacturing,* he did not use it and adopted *theory of constraints* (TOC) in 1987.

TOC recognizes that manufacturing operations are characterized by dependent events—one event must take place before another as a product moves through the production process. Statistical fluctuations and random events interrupt the dependent events. Statistical fluctuations have some pattern of variability and can be predicted to a degree. However, random events occur without pattern. Random events are the true Murphy's Law disrupters. Statistical fluctuations and random events cause the crisis nature of many manufacturing operations and interrupt the synchronous flow.

When applying TOC, a management team first identifies the constraints that interfere with the synchronous flow. For example, a job-shop steel fabricating plant in Texas first identified three of its constraints as its weld assembly area, its market, and the engineering department at the home office (Koziol 1988: 45). As bottlenecks are eliminated or eased, other areas that previously were not recognized as constraints will appear. Gradually, by eliminating as many constraints as possible, the production flow is balanced throughout the plant. One difference between TOC and JIT is that TOC permits strategically placed amounts of buffer inventories in front of constraints to keep the bottlenecks operating continuously.

As production moves through the factory in a synchronous fashion, the paradigm for the production process in TOC is the drum-buffer-rope concept. The drum is the production schedule, which maximizes the use of the constraints. However, because of statistical fluctuations and random events, there must be a time buffer. The rope controls the flow of product by controlling the schedule release points for certain critical operations. The rope determines the sequence of work at a particular work station.

TOC assists a business in making as much money as possible (the goal). The theory says that three actions are necessary in order to do this—inventories must be reduced, operating expenses must be cut, and throughput (the rate at which an organization generates money through sales) must be maximized. In fact constraints are seen as whatever hinders the organization in making money.

Goldratt once maintained that cost accounting was the number one enemy of productivity (Goldratt: 1983). He later softened that stand and said cost rather than accounting was the culprit (Jayson 1987: 18). Nevertheless he maintains the cost measurements in use today are sending the wrong signals to managers, who are trying to control inventories, operating expenses, and throughput.

SHORTENED PRODUCT LIFE CYCLES

Still another change occurring in today's manufacturing environment is the shortening of product life cycles. Whereas most products used to remain essentially unchanged over 5, 10, or even 20 years, today's products tend to have very short life cycles. To remain competitive a manufacturer must continually be developing and putting new products into production.

George Stalk, Jr., and Thomas M. Hout, authors of *Competing against Time* have pointed out that

The slower innovators, trapped in the vicious cycle of long development and introduction times, must increasingly depend on the elusive great breakthrough to recapture former glory. Clearly, the price of being a slow innovator is loss of competitive position to the fast innovator. In industry after industry, companies with faster innovation cycles have been able to move from follower positions and to seize leadership in their industries in about 10 years. (1990: 19)

Although Japanese companies generally lead the way in rapid innovation, some American companies such as Black & Decker have aggressive programs to improve product development and introduction. In a period of 18 months Black & Decker introduced more than 60 new products and is growing at twice the industry average (Stalk and Hout 1990: 23).

As a result of shortened product life cycles, research and development (R&D) has become a much more important activity than it once was. One Ernst & Young consultant who was formerly with Xerox in strategic product planning estimates that 85 percent of the cost of a new product is determined in the design stage while only 10 to 15 percent is determined by the manufacturing stage (Raffish 1991: 36–37). Clearly, any accounting system that concentrates on manufacturing operations and ignores nonmanufacturing costs is an incomplete system. The system should include the upstream costs such as R&D as well as downstream costs such as marketing.

» «

The new manufacturing environment of the 1980s was challenging and exciting, an era of change in many ways. Whether the changes will be sufficient to meet the demands of the 1990s and beyond remains to be seen. The U.S. has lost its dominance in important industries like steel, automobiles, and electronics. Some predict that this country is headed for a service economy or an information society. However, many feel that manufacturing is our real base of wealth. Robert Fox remarked back in 1986 that "if we lose our manufacturing base, we will also lose many service jobs, and we will lose our major mechanism for generating wealth, and for increasing our standard of living" (Fox 1986: 14).

Whatever the challenges in manufacturing, it is clear that managers need relevant, accurate, and complete cost information. Without such information, they will be unable to make the important decisions they face. In the chapter that follows some ways to upgrade cost information systems are discussed.

REFERENCES

Calvasina, Richard V., Eugene J. Calvasina, and Gerald E. Calvasina. "Beware the New Accounting Myths," *Management Accounting.* December 1989, pp. 41–45.

Fox, Robert E. "Coping with Today's Technology: Is Cost Accounting Keeping Up?" *Proceedings, Cost Accounting for the 90s: The Challenge of Technological Change,* National Association of Accountants, Boston, April 28–29, 1986.

Goldratt, Eliyahu M. "Cost Accounting Is Enemy Number One of Productivity." *International Conference Proceedings, American Production and Inventory Control Society,* October 1983.

Goldratt, Eliyahu M., and Jeff Cox. *The Goal: A Process of Ongoing Improvement.* New Haven, Conn.: Spectrum, 1986.

Howell, Robert A., and Stephen R. Soucy. "The New Manufacturing Environment: Major Trends for Management Accounting," *Management Accounting.* July 1987, pp. 21–27.

Jayson, Susan. "Goldratt & Fox: Revolutionizing the Factory Floor," *Management Accounting.* May 1987, pp. 18–22.

Koziol, David S. "How the Constraint Theory Improved a Job-Shop Operation," *Management Accounting.* May 1988, pp. 44–49.

Koretz, Gene. "The Surge in Factory Productivity Looks Like History Now. . .," *Business Week.* October 8, 1990, p. 24.

McEachern, William A. *Economics: A Contemporary Introduction.* Cincinnati, Ohio: South-Western, 1988.

Raffish, Norm. "How Much Does That Product Really Co$t?" *Management Accounting.* March 1991, pp. 36–39.

Stalk, Jr., George, and Thomas M. Hout. "Competing against Time," *Research Technology Management.* March–April 1990, pp. 19–24.

Turney, Peter B. B., and Bruce Anderson. "Accounting for Continuous Improvement," *Sloan Management Review.* Winter 1989, pp. 37–47.

Umble, Michael, and Mokshagundam L. Srikanth. *Synchronous Manufacturing: Principles for World-Class Excellence.* Cincinnati, Ohio: South-Western, 1990.

Zipkin, Paul H. "Does Manufacturing Need a JIT Revolution?" *Harvard Business Review.* January–February 1991, pp. 40–50.

CHAPTER 2

Tailoring Cost Accounting Systems to the New Manufacturing Environment

When it became apparent that U.S. industry was no longer competitive with much of foreign industry in the 1980s, managers looked for the source of the trouble. Two early favorites to blame were unions, because of the higher U.S. wages, and the federal government, because it did not maintain protectionist policies. A third favorite was accountants because their manufacturing cost systems did not provide information needed in the new environment. From the time of Goldratt's statement that cost accounting was the number one enemy of productivity (Goldratt 1983; Jayson 1987: 18), cost accounting was the main whipping boy for management's poor decisions.

THE FAILURE OF MANAGERIAL ACCOUNTING

Although cost accounting was not the sole reason, or even the main reason, for the decline of American industry, accountants must accept some share of the blame. Why were there no red flags that told managers they must change their approaches or lose out competitively? Two reasons were primary—one was that accountants in industry were geared to thinking in terms of financial rather than managerial accounting. The other was that accountants in academia concentrated on the wrong research problems.

Accounting can broadly be divided into two areas, financial and managerial. Financial accounting is concerned with preparing reports for stockholders and other external parties such as the government. Managerial accounting is concerned with providing information to managers for internal decision making. Obviously, the orientations of the two types are quite different. Financial accounting is a stewardship function that essentially looks to the past. Managerial accounting is forward-looking, concerned with estimates and probabilities of future events.

Most accountants by training are more versed in financial accounting because that is what business schools typically emphasize. Moreover the standard for excellence among accountants is passing the CPA examination, which stresses financial accounting. The CPA examination has been given since 1916, but it was not until 1972 that the Certified Management Accounting (CMA) examination was administered. In 1989 slightly fewer than 5,000 candidates sat for the CMA exam while more than 142,000 sat for the CPA exam (Gleim and Flesher 1990: 20).

As a result of this emphasis, the accounting function in most businesses is driven by financial accounting with managerial accounting a poor second. Accounting managers by interest and skill worry about the financial statements while managerial concerns go unnoticed. In their landmark book *Relevance Lost: The Rise and Fall of Management Accounting,* Johnson and Kaplan point out that

By 1925, American industrial firms had developed virtually every management accounting procedure known today. . . . Until the 1920s, managers invariably relied on information about the underlying processes, transactions, and events that produce financial numbers. By the 1960s and 1970s, however, managers commonly relied on the financial numbers alone. Guided increasingly by data compiled for external financial reports, corporate management — the "visible hand" — has "managed by the numbers" since the 1950s. We wait for future historians to explain fully the complex forces that caused this transition. (1987: 125–126)

While accountants in industry concentrated on financial accounting and largely ignored managerial concerns, accountants in academia addressed research topics that had little practical value. One would expect that if industrial accountants were too close to the problems to see them or too mired in day-to-day operations, at least accountants in education could take the longer view. Unfortunately, this was not the case. Both accountants in industry and those in education seemed to stay as far away from the realities of the manufacturing world as possible.

Accounting research in the 1970s and 1980s tended to be dominated by empirical studies of financial accounting concerns such as the effect of the latest Financial Accounting Standards Board pronouncement on financial statements or stock prices. When studies were done in the area of management accounting, such as cost-volume-profit models, the authors tended to apply them to single-product firms and to assume such factors as price elasticity of demand and productivity changes were irrelevant. The real problems of manufacturing and the effect of foreign competition on U.S. industry were largely ignored.

Virtually no academic journals focused on management accounting. The main periodical for management accounting was the National Association of Accountants' practitioner-oriented *Management Accounting;* Kaplan estimates that this journal published no startling innovations in practice between 1955 and 1980 (1981: 57–76). However, since 1980 that journal has been a major source of information on accounting in the new manufacturing environment, and at least one new academic journal in management accounting has been added.

PROPOSED NEW ACCOUNTING SYSTEMS

When it became apparent in the 1980s that managers in industry needed better managerial accounting information to stay competitive, consultants began to fill the gap by recommending a variety of replacements for the outdated cost systems. The three proposals that gained the most prominence were using various performance measures not tied in to the accounting system, backflush costing, and activity-based costing.

Performance Measures

Using various performance measures not tied in to the accounting system was a proposal that came mostly from production and quality control managers and engineers. For the most part they seemed unaware that accounting could and should be providing them with the information they needed. When they were aware of the accountants, they usually advocated actively ignoring them.

The performance measurement systems that were devised tended to be tailored to the needs of a particular business or mirrored the concerns of a particular consulting group. They were fragmented and did not articulate with the accounting system.

Hall recommends a system that includes the ratio of the total number of value-added operations to the total operations, warranty return rates, trend in overall process yield, total system production lead time, customer lead time, total actual unit cost, increase in value-added per person, and suggestions implemented per person (1990: 110). Green, Amenkhienan, and Johnson recommend number of defectives, first pass quality percentage yield, on-time percentages shipped, manufacturing intervals, shop work in process (WIP) inventory, WIP turnover, finished goods turnover, WIP and finished goods turnover, cost of scrap, scrap percentage of output, line disruptions, percentage cross-trained, and percentage completion of just-in-time/total quality control checklist (1991: 53).

Backflush Costing

Backflush costing was another proposed alternative to the traditional cost accounting system. Backflush (BF) costing grew out of the JIT philosophy. Its simplicity mirrors the simplicity of the production system. Reasoning that the accounting system does not need to account for inventories that are not there, BF costing makes only two entries in the accounting records — one entry when production is started to show the purchase and use of raw materials and one entry when production is finished to show the application of conversion cost and the transfer to finished goods. The only inventory accounts are a raw material-in-process (RIP) account and a finished goods account.

Activity-based Costing

Probably the most popular proposal to upgrade the traditional cost accounting system is activity-based costing (ABC). ABC seeks to identify activities that cause or drive costs. Once these activities are identified, product costs are assigned according to the activities consumed. Typical activities would be storage time, wait time, number of setups, number of engineering changes, and move time. The traditional cost system usually assumes that the only relevant activities are volume (measured in units of product), direct labor hours, or direct labor dollars. ABC expands these activities and claims better assignment of overhead as a result.

REVISED ACCOUNTING SYSTEMS

While some authors and consultants in the 1980s recommended that firms dismantle their accounting systems and start completely new systems, others advised caution. As Tatikonda pointed out:

No system is perfect. All systems evolve with time and changing needs. If the current system is inadequate for the needs it should be changed. But, before a system is changed it is very important to find the real causes for the existing problems. Failure to do so will result in designing the new system with all the past problems intact. In other words, the system may be changed without any regard to the real needs, and as a result the same old problems will continue. (1987: 29)

While some advocated the radical changes of completely new systems, others felt that solution for cost accounting's problems was disruptive and eliminated much of the good along with the bad. They believed that modifications to current systems would accomplish more than throwing the baby out with the bath water.

Don Baker, chairman of the National Association of Accountants' research committee (later president of that organization) commented in a 1989 interview, "We recognize that our environment is changing. I'm not ready to say that all our systems are outdated and that accountants are behind the times . . . but we do need to examine cost management systems more closely" (Semich: 75).

Whether advocating new or revised systems, most managers and accountants do see a need for change in manufacturing accounting. They want an information systems that will provide data on such issues as

- which products should be produced.
- what size batches should be produced.
- which departments and managers are doing the best job.
- whether the cost of automation can be justified.
- the benefits of increased quality, better flexibility, and shortened lead times.
- the cost of product line diversity.
- whether the company is performing better than last week, last month, or last year and how it compares with similar companies.

The advent of computer systems has allowed accounting departments to produce a wealth of data, but most of the needs in the preceding list would go unmet in today's manufacturing companies. In order to provide such information, any system must be able to identify the true cost drivers, promote continuous improvement, measure the right variables, identify the costs and benefits of automation, and consider the entire product cost.

NEED TO IDENTIFY COST DRIVERS

Cost drivers are the causal factors in cost. It is important to know what the cost drivers are because controlling the drivers allows a company to control cost. Traditional cost accounting systems, which evolved in the early part of the century, tended to assume that volume of production was the only cost driver. Volume of production in a one-product firm could be measured by units of production. If more than one product were produced, direct labor hours or direct labor dollars were used as proxies for the number of units.

When firms were highly labor-intensive, this simple assumption about cost drivers did not significantly distort product costs. The major costs involved in production were materials and labor, both of which could be traced directly to the units. Overhead, the catchall or "everything else" category of manufacturing cost, was insignificant because there were few machines to depreciate and few service costs. If overhead expenses were applied to production by number of units or by a labor base, there was little to cause distortion.

Today's highly automated factory environment is vastly different, with most manufacturing cost falling in the overhead category. Estimates are that direct labor may be as little as 5 to 10 percent of manufacturing costs (Ellis and McDonald 1990: 30). Overhead, on the other hand, can be 35 percent of manufacturing cost (Semich 1989: 74) or higher, depending on the amount of automation. Assuming that labor is driving overhead is absurd when there is so little labor in comparison to overhead.

Johnson and Kaplan tell of one company whose direct labor-based accounting system indicated that most products were making profit margins of greater than 40 percent. However, a more accurate tracing of overhead costs revealed that 77 percent of the products were actually losing money — the remaining 23 percent produced 400 percent of the profits (1987: 240).

An electronics manufacturer producing product line L (older with high labor content) and product line A (newer with more automation) thought that the cost of L was $350 while A was $240. After a more accurate reallocation of costs and identification of technology costs, the cost was found to be $300 for L and $450 for A. In another company some products were found to be overcosted by as much as 100 percent while others were undercosted by as much as 80 percent (Raffish 1991: 39).

Identifying cost drivers allows a company to more accurately allocate overhead costs, giving a better estimate of product line costs. Determining cost drivers also permits a company to more adequately control costs by controlling the drivers or activities that are the causal factors.

NEED FOR CONTINUOUS IMPROVEMENT

Another goal of the new manufacturing environment is continuous improvement. The charge has been made that standard cost systems do not foster continuous improvement because standards typically are static.

This charge deserves closer examination. First, standards in a standard cost system should not be static and were never intended to be so. Practitioners and theorists alike advocate revising standards as needed. If some companies have not chosen to spend money on new engineering studies to revise standards, the decision cannot be assumed to be a flaw in the system itself.

Budgets are also targets that manufacturers try to attain, and they are automatically revised at least annually. If there is reason to think that budgets have become outdated, the recommendation has always been to revise more frequently. Indeed quarterly or monthly adjustments are not unusual. It may be charged that budgets typically are revised because a company failed to reach its goals, not because it bettered them. However, this is not a flaw in the system but merely in the way it is applied.

Even though it may be argued that standard cost systems and budgets are revised periodically, perhaps this is not sufficient to meet the goal of continuous improvement. In such cases standard cost systems and budgets can be revised on an almost continuous basis by using last period's results as the standard. If last period's results are not good enough, the best performance to date can be used.

Some companies have gotten very involved in a process called *benchmarking*. Benchmarking is measuring the firm's performance against the performance of best-in-the-industry companies. Such heavyweights as DuPont, AT&T, Eastman Kodak, and Digital Equipment use benchmarking to encourage continuous improvements in quality and other areas.

Market-driven cost goals are frequently used by Japanese firms. They set a target price and then determine what manufacturing costs must be to achieve the consumer price. Typically, the cost goals are significantly below what is currently attainable. American firms can also use market-driven rather than engineering-driven standards.

After all, the idea behind a standard cost system or a budget is that goals are set and performance is measured against the goals. A standard is like par in golf in the sense that it is just a mark for the participant to strive to achieve. Continuous improvement may be fostered by using dynamic standards—either internal standards such as last period's or best-to-date performance or external standards set by industry leaders or the market.

NEED TO MEASURE THE RIGHT VARIABLES

Standard cost systems have been criticized in the new manufacturing environment as not measuring the right variables. It has been charged that the variables that are measured were important in the labor-intensive, production-driven environment of the 1950s and 1960s, but that these variables should not be stressed today. Moreover it is charged that emphasizing these variables is counterproductive.

The criticism of standard cost systems has centered primarily on three types of variances—labor efficiency, material price, and volume. To understand the censure of these variances, it is necessary to examine each one.

Labor Efficiency Variance

Variances are just differences between actual and standard costs. A labor efficiency variance indicates the cost of the difference between actual labor hours and the number of labor hours that should have been used for the amount of production achieved (the standard labor hours). The charge against the labor efficiency variance is that production supervisors tend to ignore quality in order to minimize the number of hours used.

To examine this charge, it should be noted that it concerns how the variance is used for control or responsibility accounting purposes, not as a criticism of the concept itself. Most critics are not arguing that efficiency is not important but that quality should not be sacrificed in the interests of efficiency.

Actually, an unfavorable labor efficiency variance may be thought of as two variances — the excess hours spent on defective units and the excess hours spent on good units. If the former is computed separately, it becomes a quality variance and what is left may be thought of as a true efficiency variance. A quality variance may similarly be pulled out of the efficiency variance for variable overhead or the efficiency (quantity) variance for materials. With a little creativity the efficiency variance becomes a tool for measuring quality, one of the variables thought important in the new manufacturing environment.

Material Price Variance

Another variance the critics dislike is the material price variance. An unfavorable material price variance is the excess paid over the standard price for the material units purchased or used. Again the criticism concerns quality. It is believed that quality is sacrificed in the interest of buying less expensive materials to achieve a favorable price variance.

As with the efficiency variance, it is not that price is not a legitimate concern. Doubts center on the fact that price is the only or even the primary concern. Part of the problem is that the material price variance is usually, although not always, computed on the units purchased. Employing units purchased rather than those used in production historically has been considered by most authorities the best way to compute the variance — it isolates it at the point of the problem, the purchase point, and at an earlier point in time.

Unfortunately, when the price variance is computed on units purchased, it makes the base for this variance different than the quantity variance, which is computed on units used in production. There is no way that the trade-offs between price and quantity (or quantity/quality as discussed earlier) can be evaluated. Furthermore the responsibility for the two variances is divided, with the purchasing manager usually held responsible for the price variance and the production manager for the quantity variances.

To deal with the problem of the different bases for computation, price, quantity, and quality can all be evaluated on the basis of units of material used in production. This way, trade-offs between price and quantity or price and quality can be evaluated. Furthermore responsibility for variances can be rethought, with the purchasing manager reaping some of the praise for favorable quantity or quality variances when they occur.

It may be argued that units of material purchased and units used should be the same in a bona fide JIT environment. This is true. It may also be argued that price variances do not have much meaning when all purchases are made according to an advance delivery schedule at prenegotiated prices. However, most companies are not yet operating in this environment for all their purchases. For some companies it will not be feasible to do so in the foreseeable future. Therefore it is important that price variances be computed and evaluated in a meaningful way.

Volume Variance

Still a third variance that has come in for a great deal of criticism is the volume variance. The volume variance exists because of the attempt to allocate fixed overhead to all units of production. Using an estimated number of units or other activity measure, accountants construct a rate for what fixed overhead should be per unit of volume, which is then applied to all units produced during the year. This procedure is considered necessary for units to carry the full manufacturing cost for financial accounting purposes — that is, to value inventories and cost of goods sold. The volume variance is the difference between what is applied to units using the estimated rate and the total budgeted fixed overhead. The variance exists because the estimated number of units used to construct the rate is different than the actual number produced.

The main problem with the volume variance is how it is interpreted. Instead of accepting that the rate was based on a predetermined estimate, which should be subject to change, the estimate becomes the standard. Not producing as much as the estimate results in an unfavorable variance, and explanations must be made. More production results in a favorable variance and actually increases net income. Obviously, the motivation is to produce as much as possible, which is in opposition to the new manufacturing environment thinking about minimal inventories.

As far as operations and managerial accounting are concerned, the volume variance really has no value and should be ignored. Variable (direct) costing advocates have said for years that fixed overhead should be treated like other fixed expenses and should not be applied to products. If this is done, there is no volume variance.

Instead of a volume variance, it makes more sense to compute a production variance that uses the *variable* overhead as well as all other variable manufacturing expenses. A production variance is computed by multiplying the excess or shortage of units produced by the variable manufacturing cost invested. If too many units are produced, the result is an unfavorable variance, which is the opposite of the direction of the volume variance. The production variance can then be used to evaluate the excess investment in inventories. Actually, some companies that use production variances consider either an excess or shortage of units to be unfavorable. Their target is to hit their short-run production goals, and being off either way is objectionable.

Years ago the goals that made a manufacturer successful were maintaining labor efficiency, purchasing reasonably priced materials, and keeping production volume high. These goals have changed, and standards should also change. If quality and minimal inventories are the new goals, they can be incorporated into a standard cost system, along with other objectives.

NEED TO IDENTIFY THE COSTS AND
BENEFITS OF AUTOMATION

A great deal of the automation that took place in the 1980s was in spite of, rather than because of, the findings of accountants using traditional capital budgeting techniques. Russell and Dilt's findings were probably typical:

While at Michigan State University, we had a number of people who had installed flexible manufacturing systems come and visit. During that time we chatted with them, my immediate question to all of these engineers was, where was the accountant when you were putting this together? What I got back when I asked that question was an almost standard reply: "We tried to keep this as far away from the accountant as we could." (1986: 27)

The problems with the usual capital budgeting techniques were that they often understated the benefits to be received from automation, they had to be triggered by external events or a machine breakdown, and they tended to evaluate manufacturing equipments on a piecemeal basis rather than on a systems basis.

The benefits from automation are often elusive and hard to quantify. Consider the case of Boston Metal Products, a relatively small firm with $7 million in sales and 65 employees. This manufacturer of metal shelving for supermarkets decided to buy a robot to weld its cooler shelving for freezers. The president had seen robots used in Europe and was eager for the company to start using the technology. Even though officials could not quantify what they believed to be the benefits, they went ahead with the $220,000 purchase.

Company sales representatives began talking to customers about their "robotics" and carrying a sample bracket of cooler shelving with a manual weld on one side and a robot weld on the other. Sales in cooler shelving doubled. Furthermore finding applications for the robot caused company engineers to rethink and redesign some products so that cost savings were also reaped from the improved processes (Greenberg 1986: 57–61).

Although Boston Metals' benefits were somewhat unpredictable and could not be duplicated in other companies, automation has many advantages. Efforts need to be made to identify these benefits and quantify those that can be quantified. The responsibility for this identification and quantification should be shifted to engineers and production managers. Accountants may be able to perform some evaluation of increases in capacity and cost savings, but other benefits are beyond their area of expertise.

Tatikonda makes the excellent point that "With more workable data the so-called 'intangible benefits' can be incorporated into the cost justification. . . .

They [engineers and production managers] should not expect the accounting department to fully understand new engineering designs, machine perform-ance, and intangible benefits such as flexibility" (1987: 28).

Besides improving the evaluation of the benefits of automation, the whole capital budgeting process needs a more systematic approach. The evaluation of new equipment should not be triggered by external events or a machine breakdown; review of plant and equipment should be continual. Furthermore this review should look at the system as a whole. Instituting a flexible manu-facturing system or other fully integrated factory system necessitates a com-prehensive evaluation.

NEED TO CONSIDER THE ENTIRE PRODUCT COST

The increased pace of innovation with the expansion of R&D, market development, and other "front-end" costs has generated several accounting questions. One question is whether a company should incur these expenses. A second question relates to whether the front-end costs should be expensed immediately or spread over the life of the product. A third question concerns controls over these costs and how the cost of a product is viewed.

New Product Decisions

The decision to invest in a new product is probably more complex than nonresearch executives would expect. What nonresearchers would lump to-gether as product design is actually a complex process involving the design concept, engineering, review, detailed design, field test, and prototype. Add to this market testing and development for a new product and there is a sizable investment. The decision to invest in a new product is like the decision to in-vest in plant and equipment — the investment will affect several time periods, and the benefits are hard to quantify.

The research executives who present proposals for new products to upper-level management have perhaps an even harder task than those trying to jus-tify decisions to automate because the benefits are equally hard to define and the risks are probably greater. In addition, instead of justifying projects on the usual capital budgeting measures of net present value or internal rate of return, R&D projects are typically evaluated on the basis of return on in-vestment (Mitchell and Hamilton 1988: 15). Using nontime-adjusted criteria results in selection of short-term, minimal risk ventures.

Expensing versus Capitalizing of R&D Expenses

The financial accounting treatment of R&D expenses is another reason for selecting short-term, minimal risk ventures. Since its *Statement No. 2* in 1974, the Financial Accounting Standards Board has mandated that R&D

costs be expensed as incurred. The only exception is computer software, which may be capitalized after technological feasibility has been established. The tax law also permits R&D costs to be expensed as incurred.

Those who advocate capitalizing R&D feel such costs can be more easily justified if they are spread over the life cycle of the product. They would expense the expenditures for tax purposes to reap the tax savings, but use the capitalization treatment for financial statement purposes. Proponents of *product life cycle accounting* also believe that the profitability of a product should be evaluated according to the phase of its life cycle, with the performance of emerging products measured differently than that of mature products.

If Stalk and Hout's observations about fast innovation are correct in *Competing against Time,* capitalization may actually retard product development. They make the point that American companies have tended to invest large amounts in order to make breakthroughs, whereas Japanese companies use "incremental experimentation" to make small changes (1990: 19). (It has also been argued that they use U.S. technology.) Allowing companies to capitalize R&D may foster the breakthrough concept, which seems to be counterproductive. It may also be argued that if R&D is an ongoing process rather than an occasional emphasis, the costs of operating an R&D segment can logically be expensed.

Cost Controls for R&D

Still another question relates to the responsibility for R&D costs. While manufacturing costs are meticulously recorded and analyzed, R&D costs may be written off with very little accountability from the researchers involved. The reason for ignoring the control function is that the benefits are so intangible and hard to quantify. R&D costs for a new product are typically 80 percent of the cost of the product, with manufacturing and other costs only 20 percent. It appears that the 80/20 rule applies to accounting for R&D cost because at least 80 percent of the accounting effort is applied to the 20 percent of nonresearch costs.

It seems clear that greater accountability for R&D costs is in order and that the definition of *product cost* needs expansion. Stalk and Hout have observed that companies that are rapid innovators tend to have their new product development organized across functional lines. They point out that

A company with a rapid new product development cycle functions much like a fast response factory. It gathers all development resources for one product in one group — including marketing, design, manufacturing and, in some situations, finance and sales. The participants in these functional areas work together on a full-time basis. Often, they are physically located at the site where the new product is to be manufactured. (1990: 20)

For companies that have moved to the system of product innovation described by Stalk and Hout, calculating complete product cost will be facilitated because all costs can be traced to a particular product. Companies that use a separate R&D function need greater accountability in terms of productivity and yield.

$$\gg \quad \ll$$

When it became apparent that U.S. industry was falling behind foreign competitors in the 1980s, managers looked for the source of the trouble. One group they blamed was accountants because their accounting reports did not warn them of the problems. Although the depth of this criticism was probably unjustified, there was a deficiency in accounting. This was particularly true in the area of managerial accounting, the type of accounting that should give managers the information they need for decision making. While accountants in industry concentrated on financial accounting and academic accountants pursued research interests with little practical value, managerial accounting was ignored.

Managerial accounting needs to be upgraded in the 1990s to assist managers in firms that have entered the new manufacturing environment. To do this, accounting systems need to be developed to identify the real cost drivers in a company, promote continuous improvement, and measure important variables such as quality and productivity. Managerial accounting systems need to be capable of assessing the costs and benefits of automation and new product development. When these goals are reached, managers will have a useful competitive tool for making decisions in the 1990s and beyond.

REFERENCES

Ellis, Lynn W., and Robert G. McDonald. "Reforming Management Accounting To Support Today's Technology," *Research Technology Management*. March–April 1990, pp. 30–34.

Financial Accounting Standards Board. *Statement of Financial Accounting Standards, No. 2*. Stamford, Conn., 1974.

Gleim, Irvin N., and Dale L. Flesher. *CMA Examination Review, Volume 1*, 4th ed. Gainesville, Fl.: Accounting Publications, 1990.

Goldratt, Eliyahu M. "Cost Accounting Is Enemy Number One of Productivity." *International Conference Proceedings, American Production and Inventory Control Society*, October 1983.

Green, F. B., Felix Amenkhienan, and George Johnson. "Performance Measures and JIT," *Management Accounting*. February 1991, pp. 50–53.

Greenberg, David A. "Robotics: One Small Company's Experience." *Proceedings, Cost Accounting for the 90s: The Challenge of Technological Change*, National Association of Accountants, Boston, April 28–29, 1986.

Hall, Robert W. "World-Class Manufacturing: Performance Measurement." *Proceedings, Performance Excellence in Manufacturing and Service Organizations.* Third Annual Management Accounting Symposium, American Accounting Association, San Diego, March 10–11, 1989, pp. 103–110.

Jayson, Susan. "Goldratt & Fox: Revolutionizing the Factory Floor." *Management Accounting.* May 1987, pp. 18–22.

Johnson, H. Thomas, and Robert S. Kaplan. *Relevance Lost: The Rise and Fall of Management Accounting.* Boston: Harvard Business School Press, 1987.

Kaplan, R. S. "The Impact of Management Accounting Research on Policy and Practice," in John W. Buckley, ed., *The Impact of Accounting Research on Policy and Practice, 1981 Proceedings of the Arthur Young Professors' Roundtable.* Reston, Va.: Council of Arthur Young Professors, 1981, pp. 57–76.

Mitchell, Graham R., and William F. Hamilton. "Managing R&D as a Strategic Option." *Research Technology Management.* May–June 1988, pp. 15–22.

Raffish, Norm. "How Much Does that Product Really Co$t?" *Management Accounting.* March 1991, pp. 36–39.

Russell, Grant, and David M. Dilts. "Are Accountants Delaying the Automation of America?" *Proceedings, Cost Accounting for the 90s: The Challenge of Technological Change.* National Association of Accountants, 1986.

Semich, J. William. "Accounting for Quality," *Purchasing.* January 19, 1989, pp. 74–77.

Stalk, George, Jr., and Thomas M. Hout. "Competing against Time." *Research Technology Management.* March–April 1990, pp. 19–24.

Tatikonda, Lakshmi U. "Production Managers Need a Course in Cost Accounting." *Management Accounting.* June 1987, pp. 26–29.

CHAPTER 3

Benefits of Updating versus Installing a New Cost System

The new manufacturing environment has had an impact on the human side of business as well as the physical side. Stress on new values such as quality and rearrangement of long-established work centers has altered corporate culture. Accounting has been affected less than the manufacturing area in most companies. However, the changes will also affect the financial area as accountants struggle to establish a cost management system that will keep up with the changes in manufacturing. The key to acceptance of new or revised cost systems is to work with the cultural revolution going on in the rest of the company, not fight it.

Generally speaking, cultural change is a difficult process. The accounting function is as resistant to change as any other part of the organization, and some would say more so. As alterations are made in the accounting subculture it is important to keep the changes, or at least the perception of change, as limited as possible. For this reason updating the current cost system stands a better chance of gaining acceptance than introducing a new one.

CORPORATE CULTURE AND THE NEW MANUFACTURING ENVIRONMENT

The new manufacturing environment has left some companies reeling from the changes in their corporate cultures. Corporate culture, or more broadly *organizational culture,* is the "interrelated set of beliefs, shared by most of the [organization's] members, about how people should behave at work and what tasks and goals are important" (Baker 1980: 8). Corporate culture includes the values and beliefs, the rites and rituals, and the heroes and myths of an organization.

Values and Beliefs

Values and beliefs are at the very heart of a company's culture. Values and beliefs are the underlying basis for actions and day-to-day behavior. Honda, for example, stresses dreams and youthfulness. Top managers retire at fifty-five, and product innovation is emphasized (Kono 1990: 14). Johnson & Johnson's credo stresses being morally responsible to all its constituencies, including "doctors, nurses and patients, to mothers and all others who use our products and services" (Collins 1986: 15). This credo served as a guide throughout the Tylenol crisis when capsules were withdrawn from the market at a cost of some $85 million. McDonalds has a strong corporate culture in spite of its widespread franchising, emphasizing "Quality, Service, Convenience, and Value" (QSCV) as taught at its Hamburger University (Deal and Kennedy 1982: 193).

The new manufacturing environment has affected the value structure of many companies by calling even their basic beliefs into question. Manufacturers that stressed low cost with acceptable quality are revising their values to include high quality. Companies that were not competitive because of their outdated product lines are struggling to become rapid innovators. Static organizations are changing their philosophies to include continuous improvement.

An illustration of the impact is the introduction of a total quality effort at Corning Glass Works in 1983. Its policy is that every employee, whether hourly or salaried, must be trained in quality improvement. In the first two years of the program, 20,000 people speaking six languages were trained. A special Corning Quality Institute was developed to train 150 quality improvement teams.

Corporate cultural barriers that had to be overcome included supervisors' beliefs that they were losing authority and control and union officials feeling that their positions were being threatened. However, two years into the program David Luther, corporate director for quality, was able to comment that "So far, the total-quality program has made a substantial impact on our company, on the way people think, and on the way we deal with one another and with our customers. Our job now is to go fast enough to keep up with the rest of the world." Michael J. Collitti, manufacturing and engineering manager of the Science Products Division, attributes the success of the program to the massive education effort, as well as developing team skills among lower-level employees, making management's commitment highly visible, complete participation by all employees, focusing on the right goals, and allowing enough time for the changes (Luther, Collitti, and Howe 1986: 29–32).

Rites and Rituals

Rites and rituals are the visual manifestations of corporate culture. They play an important part in reaffirming the existence and strength of the culture. Rites and rituals include informal gatherings around the coffee pot, a group of co-workers going to lunch together, and the more formal staff meetings or a planned company picnic.

The 1970s brought changes to the rites and rituals as more women and minorities were brought into the corporate structure. With no established codes of behavior workers felt awkward or resistant to admitting the newcomers to the rites and rituals. It took a period of adjustment before the new groups were assimilated.

The 1980s brought more adjustments to manufacturing companies as work cells and automation led to reorganization of work groups. Interdisciplinary teams of management and workers affected the hierarchical structure of the organizations. As groups were realigned, new rites and rituals had to be formed.

Grand Rapid Spring and Wire Company (GRSW) officials used the corporate culture rather than resisted it when they undertook to reorganize operations along the lines of the principles espoused in Goldratt and Cox's *The Goal*. With a "four + one program" they focused on five major constraints. Employees and management worked together to find solutions to the problems. Employees met in "Herbie" sessions to discuss the problems (the Boy Scout Herbie was the constraining factor in *The Goal*).

Physical results of the improvement program at GRSW were remarkable. On-time shipments rose to 97 percent from 60 percent, parts defective per million improved 1,000 percent, and cost of quality dropped to 2.7 percent of sales from 6 percent. In the process, machines were rearranged, setup and cycle times were reduced, and preventive maintenance and housekeeping improved. Cultural results were just as impressive. Rather than waiting for quitting time, workers began to stay overtime without being asked if it was necessary to finish a job.

Rites and rituals also were strengthened by providing workers with the opportunity to participate in company-provided weight loss, no smoking, and nutrition programs as well as CPR training. Management introduced tuition rebates, apprenticeship programs, and a film library. GRSW management emphasizes "the role that trust played in the conversion process. The trust that developed between management and their employees formed the connecting link between the production and cultural changes that were necessary to create a WCM [world-class manufacturing] environment" (Roehm, Klein, and Castellano 1991: 44).

Heroes and Myths

Corporate culture also includes myths such as the stories told around the water cooler and the heroes whose deeds are related. Myths may include tales of performing huge amounts of work in a short period of time or beating out the competition as well as the after-hours action at the last convention.

Heroes may be prominent in either the formal or informal hierarchical structure, all the way from the secretary whose network can get anything done to the young engineer who advances rapidly through the ranks to the old-time manager who knows where all the bodies are buried.

Typical of the strong leader-hero was S. C. Allyn of NCR. In August 1945, Allyn was one of the first Allied civilians to enter Germany after the war. There he found two former NCR employees cleaning out the rubble of a burned-out NCR factory. Their first response was "We knew you'd come." A few days later a GI in a tank rumbled up and said, "Hi. I'm NCR, Omaha. Did you guys make your quota this month?" The story says a lot for Allyn as a company hero as well as NCR's hard-driving, sales-oriented culture (Deal and Kennedy 1982: 3).

Wise managers know that heroes become role models. In shaping heroes they also shape the actions of the firm. Heroes can be molded by placing individuals in certain roles of responsibility. Many management structures have a position that is reserved for the heir apparent to the top job. Heroes can also be the top salesperson, the star regional manager, or employee of the month. They can be recognized by bonuses, by having their pictures in the organization newsletter, or by getting reserved parking slots.

The new manufacturing environment tends to work through a committee structure, and it is difficult to make a hero out of a committee. However, one group that has really come into its own in the new environment is the lowest-level production workers, those who used to be assembly line workers but now are likely to be members of a work-cell team. These workers are real candidates for heroes. Their intimate knowledge of their particular jobs fosters continuous improvement if their suggestions are encouraged and heeded.

At GRSW an employee suggested that a portable oven be placed next to the spring machine rather than moving the springs to the heat-treating process. The suggestion was adopted, which meant an employee who was leaving did not need to be replaced and considerable factory space was saved (Roehm, Klein, and Castellano 1980: 43). Employees like these can be encouraged through various incentives to make innovative suggestions and should be recognized as heroes when their ideas help the company.

Corporate Culture and the Accounting System

The accounting function generally has been a follower rather than a leader in the changes that have taken place in the new manufacturing environment. Some would say it has not even been a good follower. In some cases manufacturing managers have actively avoided the accounting department as changes were made. In other cases accountants showed no interest in the physical reality they were accounting for.

The accounting function needs to adapt to the changing culture as the manufacturing function has. If meeting production quotas and stressing efficiency over quality are outdated values, accounting needs to change the accounting system to measure new values. If rites and rituals include committees to steer the company through the new procedures, accountants need to make sure they are a part of the committees. If there are heroes to be made in the change process, accountants need to be innovative enough to be contenders for the distinction. The change in manufacturing in the latter part of this century is comparable to the Industrial Revolution of the latter part of the last century. Accountants should be a part of the process.

USING CORPORATE CULTURE TO EFFECT CHANGE IN ACCOUNTING

Within the context of the corporate or overarching culture are subcultures unique to a geographic area or function. Deal and Kennedy discussed the subculture in their groundbreaking book *Corporate Cultures* in 1982: "In any company, there will be strong variations in the behavior of different parts of the company. For example, different divisions will have different cultures to some extent, depending on the different requirements for success in their basic businesses. In addition, different functions will have different subcultures" (p. 138).

Accounting forms a distinct subculture in most companies. Accounting managers may perpetuate the status quo by hiring in their own image and by reinforcing what they believe is correct behavior with rewards and punishment. Due to the organizational structure and sometimes by choice, accounting is somewhat isolated from the mainstream culture and may become reactionary.

One danger of subcultures is that a group may develop goals and behaviors that are dysfunctional for the main organizational culture. The subculture pulls in one direction while the rest of the company goes another. While engineering, quality control, and production march off in the mainstream direction of progress, accounting in many organizations is dragging its feet. Accounting needs to come into the mainstream if this is the case.

Getting the accounting function back on track will require some adjustment in the subculture. The process of changing the accounting subculture is not without pain, both to accounting and to the company as a whole since no subculture works in a vacuum. In discussing the installation of new accounting systems, one Arthur Andersen partner comments that "changing cost-management systems really rips the culture up in an organization. The company has got to be ready for that" (Port, King, and Hampton 1988: 104).

How is change effected? The classic paradigm for bringing about cultural change is Lewin's three-phase model of unfreeze, move (or change), and refreeze (1958). In other words, identify the undesirable elements in a culture and attempt to nullify them, introduce desirable elements, and then reinforce the changes. However helpful Lewin's model may be in understanding the theory of change, it may not be tangible enough to help alter a subculture.

If Lewin's model is not practical enough, perhaps the "CAREFUL" model would be of help. This model is gleaned from a wide variety of sources on corporate culture and organizational change. Managers wishing to effect change in their units should:

- *C*ommunicate the need
- *A*llow enough time
- *R*earrange the relationships
- *E*mphasize the reasons
- *F*ocus on the task
- *U*nderstand the personalities
- *L*essen the magnitude

Communicating the need is necessary. For a manager, this probably means calling a meeting or series of meetings. For a lower-level member of the accounting department, it probably means convincing someone with more authority. Memos and phone calls also may be necessary, but some face-to-face contact is desirable. Corporate culture deals with personalities, not slots on an organizational chart. To get people's reactions some personal contact is necessary.

Robert Gilbreath, president of Change Management Associates, counsels, "The more that's known about change, the more we're involved in its design, the less we resist. It's natural for people to be afraid of the dark. Turn on the light. Communicate relentlessly. Secrecy is a game for losers" (1990: 2).

Allowing enough time is also important. The corporate culture did not get to its present state overnight, and changes will not come about overnight. It is better to move slowly and let people come to their own conclusions about the need for change rather than offend them.

Rearranging the relationships may be necessary to work around those who resist change. Others may benefit by being with leaders in the drive to change. Skillful creation of committees and subcommittees will assist the process.

The authors of *The Critical Path to Corporate Renewal* did a four-year study of change programs in six companies. One finding was that the most successful change agents are usually cross-functional teams (Beer, Eisenstat, and Spector 1990: 158–159). Forming a team of individuals from the different functional areas is a good starting point for deciding what changes are needed in an accounting system and how these changes should be implemented. Appointing key accounting personnel to plantwide change committees can give them a new perspective.

Emphasizing the reasons for change is usually a prerequisite to effecting change. Research shows that cultural changes are not made unless there is a pressing reason to do so, usually a financial crisis. Accountants who are used to reading financial statements should be able to recognize the effects of increased competition from companies that are using the new manufacturing techniques. However, they may have difficulty understanding how outdated cost systems can lead managers to make incorrect decisions about such things as automating and optimizing the product mix.

Focusing on the task is probably more productive than trying to change the attitudes of the people involved. A further insight from the *Critical Path* study was that change usually was not brought about by such abstractions as modifying attitudes. Rather, change was brought about by concentrating on the task of solving the problem. Working on changing attitudes was typically unsuccessful and took energy away from the real task.

Understanding the personalities involved is important in deciding how relationships and responsibilities should be arranged. Management development consultant Donna Deeprose characterizes people in their attitudes toward cultural change as being *drivers, riders,* or *spoilers.* Drivers "take advantage of a changing environment to lead their work units in new directions," while riders go along for the ride and only react to changes as they occur. Spoilers actively resist change (1990: 3). One advantage of communicating face to face in meetings is that the feedback allows the manager to determine who the drivers, riders, and spoilers are. Team selections may depend on strategic placement of the drivers (as well as the spoilers).

Lessening the magnitude of the change helps to bring about its acceptance. Researchers distinguish between the adaptations of a stable system to its environment (first-order change) and the more drastic changes that transform fundamental properties of the system (second-order change) (Meyer, Brooks, and Goes 1990: 94). If a change appears to be of the first order, it is easier to manage than second-order change.

Changing the cost management system by changing the standard cost system in place is a change of the first order. Changing to a completely new system may be perceived by those in the accounting department as a second-order change because it alters the accounting structure. Changing the standard cost system is likely to be more acceptable because the changes are within the context of the existing structure.

ADVANTAGES OF UPDATING THE STANDARD COST SYSTEM

Some authors believed that cost accounting systems of the 1960s and 1970s were so flawed that manufacturers would be better off if they returned to the simple systems of the 1920s. Howell and Soucy, for example, predicted that "Instead of standard, full-cost, process oriented systems, the new manufacturing environment will use *actual, differential cost and asset, job order systems*" (1987: 48).

Others advocated completely new systems. Activity-based costing and backflush costing fell into this category. Still others recommended new performance measures. The new performance measures were not tied in to the financial accounting records and were not a complete accounting system. All these new systems are compatible with a standard cost system. However, their advocates generally saw these measures as replacing the function of a standard cost system.

Still others believed that accounting systems that were in place, including the standard cost system in use in most companies, could be updated and redesigned to meet the needs of manufacturers facing the new environment. Those who advocated changing rather than replacing cost accounting systems pointed out that the new manufacturing environment had affected companies to different degrees. Some were deeply into JIT systems with minimal inventories, high quality goals, significant automation, and a commitment to continuous improvement. Others had moved in this direction but the changes were not as complete and pervasive. Proponents believed the latter group would benefit from modifying their existing systems.

In addition to being more acceptable to the corporate culture, other advantages of updating rather than scrapping the standard cost system are:

- better integration of the financial, managerial, and operational information systems;
- less cost and disruption to the organization; and
- maintenance of comparability with previous data.

Integration of the Financial, Managerial, and Operational Information Systems

In many companies the financial accounting and production functions have very little contact, and the managerial accounting function is weak or nonexistent. The accounting department is concerned about gathering sufficient information to prepare financial statements. Operations may develop a series of its own performance measures to guide its actions. The two do not relate, and the functions ignore each other. About the only integrating factor in many organizations is the standard cost system.

The standard cost system is interfunctional in that the inventory figures and the cost of goods sold data are outputs of the system that affect financial accounting. The variances of the system are used by operations to gauge performance, and management uses the system for control and responsibility accounting purposes.

If the standard cost system is eliminated, the integrating factor is also eliminated. None of the proposed new systems cuts across functional lines as well as a standard cost system. In regard to activity-based costing, one consultant comments:

At this stage of acceptance and development, many consider it an advanced analytical tool for management as opposed to an official set of records. It certainly may not yet be robust enough to replace our day-to-day systems. Each implementation of ABC at this point probably will be tailored to each user's objectives. (Raffish 1991: 39)

New Systems May Be Costly and Disruptive to Install

Data on the explicit and implicit costs of installing new manufacturing cost systems are difficult to obtain. Most new systems proposed in the 1980s are in the early stages, and it is too soon to see if long-run benefits will outweigh the costs. The wealth of journal articles on new systems, particularly activity-based costing, tend to extol the virtues and ignore the problems. It will probably be some time before the romance factor wears off and a few souls are willing to admit there are difficulties.

Nevertheless installing a new system is not a simple process, and disruption is to be expected. Systems have life cycles that may be divided into stages. Authorities on systems development differ in their terminology and grouping for such stages. However, a general outline would include:

1. Problem identification. At this stage the organization identifies that a problem or problems exist and tries to define them.
2. Analysis. The existing system is examined and analyzed.
3. Design. A new conceptual design is proposed and feasibility studies are done to determine whether it would be cost beneficial.
4. Development. Databases and programs are designed. Flow charts are made of work flows. Procedures are developed.
5. Implementation. Personnel are trained. The system is tested. Pilot operations may test the system in one segment, or parallel operations may be used by operating both the old and new systems until the bugs are worked out of the new system. Systems conversion occurs.
6. Maintenance. Systems maintenance requires correction of defects found subsequent to implementation, as well as updates as conditions change.
7. Post audit. An evaluation of effectiveness is made after the system has been in operation a year or more.

Most managers who want to install a new accounting or management information system do not understand the complexity of the task. Therefore they underestimate both the cost and time involved. Likewise, they do not understand the disruption that will occur. The information given at seminars and in journal articles on new cost systems typically glosses over many steps in the process.

There are two reasons why steps often are omitted. One is that advocates may be oversimplifying the actual process, and the other is that some new systems are only partial systems. These can lead to information deficiencies if the traditional standard cost system is abandoned prematurely. Another less drastic result is that redundancy may occur if the old system is not abandoned.

Maintaining Comparability with Previous Data

A final reason why it is better to update than to install a new system is to maintain comparability. New systems may be so minimal or so different that there is no way to compare the results achieved before the new system and after its installation. It is said that one sign that a new accounting system is needed is that production and other functional groups have to maintain their own records in order to know what is going on. This also may be a sign a newly installed system is not operating as it should.

Hewlett Packard eliminated receiving reports, material requisitions, and work orders and started using a combined raw materials and work in process accounts (backflush) system. Because they had no figures from accounting on inventories, managers had to interrupt production for a count of certain critical items (Calvasina, Calvasina, and Calvasina 1989: 45).

This is not to say that most businesses would not benefit from simplifying their accounting procedures. Most businesses have unnecessary reports that started out with some useful purpose that has now disappeared into history. The reports have become an institution and are not eliminated even though they are filed routinely without being read. Some advantages claimed for newly instituted systems are merely the benefits received from an unbiased evaluation of such reporting procedures. Personnel within the company could eliminate such reports and simplify the system if given the incentive to do so.

WHAT ABOUT ACTIVITY-BASED COSTING (ABC)?

The two new cost accounting systems that are most discussed in the new manufacturing environment are activity-based costing and backflush costing. Both are appropriate in certain circumstances but neither represents a complete managerial accounting system.

A textbook definition of ABC is "A costing method that creates a cost pool for each event or transaction (activity) in an organization that acts as a cost driver. Overhead costs are then assigned to products and services on a basis of the number of these events or transactions that the product or service has generated" (Garrison 1991: 96). Garrison further refers to ABC as Level Three in the complexity of overhead assignment, with a plantwide rate as Level One and a departmentalized rate as Level Two.

In other words, the first level of complexity in overhead assignment is to assign overhead to products on a plantwide basis using some measure of volume such as number of products produced, direct labor hours, direct labor cost, or machine hours. This level sufficed through the middle part of this century when overhead charges were small and directly related to the volume of products produced or to a proxy for the volume of products such as direct labor hours.

In some companies it became apparent, even in the early part of this century, that a plantwide basis was inappropriate because different departments or processes had different characteristics. If the products spent unequal amounts of time in the different departments, the plantwide rate could be misleading. Therefore overhead rates for the different departments were developed. This necessitated a two-stage process of overhead allocation because certain expenses of the factory were plantwide, such as plant utilities, building maintenance, and operation of service departments that did not produce products. These indirect expenses had to be allocated first to producing departments; then a rate was computed for all the expenses of each producing department, including both direct and indirect expenses. However, even after this process was complete, the rate itself still was usually based on production volume, using one of the traditional measures of number of units, direct labor cost, or direct labor or machine hours.

It is also necessary to allocate indirect expenses first in ABC. However, these indirect expenses are allocated to cost pools. The pools relate to the activities performed by the firm rather than departments or processes. For example, activities of a typical manufacturing firm would include purchasing, setups, material handling, and inspection. These are the cost pools. An overhead rate is then based on the cost drivers, or causal factors, for each cost pool. For example, cost drivers could include number of purchase orders, setups, material movements, or inspections. Frequently, the cost pools and drivers in ABC are analyzed in great detail and then reaggregated in some kind of manageable group. The advantage of such a system is more precision in assigning overhead to products than the plantwide or departmental overhead rate permits.

Most of the work in setting up an ABC system is involved with identifying the appropriate cost pools and related cost drivers. The process of analyzing overhead costs in this manner is beneficial in itself. While company managers, including accounting managers, have tended to ignore the overhead "glob"; it has grown like some kind of monster to take over most of the cost of the products produced. Taking a serious look at this "glob" is a first step toward managing it.

However, identifying cost pools and cost drivers is also an expensive and time-consuming part of the process. The results obtained may be little better than what would be obtained if production and financial managers used their informed judgment. Furthermore the reaggregation process may result in use of a very simplified version of the cost pool/cost driver analysis. One plumbing fixture manufacturer started out with a cost matrix that included 26 overhead cost pools for each department. As finally applied, the firm accumulated the costs in 2 pools for each department and used volume (earned labor dollars) and number of transactions as cost drivers (O'Guin 1990: 37–39).

At Cal Electronic Circuits, Inc. (CECI) the analysis resulted in the identification of 23 cost pools and 19 cost drivers. The reaction of the senior cost accountant was that "We should compromise as to the level of detail.

Finding cost drivers is one thing, but based on the number of possible drivers, I don't know how our current cost accounting system can be adapted to handle product costing. It will be virtually impossible to track all drivers on a part data set" (Lee 1990: 37). The result was that CECI used 10 cost pools and 8 drivers, still a considerable group with which to deal.

As ABC is introduced in more companies, the selection of cost pools and drivers is likely to become more generalized from company to company. A variation on Beaujon and Singhal's 5 cost pools (costs that vary with units produced, the batches, the different products, the number of processes, and the plant [1990: 51–72]) may become the norm.

Some ABC consultants and authors appear to identify value analysis with ABC. *Value analysis* is the further step of analyzing the identified activities to determine which add value to the product and which do not. Although it is a logical extension of ABC, it is not inherent in ABC. When process value analysis is performed, it does give further front-end benefits to instituting ABC.

The main disadvantage of ABC is that its proponents appear willing to discard the standard cost system for ABC when ABC is not a complete cost system. There is much good in ABC in its more precise allocation of overhead and its better determination of product costs. When used with the traditional standard cost system, rather than in place of it, ABC has much to recommend it. Some drivers may not lend themselves to being standardized, but some do. Even if standards cannot be built for all drivers, there is still benefit from ABC in terms of overhead analysis.

In summary, the limitations of ABC are that:

- it is not a complete system,
- many benefits are front-end rather than sustained,
- precision may be lost if cost pools and drivers are reaggregated,
- cost and time are involved in the installation, and
- the corporate culture is affected.

The advantages of ABC are

- more precise overhead allocation,
- better product costing,
- easier identification of nonvalue-adding activities, and
- compatibility with a traditional cost system.

WHAT ABOUT BACKFLUSH COSTING?

The other major system proposed in the new manufacturing environment is backflush costing. Backflush costing is designed to mirror the simplicity of a JIT production system with simplicity in accounting. Although there are variations, the backflush system generally makes two entries for production. The first entry shows the purchase and use of raw materials by placing the cost in a raw materials in process (RIP) account. The second entry shows the addition of labor and overhead cost and transfer to finished goods. The term *backflush costing* comes from the fact that the manufacturing costs are "flushed" out of the system once production is completed.

Backflush is intended to be a minimal accounting system because there are minimal inventories to account for. The problem with the backflush system occurs when it is inappropriately applied to companies that do not have a true JIT production system. If inventories are present, they need to be recorded and controlled. If the accounting system does not perform this function, the production department has to resort to physical counts. Physical counts interrupt the production process and are expensive.

Furthermore backflush costing has no mechanism for controlling the cost of materials, labor, and overhead. There are no standards for what these costs should be, and the costs are not tracked through the manufacturing process. If a company operates in a true JIT environment with advance delivery schedules for materials, very little labor, and correctly identified cost pools, there may be no need to track and control these costs. However, if the company does not operate in a true JIT environment, it will need closer monitoring of manufacturing costs.

As Garrison points out in his textbook:

We must emphasize, however, that backflush costing is appropriate *only* in those situations where a *true* JIT systems is in operation. . . . When inventories are present, frequent and expensive physical counts of inventory will be necessary to determine the amount of materials and the amount of partially completed goods still on hand. Moreover, with no requisition slips or work orders available, it will be difficult to identify how much cost should be applied to raw materials and work in process inventories and how much should be applied to completed output. Thus in the absence of a *true* JIT system, backflush costing may result in less timely, less accurate, and more expensive data than a conventional costing system. (1991: 99)

» «

The corporate culture in many manufacturing firms has been hit hard by the changes in the manufacturing environment. To some degree the accounting function has been insulated from these changes. However, if accountants are to accurately account for the physical realities in their firms, they must plan and execute changes in the accounting system that will reflect the new manufacturing environment. To do so, changes may have to occur in the accounting subculture.

One advantage of updating the traditional standard cost system rather than scrapping it for a new system is that there is less disruption to the accounting subculture. Other advantages are that the integrating function of the standard cost system (SCS) is maintained, there is less cost and disruption to the company, and comparability with previous periods' data is maintained.

Two new accounting systems are ABC and backflush costing. ABC is not a complete system as such and therefore should not be viewed as replacement for the SCS. ABC does provide more precision in analyzing overhead and as a result improves product costing. Backflush costing is a simplified system that should be used only in companies that have a true JIT manufacturing environment.

REFERENCES

Baker, E. L. "Managing Organizational Culture," *Management Review.* July 1980, pp. 8–13.

Beaujon, George J., and Vinod R. Singhal. "Understanding the Activity Costs in an Activity-Based Cost System," *Journal of Cost Management.* Spring 1990, pp. 51–72.

Beer, Michael, Russell A. Eisenstat, and Bert Spector. "Why Change Programs Don't Produce Change," *Harvard Business Review.* November–December 1990, pp. 158–166.

Calvasina, Richard V., Eugene J. Calvasina, and Gerald E. Calvasina. "Beware the New Accounting Myths," *Management Accounting,* December 1989, pp. 41–45.

Collins, David E. "Cultural Heritage and Crisis Management," in Melissa A. Berman, ed., *Corporate Culture and Change.* The Conference Board, New York, 1986, pp. 13–19.

Deal, Terrance E., and Allan A. Kennedy. *Corporate Cultures.* Reading, Mass.: Addison-Wesley, 1982.

Deeprose, Donna. "Change: Are You a Driver, Rider, or Spoiler?" *Supervisory Management.* February 1990, p. 3.

Garrison, Ray H. *Managerial Accounting: Concepts for Planning, Control, Decision Making.* Homewood, Ill.: Richard D. Irwin, 1991.

Gilbreath, Robert D. "The Myths about Winning over Resisters to Change," *Supervisory Management.* January 1990, pp. 1–2.

Goldratt, Eliyahu M., and Jeff Cox. *The Goal: A Process of Ongoing Improvement.* New Haven, Conn.: Spectrum, 1986.

Howell, Robert A., and Stephen R. Soucy. "Cost Accounting in the New Manufacturing Environment," *Management Accounting.* August 1987, pp. 42–48.

Kono, Toyohiro. "Corporate Culture and Long-range Planning," *Long Range Planning.* August 1990, pp. 9–19.

Lee, John Y. "Activity-Based Costing at Cal Electronic Circuits," *Management Accounting.* October 1990, pp. 36–38.

Lewin, Kurt. "Group Decisions and Social Change," in Eleanor E. MacCobby, Theodore M. Newcomb, and Eugene L. Hartley, eds., *Readings in Social Psychology.* New York: Holt Rinehart & Winston, 1958.

Luther, David B., Michael J. Collitti, and Thomas Howitt, Jr. "The Corporate Vision at Corning Glass Works: Total Quality," in Melissa A. Berman, ed, *Corporate Culture and Change.* The Conference Board, New York, 1986, pp. 29–35.

Meyer, Alan D., Geoffrey R. Brooks, and James B. Goes. "Environmental Jolts and Industry Revolutions: Organizational Responses to Discontinuous Change," *Strategic Management Journal.* Summer 1990 (special issue), pp. 93–109.

O'Guin, Michael. "Focus the Factory with Activity-Based Costing," *Management Accounting.* February 1990, pp. 36–41.

Port, Otis, Resa King, and William J. Hampton. "How the New Math of Productivity Adds Up," *Business Week.* June 6, 1988, pp. 103–113.

Raffish, Norm. "How Much Does that Product Really Co$t?" *Management Accounting.* March 1991, pp. 36–39.

Roehm, Harper A., Donald Klein, and Joseph F. Castellano. "Springing to World-Class Manufacturing," *Management Accounting.* March 1991, pp. 40–44.

CHAPTER 4

The Traditional Standard Cost System

The traditional standard cost system has been highly criticized by engineers and production managers, as well as writers, in the new manufacturing environment. The criticism has centered on the use of variances for control purposes—primarily the material price variance, the labor efficiency variance, and the volume variance. To a lesser degree standard cost systems have been disparaged for not promoting continuous improvement for allowing adherence to static standards.

Before addressing remedies for the problems of today's standard cost systems, it is necessary to examine the systems. A little historical background is useful.

HISTORICAL BACKGROUND OF STANDARD COST SYSTEMS

Systems for accounting for costs date back several centuries. Indeed it might be pointed out that cost systems were of greater concern to early merchants and craftsmen than what is now called financial accounting. When there were no income taxes or regulatory government agencies to demand the preparation of financial statements, all accounting was managerial accounting—accounting done for management to meet its information needs.

Standard cost systems did not evolve until about 1900. Standard cost systems were distinguished from earlier cost systems in that they prescribed what costs ought to be rather than merely recording what they had been in the past. Estimates or standards for future costs were constructed, and actual costs were compared to these predetermined benchmarks to determine the effectiveness of performance. Setting up standards for what performance should be was the tricky part of this process, and that had to wait for the scientific management movement headed by Frederick Taylor.

By the time Taylor put forth his article on shop management in 1903, the Industrial Revolution had occurred; mass production methods were replacing the labor of individual craftspeople. Taylor's purpose was to increase efficiency in the factory by determining the best way to do a task and then to set standards for its performance. Taylor and his followers were engineers and efficiency experts rather than accountants, but their work formed the basis for the standards that accountants would later use.

The idea of standard costs is difficult to trace to any one individual. However, four names stand out in the evolution of standard cost systems — Alexander Hamilton Church, John Whitmore, Harrington Emerson, and G. Charter Harrison.

Alexander Hamilton Church did not describe a standard cost system as such, but his ideas planted the seeds for what was to follow. His six articles on "The Proper Distribution of Establishment Charges" appeared in *Engineering Magazine* in 1901. Church perceived that the really difficult area in manufacturing cost is overhead. He proposed that a machine hour rate be used to apply overhead and that the rate be based on predetermined estimates. He also proposed that the rate be applied to production centers rather than to the factory as a whole, and he recognized the effect of idle capacity.

John Whitmore, a disciple of Church's, is credited with giving the first specific description of a standard cost system in a lecture at New York University in 1908. The lecture was later published in the *Journal of Accountancy* and contained detailed journal entries for a shoe factory. The entries for leather clearly show an account for sorted leather at its "proper" cost and a variation account for the difference between the "proper" cost and the actual cost.

Harrington Emerson, an efficiency engineer, published a series of articles on "Efficiency as a Basis for Operations and Wages," in *Engineering Magazine* in 1908 and 1909. He advocated use of standard costs to eliminate waste and inefficiency. Emerson saw the engineer as setting and revising standards with the eventual objective of eliminating the differences between actual and standard costs. He saw the accountant's responsibility as that of keeping good records so the engineer could carry out this purpose.

G. Charter Harrison is credited with designing the first full-fledged standard cost system, which he installed at the Boss Manufacturing Company in Kewanee, Illinois, in 1911. Unlike his associate Emerson, he was an accountant by trade, which is evident in his detailed standard cost cards, daily progress reports, and stress on managerial decision making. He published his system in a series of articles on "Cost Accounting to Aid Production" in *Industrial Management* in 1918 and 1919; these articles were later published as a book. His term *standard cost* predominated over a host of similar terms floating around at the time, and he is considered by accounting historian Nathan Kranowski as the "father of standard cost accounting" (1979: 216).

Spurred by a need for better cost control for mass production methods and aided by the development of engineering standards, the standard cost idea was conceived shortly after the turn of the century. Practical applications followed in the 1920s until almost every manufacturing operation of any size used some variation of the method.

THE CONCEPT OF STANDARDS FOR PRODUCTION

Engineering studies continue to be the usual source of information for most efficiency standards today, including the material quantity variance. Price standards are usually set by the accounting department in conference with the purchasing department, personnel department, or whatever department is affected. The basis for information may be contracts, current prices, or historical data.

There are various ideas of how "tight" standards should be. Some believe that high standards of performance motivate supervisors and workers to perform better. In these companies it is expected that most variances will be unfavorable. Others feel that realistic standards are better motivational tools and provide a more reasonable figure for product cost that is easier to use when bidding on orders or estimating costs. In either case investigation is not usually warranted unless the variances indicate costs are off by some predetermined percentage.

Wise supervisors investigate unusually high favorable variances as well as unfavorable variances because these also may indicate a problem. An unusually high favorable material price variance may indicate the purchase of substandard materials, for example.

Volume variances are determined by estimating the level of production used to set the fixed overhead rate. These are various philosophies of how this estimate should be determined. Projections range from the theoretical maximum production that a plant could obtain if it operated around the clock with no interruptions to the expected production volume for the coming year.

Most companies base their fixed overhead rate on either practical capacity or normal capacity. Practical capacity allows for normal time worked, which excludes holidays and weekends and considers the number of shifts used. Practical capacity also allows for the usual production delays due to machine breakdowns, material delays, and scheduling problems. However, lack of sales orders is ignored.

Normal capacity permits all the delays and unscheduled time that practical capacity does. It also considers sales orders. For example, a plant may be capable of producing 100,000 units a year according to its practical capacity, but it may be able to sell only an average of 80,000 units. Normal capacity would be 80,000 units. Normal capacity is not an estimate of sales orders for the coming year but is an average over a period of years, usually about five. Obviously, if a company can sell all it makes, capacity is estimated at the practical capacity level because production puts a cap on what sales can be.

TRADITIONAL VARIANCE MEASURES

There are basically two types of variances for costs that vary with volume — price and efficiency variances. Price variances show the difference between the actual and standard cost of the units produced caused by price variations in inputs. Efficiency variances show the difference caused by deviations in the quantities of inputs used.

Besides price and efficiency variances, a producer may incur mix and yield variances for variable costs. Mix variances apply if the producer can alter the mix or proportion of inputs. If a meat packer is making sausage, for example, one meat could be traded for another within certain limits. On the other hand, if a manufacturer is making can openers there is little opportunity to trade one component for another. A mix variance for materials would be appropriate in the case of the sausage but not in the case of the can opener.

Yield variances can be computed along with mix variances as part of the breakdown of the efficiency variance. Yield variances can also be computed in situations in which there is some shrinkage in production in order to compare the actual yield from the inputs with the standard yield.

The only type of fixed cost in the traditional system is the cost of fixed overhead. This group of costs may be treated in a variety of fashions. It may be combined with some variable overhead costs, or it may be treated separately, depending on whether the manufacturer breaks the actual cost of overhead into its fixed and variable components. However, whether broken out separately or combined with variable overhead, there are two basic types of fixed overhead variances — budget variances and volume variances. The volume variance shows the over- or underabsorption of the fixed overhead into the units produced; the budget variance shows the difference between the fixed overhead budget amount and the actual amount spent on fixed overhead items.

A Standard Cost Example

With the general background in mind, it is possible to illustrate a standard cost system using a simple product with two types of materials. If a firm produces more than one product, the variances may be computed for each product or combined.

Assume a cat food canner with the following standard costs:

Standard Costs for Tory Cat Food

Standard output: 9 pounds (24 cans)

Liver 9 pounds @ $.25	$ 2.25
Bacon 3 pounds @ $.50	1.50
Cans 24 cans @ $.02	.48
Labor .5 hour @ $5.00	2.50
Variable Overhead .5 hour @ $4.00	2.00
Fixed Overhead .5 hour @ $2.00	1.00
Standard Cost Per Case	$ 9.73

Actual Production for July   100 cases (2,400 cans)

Materials. Assume the company used 1,000 pounds of liver at a cost of $.27 per pound to produce its 100 cases of cat food. The standard cost of liver for 100 cases of cat food would be $225 (100 cases multiplied by the standard cost of $2.25 per case). Actual cost was $270 (1,000 pounds at $.27) while standard cost was $225. Why was the actual cost $45 higher than the standard cost?

One reason might be the price paid for the liver was higher than standard. If the company pays $.27 for liver instead of the standard $.25, it causes a $.02 per pound difference. For the 1,000 pounds used the difference is $20. Another reason might be that the company used too much liver. The standard calls for 9 pounds of liver per case or a total of 900 pounds for the 100 cases. Unfortunately, workers used 1,000 pounds, which was 100 pounds too much. The 100 extra pounds at $.25 per pound account for another $25 difference. The $45 difference between standard and actual cost is made up of a $20 unfavorable price variance and a $25 unfavorable efficiency or quantity variance.

The price variance could also be computed on the amount of liver purchased during the period. If the company purchased 1,200 pounds during the period at $.27, the price variance on the purchases would be the $.02 above standard multiplied by 1,200 pounds or $24. The variance would be unfavorable since the company paid more than standard for the liver. This is supposedly the better way to compute the price variance because it isolates the variance at an earlier point in time when it presumably could be corrected more quickly.

Suppose the company purchased and used 260 pounds of bacon at $.50 per pound for this 100 cases of cat food. There would be no price variance for the bacon because the standard price was paid. The efficiency or quantity variance would be favorable by $20 because the standard amount of bacon for 100 cases of cat food is 3 pounds per case or 300 pounds. It appears the company used 40 pounds less than standard at $.50 per pound for a favorable variance of $20.

Assuming a price variance computed on quantities used rather than purchased, the variances so far may be summarized as follows:

Actual Quantities × Actual Prices	Actual Quantities × Standard Prices	Standard Quantities × Standard Prices
1000 × .27 = 270	1000 × .25 = 250	900 × .25 = 225
260 × .50 = 130	260 × .50 = 130	300 × .50 = 150
400	380	375

Price variance: $400 − 380 = $20 unfavorable (all due to liver)
Quantity variance: $380 − $375 = $5 unfavorable ($25 unfavorable on liver and $20 favorable on bacon)

Mix and yield variances would also be factors with a product such as this because there is some opportunity to interchange materials and some shrinkage is expected. The combined quantity variances for liver and bacon are $5 unfavorable. A further breakdown of this variance would show it is partly due to the mix of liver and bacon and partly due to the fact that too many pounds were used (a true quantity variance).

A total of 1,260 pounds of meat was used—1,000 pounds of liver and 260 pounds of bacon. If this 1,260 pounds were used in the standard proportions of 9 pounds to 3 pounds, a 3 to 1 mix, 945 pounds of liver and 315 pounds of bacon would have been used. There was a trade-off of 55 pounds of the mixture—55 pounds more than the standard amount of liver and 55 pounds less of bacon. This gives a favorable mix variance because proportionately less of the more expensive bacon was used and proportionately more of the lower priced liver. The difference in the price of the meats is $.25. If the 55 pounds are multiplied by the $.25 price differential, the result is a favorable mix variance of $13.75.

Overall the amount of meat that should have been used for 100 cases of cat food was 1,200 pounds (12 pounds multiplied by 100 cases). If the company actually used 1,260 pounds, it used 60 pounds too much. The average standard price per pound is $.3125 ($3.75 total per case for the meats divided by 12 pounds to be used). The 60 pounds multiplied by the average price of $.3125 give a "true" quantity variance or a yield variance of $18.75 unfavorable. The breakdown of the $5 unfavorable quantity variance may be summarized as follows:

Actual Quantities × Standard Prices @ Actual Mix	Actual Quantities × Standard Prices @ Standard Mix	Standard Quantities × Standard Prices @ Standard Mix
1000 × .25 = 250	945 × .25 = 236.25	900 × .25 = 225
260 × .50 = 130	315 × .50 = 157.50	300 × .50 = 150
1260 380	1260 × .3175 = 393.75	1200 × .3175 = 375

Mix variance: $380 − $393.75 = $13.75 favorable
Yield variance: $393.75 − $375 = $18.75 unfavorable

The other material to be used is cans. Assume the company used 2,400 cans at $.02 each and no price or quantity variances. Obviously there could not be any mix variances because there is no opportunity to trade cans for either meat.

Labor. For labor assume 60 hours at a rate of $5.50 per hour to produce the 100 cases of cat food. The standard cost of labor is $2.50 per case or $250. The actual wages paid were 60 hours multiplied by $5.50, or $330. The actual wages paid were $80 above standard ($330 less $250). This could be due either to the wage rate paid or to the number of hours used. In this situation it appears the wage paid was $.50 above the standard $5 rate. The wage differential of $.50, multiplied by the 60 hours, yields a $30 unfavorable price or rate variance.

The company should have used .5 hour of labor for every case of cat food, or 50 hours for the 100 cases it actually produced. If employees worked 60 hours, the company was 10 hours above standard at a standard rate of $5. This results in a $50 unfavorable efficiency variance.

Mix variances can also be computed for labor if there are two or more different rates, and there is opportunity for workers to trade jobs. In this case all workers were paid a standard rate of $5 per hour, giving no opportunity to trade.

Labor variances may be summarized as follows:

Actual Hours × **Actual Rate**	**Actual Hours** × **Actual Rate**	**Standard Hours** × **Standard Rate**
60 × 5.50 = 330	60 × 5.00 = 300	50 × 5.00 = 250

Rate variance: $330 − $300 = $30 unfavorable
Efficiency variance: $300 − $250 = $50 unfavorable

Variable Overhead. Variable overhead variances normally would not be calculated for a single batch of production such as 100 cases of cat food. Rather they would be calculated for a period of time. However, assume that the information on the 100 cases of cat food also applies to a particular time period for which management would like to calculate overhead variances. Also assume $250 was spent on variable overhead items and that overhead is applied on the basis of direct labor hours.

The standard amount to spend on variable overhead would be $200, calculated by multiplying the 50 hours of standard labor time by the standard variable overhead rate of $4. Therefore, the difference between the standard cost of the cases and the actual cost is $50. This difference may be due to efficiency factors or to spending factors. Production of the 100 cases required 60 hours of direct labor time, which was 10 hours above the standard time. The assumption is that using these 10 extra hours of direct labor time also caused use of more variable overhead—more payroll taxes, more supervision, more material handling, and so on. Ten extra hours multiplied by the $4 variable overhead rate yields an unfavorable efficiency variance of $40.

The rest of the $50 total variance is assumed to be due to spending factors. That is, even considering the extra time spent working, the spending for variable overhead was too high. Perhaps supervisors were paid higher rates, supplies cost more than usual, and so on.

To summarize, the variable overhead variances consist of:

Actual Spending	**Actual Hours** **× Standard Rate**	**Standard Hours** **× Standard Rate**
250.00	60 × 4.00 = 240.00	50 × 4.00 = 200.00

Spending Variance: $250 − $240 = $10 unfavorable
Efficiency Variance: $240 − $200 = $40 unfavorable

Fixed Overhead. Fixed overhead variances are not usually computed per batch of production. However, to use the cat food illustration to demonstrate these variances, assume actual spending on fixed overhead items was $150. Further assume that the company originally planned to produce 135 cases of cat food and had budgeted $135 for fixed overhead. Before its accounting period had begun, the accounting department would have calculated that fixed overhead should average $1 per case or $2 per direct labor hour. These predetermined rates would have been determined by dividing the $135 budgeted amount by the projected 135 cases or by the 67.5 hours that should be used to produce 135 cases.

The standard amount to be spent on fixed overhead for 100 cases would be $100, found by multiplying the $1 per case rate by 100 cases or the $2 hourly rate by the 50 standard hours. The difference between the actual amount of $150 and the standard amount is $50. This $50 may be divided into a budget or spending variance and a volume variance.

The budget or spending variance is the difference between the $150 actually spent and the $135 budget which is $15 unfavorable. With fixed overhead items the amount spent does not depend on the volume of production. Therefore, it is not necessary to adjust the budget for the hours worked or the units produced. The variance is just a simple comparison of what was spent with what was budgeted.

The volume variance shows how much of the fixed overhead was under- or overabsorbed into production. The accountant has constructed a rate of $1 per unit as an average amount of fixed overhead per unit. However, to try to apply a fixed expense item on a per-unit basis as though it were a variable expense is artificial. Unless the accountant estimates the production exactly, the overhead applied to the units will be either too high *(overabsorbed)* or too low *(underabsorbed)*. In this case production was only 100 cases and only $100 is absorbed into production. The difference between the budget and what is absorbed into production is the unfavorable volume variance of $35. In other words, production was 35 cases below what was planned, resulting in a variance of $1 per case, or $35. The variance is unfavorable because fewer cases than planned were produced; consequently, the fixed cost per case was higher than planned.

The volume variance is a much-maligned variance, as discussed in other chapters in this book. When understood as no more or no less than the over-or underabsorbed overhead, there is little problem with the variance. However, it is frequently taken as a measure of the cost to the company of underproducing. To measure the cost of underproducing it would be necessary to measure the lost contribution margins from the sales lost due to the underproduction. Lost contribution margins are very different from fixed overhead.

To summarize the fixed overhead variances, these variances consist of:

Actual Spending	**Budgeted Amount**	**Standard Hours** × **Standard Rate**
150	135	50 × 2.00 = 100

Spending or budget variance: $150 − $135 = $15 unfavorable
Volume variance: $135 − $100 = $35 unfavorable

Occasionally a company has the policy of further breaking down the volume variance into an efficiency variance and an idle capacity variance. This distinction is sometimes characterized as the difference between misused and unused capacity. Assume the cat food company used 10 hours too much of direct labor time in which it could have produced 20 cases if it produced at the standard rate of one case per .5 hour. At the rate of $2 per hour, this gives an unfavorable efficiency variance of $20, a measure of the misused capacity. The idle capacity variance is the difference between the projected 67.5 hours and the 60 actual hours multiplied by the $2 rate, which gives an unfavorable variance of $15, a measure of unused capacity.

The breakdown of the volume variance may be given as:

Budgeted Amount	**Actual Hours** × **Standard Rate**	**Standard Hours** × **Standard Rate**
135	60 × 2.00 = 120	50 × 2.00 = 100

Idle capacity variance: $135 − $120 = $15 unfavorable
Efficiency variance: $120 − $100 = $20 unfavorable

Depending on custom, theoretical persuasion, or expediency, overhead within a particular company may be treated in a variety of fashions. If a company's management does not want the refinement or cost of breaking down actual overhead into its fixed and variable components, it is not possible to compute separate variable overhead spending variances and fixed overhead budget variances. If this is the case, these two variances may be combined into one overhead spending variance. Other companies may isolate the volume variance as a separate item and combine all other overhead variances into one variance, which is usually called a *controllable variance*.

INTEGRATION WITH THE FINANCIAL ACCOUNTING SYSTEM

It is entirely possible to operate a standard cost system without integration into the financial accounting system. However, most organizations find that the simplicity of using standard costs for their main record base is desirable and that integration eliminates inconsistencies and redundancies.

If the standard cost system is used in the records, the work in process account (WIP) is carried at standard cost. Materials, payroll, and overhead control are carried at actual cost. (An exception would be when material price variances are isolated at the time of purchase, in which case materials are carried at actual quantities but standard prices.) When materials or labor is used in production, the difference between the actual and standard amounts are recorded in variance accounts. Overhead variances generally are recorded only at the end of the accounting period.

Materials. If the standard cost entries for the preceding cat food illustration were integrated into Tory Cat Food's financial accounting system, the entry to show the use the material would be:

WIP – Liver 900 × $.25	225	
WIP – Bacon 300 × $.50	150	
WIP – Cans 2400 × $.02	48	
Price Variance	20	
Yield Variance	18.75	
Mix Variance		13.75
Materials – Liver 1000 × $.27		270
Materials – Bacon 260 × $.50		130
Materials – Cans 2400 × $.02		48

An alternate (and generally preferred) method for treating the price variance is to isolate it when the materials are purchased. Liver was the only material for which there was a price variance. Its purchase could be recorded as:

Materials – Liver 1200 × $.25	300	
Price Variance 1200 × $.02	24	
Accounts Payable 1200 × $.27		324

If the price variance is already recorded at the time of purchase, the entry to record the material's use in production contains only the mix and yield variances. The credit to the materials account is for the actual quantity at the standard price.

Labor. The entry to show the use of the labor would be:

WIP — Labor 50 × $5.00	250	
Rate Variance	30	
Efficiency Variance	50	
Payroll 60 × $5.50		330

Variable Overhead. As mentioned, overhead variances normally would not be isolated until the end of the accounting period. Therefore an entry to record the actual variable overhead during the accounting period would be made:

Factory Overhead Control	250	
Various Credits		250

An entry also would be made to apply the variable overhead to production:

WIP — Variable Overhead	200	
Factory Overhead Applied		200

For the sake of illustration, assume no more entries for variable overhead during the accounting period. The entry to isolate variances at the end of the period would be:

Factory Overhead Applied	200	
Spending Variance	10	
Efficiency Variance	40	
Factory Overhead Control		250

This entry also closes out the portion of the factory overhead control and applied accounts that relate to variable overhead.

Fixed Overhead. Fixed overhead variances also are not recorded until the end of the accounting period. During the period the following entry is made to record actual fixed overhead:

Factory Overhead Control	150	
Various Credits		150

An entry is also made to record the application of fixed overhead to production:

WIP — Fixed Overhead	100	
Factory Overhead Applied		100

At the end of the period an entry is made to close the fixed overhead portion of the overhead accounts and to isolate the variances. Assuming these are the only entries for fixed overhead, the period-end entry would be:

Factory Overhead Applied	100	
Spending Variance	15	
Volume Variance	35	
Factory Overhead Control		150

If desired, the volume variance entry could be replaced by an entry for an idle capacity variance of $15 and a fixed overhead efficiency variance of $20. Alternately, the variances could be combined in a variety of fashions as discussed.

Disposition of Variances

As a result of the preceding entries, WIP now contains the standard cost of 100 cases of cat food—$973. As the cat food is completed, it will be transferred to finished goods and finally on to cost of goods sold at the standard price.

The variance accounts will be used for whatever control purposes are appropriate, and they will be closed out at the end of the accounting period. It is necessary to make some disposition of the variance accounts because the end-of-period financial statements must use the actual costs for inventory values and cost of goods sold. To not adjust to actual cost would give opportunity for all sorts of financial statement manipulations through changing of the standard costs. Therefore variances are closed out to cost of goods sold or the income summary at the end of the year. If more accuracy is desired, the variances are also prorated to the inventory accounts.

The effect of the standard cost system on the financial statements is that the three inventory accounts—raw materials, work in process, and finished goods—appear on the balance sheet as current assets; the cost of goods sold appears on the income statement. Cost of goods sold is deducted from revenue and is a major determinant of net income.

Although inventories and cost of goods sold are adjusted to actual for the year-end financial statements, interim statements may use standard cost figures. Standard cost figures are also used in estimating costs for pricing or bidding purposes. Furthermore standard costs are used as the building blocks for manufacturing cost budgets.

THE STANDARD COST SYSTEM AND OVERHEAD

The standard cost system is not really the culprit in overhead assignment. However, because so much of the debate in manufacturing accounting systems concerns overhead, this area is examined here. The discussion applies to so-called actual-normal systems as well as standard cost systems, at least as traditionally used. (An actual-normal system uses actual rather than standard costs. However, overhead is applied at a predetermined rate, which is a type of standard. The way overhead is applied is the normal part of an actual-normal system.)

Overhead is the catchall category in manufacturing. The three types of manufacturing cost are usually listed as direct materials (the materials used in the products), direct labor (the labor applied directly to products), and overhead. Overhead includes all manufacturing expenses other than the direct materials and direct labor groups. Obviously, overhead includes a variety of items such as manufacturing supplies, material handling, payroll taxes, supervision, indirect labor of various types, overtime premiums, shift premiums, idle time, depreciation on factory buildings and machinery, property taxes, rent, utilities, power, and maintenance.

Besides the indirect manufacturing expenses, overhead includes the operation of any service departments that may be devoted to manufacturing. These would include the factory office, personnel, payroll, cafeteria, maintenance, building and grounds, and quality control.

Factories in the last century were simple compared to today's manufacturing operations. They took a raw material and converted it to a finished product by applying mostly hand labor. Even labor was frequently contracted out, and a supervisor paid for delivering this factor of production. Therefore companies had a major expense of only materials or materials and labor. Overhead was minimal because there were few machines and service departments. The overhead category of production has grown exponentially as factories have become automated and added service departments, particularly in the last ten years.

When factories were less complicated, a reasonable method of dealing with overhead was to estimate the overhead for the coming year, divide by expected labor dollars or hours, and arrive at a rate to apply to products throughout the year. Any excess or deficiency at the end of the year was closed to cost of goods sold or prorated to cost of goods sold and inventories. In this fashion all units bore a share of the overhead burden. When machines became more predominant, machine hours were sometimes substituted for labor dollars or hours. It was a fair and equitable method at the time, and it made sense when overhead was a small part of the total product cost.

However, overhead has become a more major part of the factory cost. New indirect expenses have been added along with new service departments. The service departments especially complicated the process because their cost could not be captured in an overhead rate and applied to products until it was first allocated to production departments. Some allocation base that seemed to relate to the expense was chosen. Personnel department expenses might be allocated according to number of employees. The building and grounds department expenses might be allocated according to square feet of floor space. How these service expenses were allocated made a difference in how much was considered attributable to a particular production department and how much overhead was charged to the products processed in those departments.

The usual activity factor for applying these expenses continued to be direct labor cost or hours or machine hours. Great effort was expended to determine which costs were variable with these activity factors and which were not. Accountants increasingly found many expenses that did change but did not vary directly with one of the volume-related activity factors. These were usually dumped into a semivariable category that was subsequently subdivided into fixed and variable.

Accountants in some companies found that more sophisticated procedures for accounting for overhead were needed. They did not wish to treat all overhead in the same manner because so many different types of expenses were involved. Consequently, they began to break overhead down into cost pools and apply each pool on a basis that made sense for that particular type of cost. There might be, for example, a pool of material-related costs such as acquisition, warehousing, and handling that would be applied on the basis of direct material cost. Another pool of labor-related costs, such as payroll taxes, supervision, and indirect labor, would be applied on the basis of direct labor cost. Still another pool of machine-related costs, such as power and depreciation, would be applied on the basis of machine hours.

Those who would revise accounting systems for the new manufacturing environment prefer to take the pool idea a step further. They emphasize finding the causes of overhead cost — the cost drivers. They also stress controlling the cost drivers in order to control the costs. Usually multiple cost drivers are identified and then aggregated into a manageable group for applying overhead.

PERFORMANCE MEASUREMENT AND REPORTING SYSTEM

Most controversies surrounding the standard cost system stem from how the variances are used to evaluate the performance of department heads and supervisors. Variances are used to assess effectiveness in terms of how well the particular manager avoided unfavorable variances or incurred favorable variances. To understand how variances are used for this purpose, it is necessary to see how responsibility is assigned.

In most organizations responsibility is assigned along functional lines. Therefore the responsibility for material variances is divided — the price variance is considered the problem of the purchasing department while the quantity variance is assigned to the production department. If the quantity variance is subdivided into mix and yield variances, these are also considered the responsibility of production.

In the case of labor variances the rate variance is the responsibility of whoever does the hiring, which is probably the personnel department in a medium or large organization. The efficiency variance or the mix and yield variances are considered the responsibility of production.

With overhead the assignment of responsibility can differ according to item. Generally, the variable overhead spending variance and the fixed overhead spending or budget variance are thought to be the responsibility of production, but such items as indirect materials and supplies would be assigned to purchasing. The variable overhead efficiency variance and the fixed overhead efficiency variance, when computed, are usually thought to be the responsibility of production. The volume variance is generally considered the responsibility of upper-level management unless production problems cause the lack of volume.

With responsibility assigned in this manner, it is not difficult to see why department managers are frequently at each others' throats. If the purchasing manager buys inferior material to obtain a favorable price variance, this can cause excess scrap and an unfavorable quantity variance for the production manager. If the production manager overproduces to obtain a favorable volume variance, the sales manager may have more units on hand than can be sold. Trade-offs between price and efficiency are difficult to evaluate because the responsibility is divided.

As discussed in Chapter 1, functional groupings of equipment in the factory area are being replaced in the new manufacturing environment with work cells. This evolution is being followed to some degree by organizational structures.

As work cells are formed, functional groups of product design personnel and engineers are being broken up and assigned to work cells or product lines. It is not difficult to foresee a day when accounting and marketing departments could be similarly broken down into product groupings. If and when this occurs, responsibility for variances or whatever performance measures are used will be greatly enhanced. The improvement will occur because most expenses will be identified directly with a product line, and any trade-offs between efficiency and quality or price and efficiency can be determined readily.

» «

The traditional standard cost system was devised in a day when controlling material and labor costs and keeping production volume up were the main concerns. Times have changed, with overhead a far more important part of the total product cost and a new emphasis on quality, minimal inventories, and rapid throughput. However, for the most part standard cost systems have not been revised to encompass the changes. Price and efficiency variances are stressed rather than more recent concerns. Overhead is applied on the basis of simplistic activity factors such as direct labor cost or hours. Responsibility is divided along functional lines and viewed in a fragmented fashion. Although the structure and concept of a standard cost system are valid, updates for the new manufacturing environment are needed.

REFERENCE

Kranowski, Nathan. "The Historical Development of Standard Costing Systems until 1920," in Edward N. Coffman, ed., *The Academy of Accounting Historians Working Paper Series,* Vol. 2, pp. 206–220.

CHAPTER 5

Measuring the Right Variables: Updating Variance Reporting

A major problem with standard cost systems as they exist in most companies is that the system does not measure the right variables. Rather than motivating managers to increase quality and decrease inventories, the traditional standard cost system (SCS) encourages them to deemphasize quality in favor of efficiency and to build up unneeded inventories by increasing production volume. This is not a defect in the system, but a failure to update as needed. Accountants and managers have gotten locked into believing that the only variables that can be measured are the traditional ones. However, the system is much more flexible.

A quick look at the definitions of SCS in accounting dictionaries and textbooks shows that the rigid adherence to price, efficiency, and volume standards is not an essential requirement of the system. Rayburn, for example, says that "Because historical data do not satisfy the need for determining the acceptability of performance, a system of costing on a predetermined basis—standard costing—has been developed. Cost standards are scientifically predetermined costs of production used as a basis for measurement and comparison" (1989: 437).

What is needed is a SCS that will measure the right variables, the variables considered important in the new manufacturing environment. These variables include quality, production and inventory levels, and product mix.

MEASURING QUALITY

Most quality control and production managers (and some accountants) do not realize that the much-maligned traditional SCS does have a quality measure. Unfortunately, it is buried in the quantity and efficiency variances and is not pulled out as a separate item. Suppose a producer of a machined part has a standard cost as follows:

Standard Cost for One Lot of Part 101

Lot Size: 100 parts

Materials 50 pounds @ $1.00	$ 50.00
Labor 5 hours @ $15.00	75.00
Variable Overhead 6 machine hours @ $25.00	150.00
Fixed Overhead 6 machine hours @ $15.00	90.00
Standard Cost per Lot	$ 365.00

Further assume that the company produced one lot of part 101 resulting in 95 good parts and 5 defective parts, which were found on final inspection. Fifty-one pounds of material, 7 hours of labor, and 7 hours of machine time were used to produce the parts. Traditional variance analysis would say that for 95 parts the materials used should be 45.5 pounds, the labor should be 4.75 hours, and the machine hours should be 5.7 hours—all found by taking 95 percent of the standard amount for 100 parts.

If the company used 51 pounds of material, it exceeded the standard by 5.5 pounds and had an unfavorable quantity variance of $5.50. It also used 2.25 extra hours of labor time at $15 per hour, resulting in an unfavorable labor efficiency variance of $33.75. The machine hours exceeded the standard amount by 1.3 hours, which resulted in an unfavorable variable overhead efficiency variance of $32.50. Total variable cost quantity and efficiency variances were $71.75, all unfavorable. To summarize, the usual analysis would show:

	Standard for 95 Parts	Actual Quantity	Difference	Cost per Input	Unfavorable Variance
Materials	47.50 lbs.	51 lbs.	3.50 lbs.	$ 1.00	$ 3.50
Labor	4.75 hrs.	7 hrs.	2.25 hrs.	15.00	33.75
Variable Overhead	5.70 hrs.	7 hrs.	1.30 hrs.	25.00	32.50
Total					$69.75

However, these variances are really caused by two factors—one is working on parts that later were determined to be defective and the other is expending too many inputs for the production lot. A quality variance could be computed as follows:

	Standard for 95 Parts	Standard for 100 Parts	Difference	Cost per Input	Quality Variance
Materials	47.50 lbs.	50 lbs.	2.50 lbs.	$ 1.00	$ 2.50
Labor	4.75 hrs.	5 hrs	.25 hrs.	15.00	3.75

Variable Overhead	5.70 hrs.	6 hrs	.30 hrs.	25.00	7.50
	Total (Unfavorable)				$13.75

A "true" efficiency variance, indicating extra time worked considering the total number of parts produced, could be computed as:

	Standard for 100 Parts	Actual Quantity	Difference	Cost per Input	Efficiency Variance
Materials	50 lbs.	51 lbs.	1.00 lbs.	$ 1.00	$ 1.00
Labor	5 hrs.	7 hrs.	2.00 hrs.	15.00	30.00
Variable Overhead	6 hrs.	7 hrs.	1.00 hrs.	25.00	25.00
	Total (Unfavorable)				$56.00

Rather than having an efficiency variance indicating an unfavorable difference of $69.75, the variance really consists of two parts – $13.75 was invested in defective units, and $56 was the result of using too many labor and machine hours and too many materials.

Another way of computing the quality variance is to say that a lot of 100 parts should cost $50 for materials, $75 for labor, and $150 for variable overhead – a total of $275. If 5 percent of the parts turn out to be defective, 5 percent of the usual cost represents an unfavorable quality variance. In this case, 5 percent of $275 is $13.75.

Besides separating the quality variance from the efficiency variance, the method of computing the quality variance used here motivates managers to detect defects as early as possible in the production process. This is done by using equivalent units to compute the variance if the units are only partially finished. If the defects were discovered when the units were only half finished as to materials, labor, and overhead, the 5 lost units would count as only 2.5 equivalent units. Instead of an unfavorable quality variance of 5 percent of $275, the quality variance would be only 2.5 percent of $275, or $6.875. This is not a particularly novel approach to variances because production is always computed on the basis of equivalent units when fractional units are involved. Nevertheless it does work to decrease an unfavorable quality variance.

Fixed overhead is not considered a factor in either efficiency or quality variances because the total amount of fixed overhead should not change with the number of machine hours used or other activity factor. Although a fixed overhead efficiency variance can be computed as discussed in Chapter 4, it is recommended that only fixed overhead budget variances be used.

EVALUATING PRODUCTION LEVELS

Another consideration in the new manufacturing environment is the level of inventories. Instead of a SCS with a volume variance that motivates managers to overproduce and build up inventories, a system that encourages production levels that match sales orders is needed.

The problem with the old volume variance is that producing more than planned results in a favorable variance; it should result in an unfavorable variance. Moreover the old volume variance is concerned with fixed overhead costs. The real harm in overproducing is that the firm incurs excess variable costs. Fixed costs remain the same, at least in theory, when production levels are increased.

Assume a firm produces lawnmowers with the following costs:

Standard Cost for 21-inch Mower

Materials	$ 30.00
Labor 2 hours @ $12.00	24.00
Variable Overhead 5 machine hours @ $15.00	75.00
Standard Variable Cost	$ 129.00

Also assume the firm uses an estimate of 6,000 mowers to set its fixed overhead rate. If a volume variance were computed, it would show an unfavorable variance if the firm produced fewer than 6,000 mowers during the year. However, suppose sales orders totaled only 5,200 mowers for whatever reasons—competition, poor economic conditions, and so on. There is no point in producing more than 5,200 mowers unless there is reason to believe there will be a large inflow of orders in the next few weeks.

A production variance uses a more short-range estimate of production levels. For example, say that for the first week in February, scheduled production is 120 mowers. This production target is set because of sales orders already received or anticipated in the near future. Suppose that actual production is 150 mowers. There is a production variance of 30 mowers. At a variable cost of $129 per mower, the 30 extra mowers would cause an investment of $3,870. This would be the production variance, and it would be unfavorable because of the excess cost invested.

The real penalty for the excess production is the interest cost on the money invested in units that cannot be sold immediately. If these units have to be held for a month before they are sold and the interest cost is 1 percent per month, it is costing the company $38.70 to hold the mowers. There also are storage and handling costs that may be as much as the interest. Management should determine a reasonable interest figure and apply it to excess production to compute the penalty for holding the inventories. These figures should be included in management reports, and responsibility for this cost should be assigned.

A NEW LOOK AT PRICE AND EFFICIENCY VARIANCES

Price and efficiency variances have come under fire because many production people have come to believe that concentrating on price and efficiency has led manufacturers to ignore quality. Price, efficiency, and quality are all interrelated concerns. They are like a three-legged stool. If any one is ignored, the stool is likely to tip over. By ignoring quality the production process is out of balance. However, to ignore either price or efficiency or both will likewise tip the balance.

Price is a legitimate concern. A manufacturer cannot pay too much for materials, wages, or variable overhead factors such as supplies and indirect labor without charging customers more for the finished product. If they refuse to pay the price, the manufacturer will go out of business. Likewise, efficiency is a legitimate concern. A manufacturer cannot use too many materials or too many labor or machine hours without charging customers for the excess materials and hours. If they refuse to pay, the company will go out of business.

The problem with the way price, efficiency, and quality variances are evaluated is that they are considered separately without regard for the trade-offs involved. As a first step, the quality variance must be pulled out of the efficiency variance to indicate where quality has been sacrificed in the interests of efficiency and vice versa.

Second, price variances need to be computed on the materials used rather than purchased in order to have a comparison. Computing price variances on purchases is usually recommended because some believe the information is more timely. However, it provides no way to evaluate the trade-offs in price, quality, or efficiency. Many companies are working toward a true JIT environment in which material purchased is immediately used. When this becomes a reality, it will make no difference whether price variances are computed on materials purchased or used. However, in the meantime the differences can be significant.

Rational decisions need to be made about price, efficiency, and quality. Suppose a company can get less expensive materials but their purchase results in more defective units and more machine time spent. Will the savings in price be justified? Suppose shortcuts will decrease labor time but will result in poor quality. Will the savings in labor time be justified? Suppose going from 1 percent defects to .001 percent defects can be achieved only by significantly increasing machine hours and by purchasing higher quality materials. Is the decrease in defectives worth the effort? The managerial decisions are important. Instead of trying to assess blame for who caused an unfavorable variance, managers need to work as a team to evaluate the alternatives.

What is needed is a system that fosters competition outside the company rather than within the company. The functional division of responsibility encourages purchasing, production, finance, and marketing to pull in different directions. Just as the functional divisions in the factory are being revised, the functional divisions in management need to be redesigned. The process is already underway in some companies — more managers are being assigned to product lines. Likewise, more organizations are using the matrix form of management in which members of different functional areas work together on projects. Many difficulties generally associated with the SCS will be ameliorated when managers are encouraged to work as a team rather than find fault. In such an environment the SCS will be a useful tool for decision making.

EVALUATING FIXED AND SEMIVARIABLE MANUFACTURING COSTS

The traditional method of evaluating fixed manufacturing costs is to compute a budget or spending variance and a volume variance as discussed in Chapter 4. The budget variance measures the difference between the fixed overhead budget amount, which should not change with the level of production, and the actual spending for fixed overhead items. The volume variance measures whether the budgeted amount has been absorbed into the units produced by applying the predetermined overhead rate. It is mistakenly used as an indicator of the effect of producing or not producing at the planned level. Actually, all it does is show whether treating this fixed cost like a variable cost (applying it at a rate per unit or hour) has resulted in the right accumulation of fixed cost.

The only meaningful comparison with truly fixed costs is whether they were on target as far as the budget was concerned, and the only variance that is really necessary is a budget or spending variance. Of course, the variance needs to be broken down by expenditure.

As overhead analysis is usually done, the semivariable or mixed costs are also broken down into fixed and variable categories by looking at the historical pattern of the cost. The assumption is that these semivariable costs are linear and can neatly be divided into the two categories. Most cost accounting textbooks discuss how these semivariable costs in fact are not linear. The textbook author then ignores this reality and blithely goes on to discuss ways to break them into fixed and variable categories under the assumption they are linear.

These costs are not linear because they vary in some degree with one or more activity factors that have not been identified. The usual concept of a variable cost is that it varies with production as measured by one of the traditional activity factors, such as units produced, labor cost or hours, or machine hours. Many costs do vary but not with these particular factors. The great contribution of activity-based costing is that the proponents recognize that costs vary with many different activities or drivers. These activity factors or cost drivers may include the number of different parts in a product, the number of setups, the number of engineering changes, and a host of other factors. Some costs vary with more than one factor. Material-handling costs, for example, may vary with number of units, size, weight, and number of different materials used.

The problem with the traditional SCS is that it is too simplistic for today's conditions. Overhead is too complex for a simple breakdown of fixed costs and costs that vary with production volume. A careful analysis of each type of cost must be done to determine the cost driver or drivers. Once the analysis is done, some aggregation is usually possible. One way to aggregate is to summarize the costs that vary with the units produced, the batches, the different products, the number of processes, and the plant (Beaujon and Singhal 1990: 51–72). The individual costs can be combined into overhead cost pools, and the drivers can be summarized into the most significant activities. Some accuracy must be sacrificed in order to aggregate costs and drivers, but the process is necessary to achieve a manageable and cost-effective system. Even with such summation, the system will not be as simple as the traditional SCS.

INTEGRATING THE STANDARD COST SYSTEM WITH THE FINANCIAL ACCOUNTING SYSTEM

After looking at both production and marketing variances, the question is how to integrate these variances into the financial accounting system. However, it should first be asked whether integration is really necessary at all. Most new systems of performance measurement do not articulate at all with the financial accounting records. They are stand-alone systems. If they are doing all right without integration into the financial accounting system, why worry about integrating the SCS?

The problem is that such stand-alone systems are not necessarily doing that well. They arose to meet a need that standard cost systems were not meeting; as such, they were superior to what was in place. However, the nonintegrated system tends to be redundant and sometimes conflicts with the financial accounting system. Moreover, there is no feedback to update the plans, budgets, and standards for the next period. It could be argued that the financial and managerial accounting systems need the SCS, even if the SCS does not need financial and managerial accounting.

How should the variances discussed in this chapter be integrated into the financial accounting system? In the traditional system the work in process and finished goods inventory accounts and cost of goods sold are carried at standard cost multiplied by actual units (or equivalent units for fractionally complete units). Price and efficiency variances are recognized before the units are placed in work in process.

The new system also recognizes quality and production variances. The quality variance is really a division of the efficiency variance and can be recognized before the units are placed in work in process. However, the production variance represents a difference from scheduled production rather than actual production. Likewise, marketing variances are recognized when products are sold. The problem then is that these new variances occur further downstream than the traditional price and efficiency variances.

Figure 5.1
Updated Production Cost Variances

Example:

Inputs (pounds):

Actual pounds purchased	5,500
Actual pounds used in production	4,900
Standard pounds per finished unit	2
Standard price per pound	$1.00
Actual price per pound	$1.10

Outputs (finished units):

Scheduled production	2,000
Total production	2,500
Good units produced	2,400
Defective units	100

Standard cost per unit: 2 pounds @ $1.00 = $2.00

Input analysis:

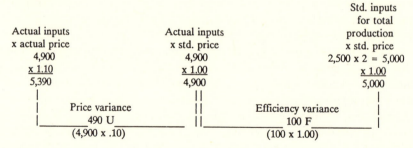

Actual inputs x actual price	Actual inputs x std. price	Std. inputs for total production x std. price
4,900	4,900	2,500 x 2 = 5,000
x 1.10	x 1.00	x 1.00
5,390	4,900	5,000

Price variance
490 U
(4,900 x .10)

Efficiency variance
100 F
(100 x 1.00)

Output analysis:

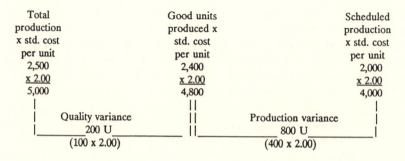

Total production x std. cost per unit	Good units produced x std. cost per unit	Scheduled production x std. cost per unit
2,500	2,400	2,000
x 2.00	x 2.00	x 2.00
5,000	4,800	4,000

Quality variance
200 U
(100 x 2.00)

Production variance
800 U
(400 x 2.00)

The difficulty can be resolved by recognizing price, quality, and efficiency variances before the products are recorded in work in process, which would require recording work in process at the standard variable cost of the *actual* units. Then the production variance can be recognized before the products are recorded in finished goods. This would require that finished goods inventory be carried at the standard variable cost of the *scheduled* units. The production variance or excess inventory can be shown in a separate account to highlight the effects of carrying unneeded inventories.

AN ILLUSTRATION OF THE SCS INTEGRATED WITH THE FINANCIAL ACCOUNTING SYSTEM

An illustration of the treatment of variable production cost variances is given in Figure 5.1. In this example inputs are measured in pounds, which would imply the illustration is for materials. However, *pounds* is intended as a generic term for any type of variable input, whether materials, labor, or variable overhead.

As discussed earlier in the chapter, the variances are updated to reflect the concerns of the new manufacturing environment. The price variance is computed on the inputs used rather than purchased (as would traditionally be done with materials) because it allows a better evaluation of the trade-offs between price and efficiency or quality. The efficiency variance contrasts the actual quantity of inputs with the required inputs for all production, whether the result is defective units or good units. In this case 2,500 total units were produced with 4,900 inputs, resulting in a favorable efficiency variance. The traditional system would have computed the efficiency variance based on the 2,400 good units produced, resulting in an unfavorable efficiency variance because the defective units were not included.

The system illustrated in Figure 5.1 highlights the quality variance by separating it from the efficiency variance. The 100 defective units result in an unfavorable quality variance. In addition there is an unfavorable production variance because 400 excess units were produced. A useful way to divide the analysis is to view the price and efficiency variances as input variances and the quality and production variances as output variances. It is necessary to compute the input variances for each element of cost, but the output variances may be computed on the basis of the total variable cost per unit, including materials, labor, and variable overhead taken together. This simplifies the computation of the output variances.

The journal entries for the variances are given in Figure 5.2. The updated system is contrasted with the usual SCS. In the traditional system the material price variance would ordinarily be computed on materials purchased and entered when the materials are purchased. The updated system computes the price variance on the materials used in production and enters the variance

Figure 5.2
Journal Entries for Variances

Traditional standard cost	Updated standard cost

Materials   5,500
Price variance   550
   Accounts payable   6,050
To record purchase of materials.
	Materials 6,050
	   Accounts payable 6,050
	To record purchase of materials.

Work in process   4,800
Efficiency variance   100
   Materials   4,900
To record materials used.
	Work in process 4,800
	Price variance 490
	Quality variance 200
	   Efficiency variance 100
	   Materials 5,390
	To record materials used.

Finished goods   4,800
   Work in process   4,800
To record completed production.
	Production variance
	   or Excess finished
	   goods inventory 800
	Scheduled finished
	   goods inventory 4,000
	      Work in process 4,800
	To record completed production.

Cost of goods sold   650*
   Price variance   550
   Efficiency variance   100
To close variances at end of
accounting period.
	Cost of goods sold 590
	Efficiency variance 100
	   Price variance 490
	   Quality variance 200
	To close variances at end of
	accounting period.

*A more accurate method would
close $60 of the price variance
to the materials account because
600 pounds remain in the materials
account for which there is a $.10
per pound variance.

as the materials go into work in process. (This is an option under the traditional system too.) The efficiency and quality variances are also computed as the inputs are used and entered into work in process. This results in an entry to work in process that represents the good units produced at the standard variable cost. The same amount would be entered in work in process under the traditional system.

The traditional SCS transfers this same amount to finished goods. The updated system only transfers the scheduled amount of production to finished goods, which is retitled "Scheduled Finished Goods Inventory." The production variance, representing the extra 400 units produced, is placed in a production variance or excess inventory account. As long as this account carries a debit balance, it is considered an asset and is listed among the inventories on the balance sheet.

When finished goods are sold, the scheduled finished goods account should be credited as long as units of a particular item are in the regular account. The excess inventory or production variance account should be used only as inventory levels are normalized. In other words, as long as excess units of an item are on hand they should remain in the excess account.

A more radical system would record the entry in the following fashion:

Dr. Finished goods	4,800	
Dr. Production variance	800	
Cr. Work in process		4,800
Cr. Excess inventories		800

This entry records the excess inventories as a liability rather than an asset. The production variance is closed out at the end of the accounting period, but the excess inventories account is carried as a liability until inventory levels are normalized. This type of entry is even more in line with the thinking of the new manufacturing environment, which views excess inventories as negative.

No matter which entry is used, the amount of the production variance in each period and the excess inventories carried should be highlighted in managerial accounting reports. Furthermore the interest cost on carrying the excess inventories should be computed and included in the reports.

The last entry in Figure 5.2 shows how the variances are closed out at the end of the year. In both cases the more expedient method of closing to cost of goods sold is used rather than prorating the variances among cost of goods sold and inventory accounts. In the updated system the production variance is not closed out as the other variances are because this variance really represents excess inventory, which is treated as an asset.

ALTERNATE APPROACH FOR MATERIAL VARIANCES

Some companies are further into the new manufacturing environment than others. For those companies that have a true JIT system for raw mate-

Figure 5.3
Updated Material Variances

Example:

Inputs (pounds):

Actual pounds ordered	5,600
Actual pounds purchased	5,500
Actual pounds used in production	5,300
Standard pounds per finished unit	2
Standard price per pound	$1.00
Actual price per pound	$1.10

Outputs (finished units):

Total production	2,500

Ordering and Price Variances:

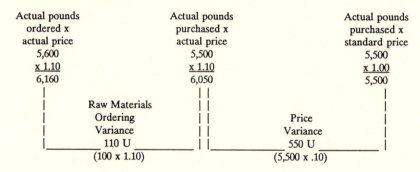

Inventory and Efficiency (Quantity) Variances:

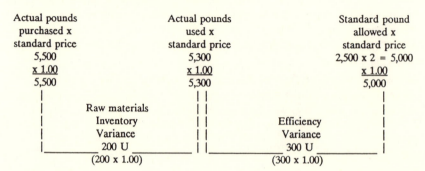

rials inventory, the approach for analyzing material input variances presented in Figure 5.3 is recommended. This format was designed by Horace W. Harrell of Georgia Southern University (1992: 33–38) and is changed here to the extent that total production rather than total good production is used to compute the efficiency (quantity) variance. This is to allow computation of a quality variance as discussed in the previous section. Harrell's approach yields a raw materials ordering variance and raw materials inventory variance in addition to the more traditional price and efficiency (quantity) variances.

The raw materials ordering variance shows the difference between the raw materials ordered and those actually delivered (purchased). Dependable deliveries are crucial to the JIT system, and this variance indicates deviations from the expected amounts. Any variance is considered unfavorable, whether too much or too little is delivered because the goal of JIT is to have exactly the right amount. Too much delivered is unfavorable because it builds up unnecessary inventories. Too little delivered is also unfavorable because delays in production may result.

The price variance shows the difference in price paid and the expected or standard price. In this case the price variance is computed on materials purchased. If a company is approaching a true JIT system, the amount purchased will be very close to the amount used; there is less advantage to computing the price variance on material used, as discussed earlier in the chapter.

The raw materials inventory variance shows materials purchased that were not used or usage of more materials than were purchased in the current period. Purchasing more than is needed for production is counter to the JIT philosophy. If the variance indicates more purchased than used, the variance is unfavorable. On the other hand, if more is used than currently purchased, the usage of excess inventories is favorable. To highlight the effects of an unfavorable raw materials inventory variance in responsibility reports, a cost of capital figure could be applied to the amount to indicate the cost to the company of maintaining excess amounts.

Finally, the efficiency or quantity variance indicates the deviation from standard quantities. In this case the computation was based on total production, including any defective units, to show true efficiency (or lack of efficiency). The effects of work on any units later found to be defective would appear as a quality variance as discussed earlier in this chapter.

INTEGRATING FIXED AND SEMIVARIABLE COST VARIANCES INTO THE FINANCIAL ACCOUNTING SYSTEM

As discussed earlier in this chapter, fixed and semivariable overhead costs present a special challenge in the new manufacturing environment. The historical view has been to quantify these costs on a per-unit or per-hour basis even when there was no reason to believe they varied with volume. To treat them as such satisfies the tax and external regulatory bodies, but it significantly lessens the value of the information for decision-making purposes. However, to the extent that semivariable costs vary with some factor, it is possible to compute price and efficiency variances as they pertain to that factor. It is also possible to compute budget variances for the fixed overhead expenditures.

In the new manufacturing environment more companies are producing only to meet sales orders. Therefore any expenses that vary with some aspect of individual orders—per-unit or per-batch expenses—can be identified with an order. In the new environment more companies also are dividing their plants into work cells with more expenses treated as direct rather than indirect. This factor works in favor of being able to identify overhead expenses with a particular order or product line.

Many actual overhead expenses can be assigned to a particular order or product line. Whether it is cost beneficial to develop standards and compute variances for semivariable overhead expenses depends upon the company and its situation. Companies with repeat orders of similar characteristics may find it beneficial to do so. Others may find the increased information is not worth the effort or cost. Many organizations are beginning new types of manufacturing operations. In this development phase, there likely will not be enough continuity to develop standards.

The best treatment of truly fixed overhead, as far as financial statements are concerned, would seem to be accumulating the actual costs and allocating these costs between inventories and cost of goods sold at the end of the period. To make other assumptions about per-unit or per-order costs that do not reflect reality is dangerous for decision-making purposes.

The traditional SCS has been criticized on the grounds it measures the wrong variables and encourages managers to take actions that are counterproductive. The updated SCS discussed in this chapter measures quality and production levels as well as price and efficiency. In addition it can measure raw materials ordering variances and raw materials inventory variances. These measures are integrated into the financial accounting system with work in process carried at the usual value of actual units at standard cost. Excess finished goods inventories are separated from scheduled inventories.

REFERENCES

Beaujon, George J., and Vinod R. Singhal. "Understanding the Activity Costs in an Activity-Based Cost System," *Journal of Cost Management.* Spring 1990, pp. 51–72.

Harrell, Horace W. "Materials Variance Analysis and JIT: A New Approach," *Management Accounting.* May 1992, pp. 33–38.

Rayburn, L. Gayle. *Principles of Cost Accounting.* Homewood, Ill.: Richard D. Irwin, 1989.

CHAPTER 6

Measuring the Right Variables: Performance Measures

The traditional standard cost system tended to be inflexible, stressing factors such as price and efficiency over quality, inventory levels, and other concerns of the new manufacturing environment. However, an updated standard cost system (USCS) or cost management system can encompass these variables as well as others that seem to be important. The standard cost system merely sets standards for what performance should be. In this context it is possible to set benchmarks or goals for any activity in the organization that needs improvement.

Within the overall framework of the USCS is room for a variety of performance measures. Classification of performance measures is difficult because many are industry-specific or even unique to particular companies, and many areas overlap. For example, a metric related to quality of incoming raw materials may be considered a measure related to quality control, material control, or inventory control. The groupings in this chapter will follow the categories in Garrison's *Managerial Accounting* textbook: (1) quality control measures, (2) material control measures, (3) inventory control measures, (4) machine performance measures, and (5) delivery performance measures (1991: 376).

After performance measures for the individual areas are examined, the chapter will present an integrated system for several measures. A final section will discuss development of an overall strategy for using performance measures.

The reader is urged to view the individual performance measures as a smorgasbord of possibilities for an organization. It is not intended that any company apply all, or even most, of the measures. It is generally counterproductive to expect any group of workers or supervisors to try to work on any more than five or six measures at any one time. For example, at the Trane Company's new plant in Pueblo, Colorado, managers selected six measures that they felt would be clearly understood, could be readily calculated, and were truly global. They selected sales per employee, inventory turnover, customer services costs as a percentage of sales, manufacturing cycle time, the on-time shipping percentage, and return on net assets (Clements and Spoede 1992: 50–52).

The measures in this chapter should be used as a starting point for developing the unique yardsticks that will measure the variables important to a specific management strategy.

QUALITY CONTROL MEASURES

Quality control costs (QCC) are not a homogeneous group of costs. QCC may be divided into five groups of costs with different characteristics. First is a group that may be classified as design costs. The product and the process should be designed and tested to prevent poor quality. These costs generally occur before the product is ever produced, although engineering changes may be made later.

Another group relates to inspection of the product during or after production. These are the costs that are more traditionally associated with quality control.

Still another group relates to product failure. These costs include the cost of scrap and rework as well as losses due to selling the poor quality units at reduced prices.

A fourth group relates to process failure. When production is interrupted or slowed because of poor quality, costs are incurred for machine down time, high setup times, implementation of engineering changes, and idle workers.

Finally, the fifth category relates to customer dissatisfaction. These costs include warranty costs, service costs, sales returns and allowances, lawsuits, and lost sales.

In traditional accounting systems all these costs are not captured in the accounting model (lost sales, for example), and many that are captured are not associated with quality (machine down time, idle time of workers, etc.). Moreover traditional performance measures are frequently counterproductive as far as quality is concerned. Production quotas and the cost of line shutdowns foster (if anything) efficiency rather than quality.

In devising new measures it is important to guard against the same mistake of designing measures that lead to counterproductive behavior as far as quality or other company goals are concerned. For example, a company seeking to measure and minimize the lead time for designing and engineering a product should not do so at the expense of quality.

Keeping this in mind, the following performance measures are suggested for the design stage: number of engineering changes, severity of engineering changes (i.e., class 1 or major), results of testing such as first pass reject rate, and parts standardization measures such as number of products, options per product, and the percentage of common parts per product. Measures relating to product complexity might include on a per-product basis the number of components, number of manufacturing operations, number of tools required, and the life/cost of tooling (McNair, Mosconi, and Norris 1988: 199–201).

Other costs are associated with the inspection process but are not to be confused with the costs associated with the rejected units. The new manufacturing environment recognizes that inspection per se is not a value-adding activity. Therefore inspection should be minimized if it can be done without sacrificing quality. Measures of the inspection process include time required for sample/test procedures, production time lost due to inspection procedures/queues, number of checkpoints, and number of returned units (McNair, Mosconi, and Norris 1988: 201).

For costs associated with product failure, some of the more traditional performance measures, such as cost of rework, cost of scrap, and loss due to defective units, can be used. Statistical quality control measures such as X-bar and R charts also are applicable. Number of defects, quantity of scrap, and first time pass rate are quality measures that can be used. Percentage of first time pass rate (yield) is also a common measure. A variation on this is measuring the time it takes to cut the defect rate in half.

Kaplan and Atkinson describe a system in which a measure called *quality scrap* was used. The measure was calculated as material issued at standard minus material scheduled for production at standard, multiplied by a labor and overhead factor. The labor and overhead factor represented the amount of labor and overhead costs incurred in the assembly up to the point at which the unit was scrapped (1989: 403).

Still another group of quality costs relates to process failure. One measure of process failure is the number of engineering change orders. Another is the estimated percentage of actual manufacturing/process engineering expenses spent on internal failure (Kaplan and Atkinson 1989: 404). Still others would include the time lost due to process failure and cost of idle time of workers. Where process failure results in high setup times, measures of setup time may be appropriate.

The final group of quality costs relates to customer dissatisfaction. Performance measures in this area include number and cost of warranty claims, cost of lawsuits and liability claims, service costs, and sales returns and allowances. Some companies survey customers to detect problems and measure satisfaction.

MATERIALS CONTROL MEASURES

The next group of performance measures relates to materials control. The emphasis used to be on material prices, and the material price variance was the main measure of success in materials acquisition. Today the emphasis is on purchasing quality materials and eliminating or drastically reducing lead time to acquire them. While not ignored, price is not considered as important as it once was. Therefore three types of performance measures relate to materials control—quality measures, time measures, and cost measures.

As to quality, suggested measures are scrap as a percentage of good pieces, scrap as a percentage of total cost, and actual scrap loss (Garrison 1991: 376). Some companies work with their vendors to establish qualified or certified vendors—those vendors whose performance histories show their quality and delivery time meet specified criteria. In those companies a quality measure is the ratio of qualified or certified vendors to total vendors. Another measurement is rejected lots to total lots, specifically, the percentage of lots rejected to total lots inspected per incoming inspection data (Duffy 1990). Returns to vendor and returns pending disposition may also be examined.

Suggested time measures include lead time from supplier, computed as the interval between placement and receipt of an order. This may be computed by supplier and by type of material (Garrison 1991: 377). Other metrics related to time would include late deliveries, on-time deliveries, back orders, and canceled orders. Transportation lead time may also be significant for some companies (McNair, Mosconi, and Norris 1988: 251–252). Flexibility of suppliers may be indicated by vendor lead times on new orders or vendor response times on increased order quantities (Brown 1990).

The cost of materials may be measured using the traditional price variance of the standard cost system. Other measures might include the cost of materials to total manufacturing cost or to total product cost. Other metrics might include average investment in raw materials inventory, investment in safety stock, and lot sizes. Material-related costs such as freight-in, receiving, inspecting, and handling can be measured in dollar amounts or as a percentage of total materials costs. For companies trying to simplify their production process, the number of stocking locations may be a metric that indicates the degree of complexity as well as cost.

INVENTORY CONTROL MEASURES

Inventory control measures are related to the investment in inventory as well as the time it is held. Investment and time are, of course, interrelated.

The longer inventory is held, the greater the cost of the investment. Other measures may relate to decreasing the number of items inventoried for the sake of simplifying the production process. Still other measures may relate to minimizing inventory-related costs.

The traditional inventory measure is turnover, and this is still valid. Days or weeks of supply in raw materials is another measure used in many companies. Safety stock in dollars, number of items, or as a percentage of total inventory are good measures of the permanent inventory investment. Weeks cost of sales in inventory is a macro measure that gives much the same information as turnover. Excess over target inventory in dollars or units may be helpful. Finished goods over 90 days is a measure of excess investment used in some companies (McNair, Mosconi, and Norris 1988: 117).

Related to simplifying the production process through inventory reduction, the number of different items in inventory may be computed. Other metrics might be the number of components per finished product, the number of options per product and the percentage of common parts per product (McNair, Mosconi, and Norris 1988: 199–200). Still other measures might be the number of stocking locations for raw materials, the number of stockpiles of work in process inventories, and the dollar investment or units of work in process stockpiled throughout the production area.

Various measures of inventory-related costs may also be computed. The cost of capital invested in inventory or in excess inventories is a significant metric that calls management's attention to the interest cost of holding these inventories. Costs of insurance and property taxes on inventories, costs of rent (real or imputed) on storage facilities and material-handling equipment, and other inventory-related costs can be viewed in dollar amounts or as percentages of sales, cost of sales, or total inventory investment.

MACHINE PERFORMANCE MEASURES

Various measures relate to efficiency in the production process. Updated efficiency variances that do not combine quality and efficiency factors can be helpful. Other than the more traditional measures, updated measures associated with productive processing time, value-adding activities, and throughput are relevant. In another section of this chapter several of these measures will be integrated into a cohesive system for evaluating the production process.

In most production processes the product spends a great deal of time in queue and being moved. A useful measure of the productivity of the process is the actual processing time divided by the available processing time to get the percentage of productive processing time or what some refer to as "up time." This metric can be applied to departments, work cells, or an entire plant's operation. Moving the product can also be measured by distance or times moved.

Eliminating nonvalue-adding activities is also a goal in many manufacturing operations. Besides minimizing idle time and queue time, time spent in activities such as setup are being reduced. Metrics such as percentage of total production time spent in value-adding activities can be determined. Percentage of time spent in total nonvalue-adding activities or percentage of time spent in specific nonvalue-adding activities can be computed. Average time per setup or other nonvalue-adding activity may be calculated.

Various measures of throughput may also be relevant. Throughput can be measured in terms of units put through the process or in terms of cycle time. Such measures can be applied to the production process as a whole or to departments or cells. In organizations coping with bottlenecks, the bottleneck capacity may be a significant variable along with the percentage use of bottleneck equipment.

For companies proceeding toward automation, an interesting statistic may be the hours of automation per product. Equipment breakdowns may be appraised by using the number of occurrences of unscheduled maintenance, productive time lost due to equipment malfunction, or mean time for repairing equipment failures. A skilled work force is also essential in an automated environment. Metrics related to the workers might include average number of jobs workers are qualified to perform and the percentage of workers qualified to perform a certain number of jobs (Brown 1990).

DELIVERY PERFORMANCE MEASURES

The two basic groups of delivery performance measures relate to time and overall customer satisfaction. Was the product delivered on time and did it meet the customer's needs? Reliability and consistency are customer considerations that relate to both time and customer needs. Can the company be counted on to consistently deliver orders on time and can it consistently meet customer needs? Obviously, delivery performance measures overlap many of the other performance measurements. The time it takes to deliver the product may depend upon materials control, inventory controls, and machine performance. Customer satisfaction may depend upon quality.

The time it takes to deliver a product to the customer may be broken down into the time it takes to receive the order, start production (some of which may be consumed in ordering and receiving raw materials necessary for the order), process the order, prepare it for shipment, and transport it to the customer. Receiving the order and transporting it to the customer may be out of the company's control. However, from the customer's standpoint these are part of the total time.

As measures of time Garrison suggests percentage of on-time deliveries, delivery cycle time (time from receipt of an order to shipment), throughput time or velocity (time to convert raw materials to completed products), order backlog, and total throughput. He also suggests use of the manufacturing cycle efficiency (MCE) measure computed as:

$$MCE = \frac{\text{Value-added time}}{\text{Throughput time}}$$

(1991: 376–380).

Other measures related to time might include late deliveries, on-time deliveries, and canceled orders (McNair, Mosconi, and Norris 1988: 206). Metrics can involve the number of orders, dollar value of orders (cost or sales prices), or invoice lines.

Analog Devices has several performance measures that it computes in terms of how long it takes to cut an undesirable rate in half (half life). Some of Analog's customer service measures related to delivery time are percentage of shipments late, early, and on time. It also uses measures related to the amount of time early or late, months to ship late backlog, excess lead times, and time to schedule an order (Lynch 1990).

Other measures suggested by Thomas Brown of Unisys include percentage of the master production schedule achieved, number of past due items per work unit or department, customer order entry and administrative time, manufacturing lead time by product line, vendor lead times on new orders, and vendor response time on increased order quantities (1990).

Customer satisfaction measures may include dollar value, number, or invoice lines of returns. Warranty costs, travel costs related to warranty costs, and liability claims may also relate to customer satisfaction. Others may include number of repeat buyers, number of customer complaints, market share, and product image among target customers (Keegan, Eiler, and Jones 1989: 48). A variety of measures may be gleaned from customer surveys.

AN INTEGRATED SYSTEM OF PERFORMANCE MEASUREMENT

Many measures related to quality, time, and machine performance are interrelated. If these metrics can be integrated in a total system, measurement becomes much easier and eliminates conflicting goals. An analogy in the financial measures area would be the system of measuring return on investment first used by DuPont, in which capital turnover, earnings as a percentage of sales, and return on investment are interrelated (Johnson and Kaplan 1987: 85).

The system presented here was devised by the authors and first published in the March 1990 *Journal of Accountancy*. It can be applied to work cells, departments, product lines, or to the production process as a whole. The interrelated measures are shown in Figure 6.1.

Figure 6.1
Throughput Measures

Productive capacity	x	Percentage of productive processing time	x	Yield	=	Throughput: good units produced per time period
Total units / Processing time	x	Processing time / Total time	x	Good units / Total units	=	Good units / Total time

Example:

Good units produced	14,700
Total units started	15,000
Processing time (hours)	500
Total time (hours)	1,000

15,000 / 500	x	500 / 1,000	x	14,700 / 15,000	=	14,700 / 1,000
30 units	x	50%	x	98%	=	14.7 units

Productive capacity is found by dividing total units started by processing time. This represents an optimistic view of what production could be if all time were productive and if all units were good units. It is related to maximum or theoretical capacity. However, maximum or theoretical capacity is a long-run concept that is applied to annual production amounts. Productive capacity is very short run. It can be related to hours, days, or weeks but would probably not be used with any longer time periods. In Figure 6.1 the company could produce thirty units an hour under ideal conditions.

Percentage of productive processing time (PPT) relates to value-adding time spent on the product. It is found by dividing processing time by total time. Processing time is time spent in actual production and excludes wait time, move time, setups, inspection, and any nonvalue-adding activities. Total time is the total processing time possible, considering the number of shifts worked, usual work week, holidays, and so on. In the Figure 6.1 the company had 50 percent PPT, which is good. Many companies spend far less time in actual processing.

Yield is found by dividing good units produced by total units started. It is a measure of quality output. Good units would ordinarily be those that passed inspection on the first try, although it could include some reworked units if they were reworked immediately and the company wanted to use this variation of the measure. The example shows 14,700 good units produced from 15,000 started, a yield of 98 percent.

Productive capacity, PPT, and yield may be multiplied together to get throughput, defined as good units produced per time period. Alternately, throughput may be obtained by dividing good units by total time. Throughput is productive capacity adjusted for nonvalue-adding activities and defective units. In Figure 6.1, 14,700 units were produced in 1,000 hours, a throughput of 14.7 units per hour.

Some may argue that they would rather work at minimizing time than maximizing throughput. Note that the inverse of throughput measured in this fashion (total time divided by good units) is average cycle time. If a company strives to increase throughput, it will automatically be reducing its average cycle time.

This system can be used to maximize the throughput by increasing any one of the other three measures. In other words, increasing productive capacity, PPT, or yield will improve throughput. Any one of the measures can be improved by either increasing the numerator or decreasing the denominator.

To increase productive capacity, for example, company management may work to adjust batch sizes, improve the plant layout, eliminate bottlenecks, increase labor and equipment efficiency, or change the product design. To improve PPT, efforts to decrease queue time, move time, or down time may be effective. Other nonvalue-adding activities such as inspection and rework may be minimized. The quality of materials and workmanship may be enhanced to increase yield. Design features and tolerances may be adjusted. The focus of responsibility may be changed from an inspection team to the workers themselves.

Goals may be set for productive capacity, PPT, and yield in terms of improvements over last period's performance, best performance to date, an external benchmark, or simply a target set by management. In this fashion a framework is provided for overall improvement.

USING PERFORMANCE MEASURES
IN AN OVERALL STRATEGY

It is generally true that you get what you measure. Therefore managers need to be careful that the performance measures selected will motivate workers, supervisors, and middle managers to take actions that will assist in achieving company goals. Using performance measures can result in dysfunctional behavior if it causes one segment of the organization to pursue one set of goals while another segment concentrates on another set. For example, if the sales department emphasizes product variety while the production department emphasizes simplifying production by decreasing the number of product lines and increasing the number of interchangeable parts, conflicts are inevitable.

Strategy Development

Developing strategy is the responsibility of upper-level management. Strategic plans should include a mission statement, overall goals or objectives, policies, and actions. Performance measures become the devices for determining whether the actions are leading to the goals that management intends.

In developing an overall strategy management should consider the environment in which the organization operates, including its opportunities and its competition. In the past many companies have had an internal focus almost exclusively. The gauge of how well they were doing included only whether they were doing better than previous time periods and were satisfying their stockholders. This focus is too narrow. Some companies that operated this way successfully for many years quickly folded when faced with aggressive competitors with new products, shorter lead times, or some other advantage.

To be effective, strategy must consider the externalities of customers and competitors. Customers must be satisfied or they will turn to competitors who can better provide for their needs. It does little good to be efficient at producing a product that customers do not want (the *buggy whip syndrome*).

Once the externalities of the market are considered, the focus can become internal to the extent that the organization must view its unique resources. Most companies do one or more things better than their competition, or they can do so if they use their resources to the greatest advantage.

Out of this process of self-examination, managers should devise particular actions that will lead their organization toward their goals or objectives. Performance measurements then become the measuring rods to determine whether the actions are being implemented and whether they are effective.

Selecting Performance Measures

Selecting performance measures is not an easy process. Developing a good system requires considerable knowledge of all parts of the business and an appreciation for the motivational aspects of performance measures. The following suggestions may be helpful in selecting the unique measures that will guide a company to a successful strategy:

Measures should correlate with the outcomes desired. In selecting performance measures, the ones that correlate best with the desired outcomes should be chosen. Earlier material in this chapter gives a wealth of ways to measure most types of performance. Some will suit a particular company better than others. For example, it does very little good to institute strict quality control measures in the manufacturing area if the problem is really in product design or in the materials purchased.

Sometimes the intuitive connection between the measure and the outcome are obvious. Other times a statistical correlation analysis may be helpful in determining the best measure.

If the company has certain sacred cow measures that have only historical significance, these should be discarded in favor of updated measures that focus on current goals.

Number of measures should be limited. An overambitious performance measurement system will diffuse efforts. The most effective systems will have any one group of workers or managers concentrating on only about five or six measures. Composite measures are useful because they measure a variety of actions without losing focus.

Sometimes the simplest measures are the best. One automobile manufacturer seeking to obtain high quality, low cost, and being first to market focused on one key performance measurement — number of part numbers. It found that more part numbers meant quality problems and a longer time to market. Furthermore number of part numbers was a significant cost driver (Grady 1991: 50).

Measures should be cost effective. The cost-benefit ratio of any measurement should be considered. If the information for the measure is so difficult or costly to obtain that it is not worth the trouble, it should be discarded in favor of another measure that will approximate the same results.

A food processor concerned with the amount of spoilage in the production process instituted a "garbage report" to be completed by the shift supervisor daily. Accumulating and measuring the spoiled food products proved to be time-consuming and was resented by the supervisors. It was discontinued, replaced later by a system that used the weights and measures of good product, most of which were already done in the usual course of the cooking and canning operation.

Measures should be timely. Measures that can only be accumulated infrequently do not motivate as well as those that are more timely. Japanese companies have put clocks on assembly lines to indicate down time. The clocks are set for 12:00 at the beginning of the shift. The clock runs whenever the line is stopped. The plant manager, supervisors, and workers can tell at a glance how long the line was out of operation (Grady 1991: 53).

Rapid feedback in the production area is essential when throughput times are being reduced to a minimum. If performance measures are not timely, they risk being of historical significance only as the batch of production to which they apply moves out of production and on to the customer. Measures that once were done on a monthly or weekly basis must be done daily or continuously to be relevant.

Of course, as measures become more aggregate and are applied to higher levels of management, the need for rapid feedback diminishes. Measuring return on investment for corporate management might be done quarterly or annually in contrast to yield or machine down time, which might be done daily or continuously.

At least some measures should be crossfunctional. One defect in standard cost systems as they used to be administered is that they fostered competition rather than cooperation. The purchasing department would strive for favorable price variances while production tried to have favorable quantity and efficiency variances. If the purchasing department bought low quality materials to obtain a favorable price variance, production had difficulty avoiding unfavorable quantity and efficiency variances. USCSs need to foster cooperation between functions.

If low cost is recognized as a company strategy, certainly the price of materials is a consideration. However, the purchasing department is by no means the only department involved. Purchasing, production, engineering, and finance are also affected. Measures that encourage cooperation would include raw materials and work in process inventory turnovers, average investment in raw materials and work in process inventories, and cost of materials to total product cost. The price variance is also valid but cannot be viewed without reference to the trade-offs between price and quality.

Most strategies will be crossfunctional. For example, a strategy to improve delivery time will involve at least production, production scheduling, purchasing, and marketing. Metrics such as on-time deliveries, late deliveries, order backlog, canceled orders, and delivery cycle time are crossfunctional. In some cases the crossfunctional measures can be supplemented by measures that target a particular area. For example, delivery cycle time can be broken down into time to schedule an order, manufacturing throughput time, and days to ship.

Measures should have a valid basis of comparison. To be motivational tools, performance measures need a valid basis of comparison. One obvious method is to track the measure over time to see if the organization has bettered its own performance. Comparisons can be made with the previous time period, the performance of the same period last year, or the best performance to date. Benchmarking has become very popular with some strong companies to compare their performances with industry leaders'. Management can also set its own goals based on any of the previously mentioned standards of comparison or on target returns to investors.

Measures should be more specific on lower levels. As in other facets of organizational control, measures at the higher levels of the organization should be more aggregate and broader in scope than at the lower levels. Lower-level measures will tend to be quite specific to the organizational area. Financial or dollar-related measures will be more prevalent at the upper levels while quantity measures will be more prevalent at the lower levels.

In an interesting article titled "Linking the Shop Floor to the Top Floor," Beischel and Smith give the example that corporate management might be interested in return on assets while the vice president of manufacturing would look at inventory days, output to equipment dollars, and output to square feet occupied. At a somewhat lower level the plant manager might consider manufacture cycle time, finished goods inventory in days, and days of vendor lead time. At the lowest level the department manager would have measures of machine down time, percentage of good output to total output, and number of unplanned schedule changes (1991: 26).

》   《

In the new manufacturing environment many production and quality control people have become so disillusioned with the traditional standard cost system that they advocate doing away with it entirely and replacing it with free-standing performance measures. Obviously, this is an extreme approach. Within the context of an updated standard cost system, performance measures have a place — some are free-standing and some are integrated into the accounting system.

This chapter contains a catalog of specific performance measures because the literature on the subject tends toward generalities. However, remember that overall company strategy needs to be considered when devising a system of performance measurement. Once the company's mission and goals have been established, performance measures can be devised to evaluate progress toward the goals.

REFERENCES

Beischel, Mark E., and K. Richard Smith. "Linking the Shop Floor to the Top Floor," *Management Accounting*. October 1991, pp. 25–29.

Brown, Thomas. "Measuring and Controlling Production Strategically." Presentation at Performance Measurement for Manufacturers Seminar, Institute for International Research, Chicago, October 24–25, 1990.

Cheatham, Carole. "Measuring and Improving Throughput," *Journal of Accountancy*. March 1990, pp. 89–91.

Clements, Ronald B., and Charlene W. Spoede. "Trane's SOUP Accounting," *Management Accounting*. June 1992, pp. 46–52.

Duffy, Betty. "Developing Performance Measures for Manufacturing: The Hill-Rom Case Study." Presentation at Performance Measurement for Manufacturers Seminar, Institute for International Research, Chicago, October 24–25, 1990.

Garrison, Ray H. *Managerial Accounting, Concepts for Planning, Control, Decision Making*. Homewood, Ill.: Richard D. Irwin, 1991.

Grady, Michael W. "Performance Measurement: Implementing Strategy," *Management Accounting*. June 1991, pp. 49–53.

Johnson, H. Thomas, and Robert S. Kaplan. *Relevance Lost: The Rise and Fall of Management Accounting*. Boston: Harvard Business School Press, 1987.

Kaplan, Robert S., and Anthony A. Atkinson. *Advanced Management Accounting*. Englewood Cliffs, N.J.: Prentice-Hall, 1989.

Keegan, Daniel P., Robert G. Eiler, and Charles R. Jones, "Are Your Performance Measures Obsolete?" *Management Accounting*. June 1989, pp. 45–50.

Lynch, Richard L. "Promoting Organizational Learning through Performance Measurement." Presentation at Performance Measurement for Manufacturers Seminar, Institute for International Research, Chicago, October 24–25, 1990.

McNair, C. J., William Mosconi, and Thomas Norris. *Meeting the Technology Challenge: Cost Accounting in a JIT Environment*. Montvale, N.J.: National Association of Accountants, 1988.

CHAPTER 7

Identifying Cost Drivers

The general definition of a *cost driver* is whatever causes a cost to occur. Romano, for example, says that cost drivers "represent the cause and effect relationship between a specific activity and a set of costs." He divides them into those used to split up resources between activity centers and cost pools within activity centers (first stage cost drivers) and those used to split cost pools between products (second stage cost drivers) (1990: 56).

Although there is agreement on the general definition of a cost driver, the definition may be viewed in a broad, theoretical sense or in a narrow sense. Raffish includes among cost drivers such items as lack of technical supervision, chemical contamination, excessive quality verification, and material review board activities (1991: 38). While these are cost drivers in the general sense, it would be difficult to use them in a cost management system. How does one measure, for example, lack of technical supervision? In order to be operational, cost drivers must be capable of being quantified. Quantifiable cost drivers include such items as number of setups, number of parts, lot sizes, engineering hours, and so on.

Some authors do not distinguish activities from cost drivers. The Garrison textbook says "an activity is any event or transaction that is a cost driver — that is, that acts as a causal factor in the incurrence of cost in an organization" (1991: 92). However, most authorities would agree with the *Computer Aided Manufacturing–International* definition of *activities* as "those actions required to achieve the goals and objectives of the function" and a cost driver as "a factor whose occurrence creates cost" (Berliner and Brimson 1988: 237, 239). An example of the distinction is an activity might be material handling while the cost drivers associated with this activity might be number, weight, and size of pieces handled, or the distance moved.

IMPROVING COST ALLOCATION BY
IDENTIFYING DRIVERS

Traditional cost systems have oversimplified the incurrence of cost by assuming that only volume is a cost driver. The classic bases for allocation of overhead have followed from this assumption—that is, some measure of volume such as units of product, direct labor cost, direct labor hours, or perhaps machine hours. However, as overhead became a larger part of product cost because automation means more overhead charges for depreciation, power, and other machine-related expenses, the classic measures no longer result in accurate product costs.

At the very least recognition of a more complex set of cost drivers allows for better overhead allocation and consequently better product costing. If cost drivers are used to apply other costs to products such as design and marketing, the benefits of better product costing extend to these costs as well.

Using proper cost drivers is enormously revealing as far as the profitability of products is concerned. The old axiom is that in most companies, 80 percent of the sales volume is generated by 20 percent of the products *(80/20 rule)*. When changing to multiple cost drivers as part of an activity-based costing (ABC) installation, many companies have also found that 20 percent of the products (or customers) generate 225 percent of the profits. Kaplan calls this the *20/225 rule*. In other words, many products are actually losing money in terms of profit, and this is undetected by traditional costing systems (Robinson 1990: 7).

Besides revealing which products are profitable, proper identification of cost drivers allows a company to effect cost reductions. Perkin-Elmer Corporation, a manufacturer of analytical instruments, found that number of parts was a major cost driver in the production of its products. New products are now designed with fewer parts—two of the newest products have 50 to 60 percent fewer parts. One new product required 70 percent less time to produce than the one it replaced. Such reductions helped the company cut inventories and material-handling requirements as well as to decrease procurement costs and simplify the MRP (material requirements planning) system (Haavind 1991: 75–77).

ISOLATING GROUPS OF FACTORS
RESPONSIBLE FOR COSTS

The traditional approach for cost allocation was based on the simple assumption that the only cost driver was volume and that all changes in total variable costs were due to changes in this factor. Since this assumption did not reflect reality, academic accountants had to devise complex procedures to make costs fit the pattern.

In the academics' eyes all costs had to be fitted into two categories—fixed costs that did not change with volume and variable costs that changed in proportion to volume. If a cost did change when volume changed but not in proportion to the volume change, it was considered a semivariable or mixed cost. Most, if not all, cost accounting textbooks carried a chapter devoted to breaking the semivariable costs down into fixed and variable elements. Using regression analysis, scattergraphs, or the so-called high-low method, the semivariable costs were analyzed down to the third or fourth decimal point while the fact that these costs could vary with some factor other than volume was ignored. Instead of looking for cost drivers, the texts resorted to mathematical techniques that might or might not result in accurate cost estimates.

In the meantime many companies did not even attempt to break down overhead expenses into fixed and variable categories. Of those that did, the majority used an account classification method, which means they merely looked at the account and decided whether it was mostly fixed or mostly variable.

In all fairness cost variability was not a complete blind spot with all authors or companies even though it was not mainstream thinking. As early as 1936, Joel Dean commented, "Since total cost is a function of many variables, cost may be regarded as marginal with respect to each of these variables. Increasing the number of new styles, for example, has a marginal cost analogous to that resulting from increasing the number of units of output" (p. 24).

In the 1940s Caterpillar abandoned the practice of applying overhead by use of a plantwide rate based on direct labor and began using a product costing system based on activities and cost drivers. A description of its system was published in the August 1951 *NACA Bulletin* by former chief executive William H. Franklin, who says there seemed to be no interest at all in the system at the time (Jones 1991: 35).

ABC consultants have frequently identified some 50 or 60 cost drivers relating to as many activities in an individual company. How can these be summarized or categorized in some manageable groups for use in a cost management system? Probably the best categories are those used by Kaplan and Cooper, pioneers in the development of ABC. Their categories include expenses at the *unit level* (the classic variable costs plus resources consumed in proportion to machine-hour processing times), expenses at the *batch,* or product-run, *level* (such as setup costs or the cost of writing purchase orders), and expenses at the *product-sustaining level* (such as costs associated with performing engineering change notices, product specification, and product enhancement) (Robinson 1990: 7–8).

To these categories may be added expenses at the *process level* (process modifications, maintenance of equipment, etc.) and the *plant level* (plant security, building maintenance, etc.) (Beaujon and Singhal, 1990: 51–72).

Once the level of variability of an expense is determined, appropriate cost pools can be formed and cost drivers chosen. Expenses at the unit level may be applied by machine hours, material cost, or labor hours, for example. Batch level expenses can be applied by number of setups or setup time. Those at the product-sustaining level can be applied by number of engineering change notices, and so on.

PROCEDURES FOR IDENTIFYING
SPECIFIC COST DRIVERS

Identification of cost drivers can be done on a quantitative basis by running correlation analyses between various drivers and related expenses. It can also be done by more subjective means, such as interviewing executives and workers involved with the expenses.

Cooper lists three factors that affect the selection of cost drivers. These include cost of measuring the cost driver, correlation of the selected cost driver to the actual consumption of the activity, and the behavior induced by use of the cost driver (1989: 45).

Without doubt the cost of measuring the cost driver is a consideration. A cost/benefit analysis is appropriate for any new cost management procedure. Measurements already in place or inexpensive to implement should be used if they do not result in cost distortions. In general Cooper recommends transaction-based drivers over duration-based drivers because they are easier to measure. For example, number of inspections is less expensive to measure than inspection hours and will give approximately the same result if each inspection is of about the same duration (1989: 43).

Correlating the cost driver with the expenses involved would seem to be a self-evident consideration. The relationship may be determined intuitively or statistically. However, cost/benefit considerations may override concern for very high correlations.

Another consideration is the behavioral or motivational aspects of the driver. Decreasing the driver will decrease the reported cost. Therefore managers are motivated to decrease the number of transactions or whatever driver is used. The question is whether the company wants to foster this behavior. For example, if number of setups is used as a cost driver, will it cause production of batches that are too large and will it create throughput and inventory problems?

The need to be open-minded and conduct innovative searches for cost drivers is illustrated by the motivational effect of a driver identified by Tektronix's Portable Instrument Division. Alert managers observed the lengthy and growing list of product component part numbers from designers making minor but frequent changes to product components. An investigation of the proliferation of part numbers showed that the quantity of part numbers was a key cost driver. Significant cost savings resulted from reducing part numbers by minimizing minor component changes (Cooper and Turney 1989: 95).

Japanese cost management systems continue to be somewhat elementary by American standards but they accomplish what the firms want in terms of behavior.

Hiromoto comments:

The Hitachi VCR plant is highly automated yet continues to use direct labor as the basis for allocating manufacturing overhead. . . . Hitachi, like many large Japanese manufacturers, is convinced that reducing direct labor is essential for ongoing cost improvement. The company is committed to aggressive automation to promote long-term competitiveness. Allocating overhead based on direct labor creates the desired strong pro-automation incentives throughout the organization. (1988: 23)

In other words, direct labor is used as a cost driver in the highly mechanized Hitachi plant because of its motivational effect. This concern apparently overrides accurate product costing and other cost management objectives.

Another consideration is how many cost drivers should be used. Companies typically go through a process of identifying many cost pools and drivers and then reaggregating the pools and selecting a limited number of cost drivers. Cal Electronic Circuits, for example, identified some 23 key processes (cost pools) and 19 cost drivers. When reaggregated into manageable groups, the company actually used 10 cost pools and 8 cost drivers (Lee 1990: 37). The number of cost drivers finally selected depends on the number of cost pools, the diversity of expenses, the desired degree of accuracy, and cost/benefit considerations.

ANTICIPATED IMPLEMENTATION DIFFICULTIES

Although glowing reports of the savings from proper cost driver identification are easy to find, certain difficulties can be anticipated. Among these are the inaccuracies introduced by the reaggregation process, the cost, and the general complexity of the task.

Reaggregation

Inaccuracies introduced by reaggregating the cost pools and the drivers can be a major difficulty. Three considerations that affect the amount of reaggregation that can be accomplished successfully are product diversity, relative cost of the activities aggregated, and volume diversity (Cooper 1989: 35).

Products are diverse if they use resources in unequal proportions. The more diverse the products, the more cost drivers are needed to detect the diversity and accurately cost the products.

Relative cost of the activities aggregated is also important. Those activities that consume a great deal of resources should have accurate cost drivers and should not be lumped together with other major activities. Correspondingly, those activities that consume few resources can be aggregated and applied by a convenient driver because there is not much potential for cost distortion.

Volume diversity is also important. If all products are produced in similar size batches, simple unit-related measures do not distort batch-related costs. However, if there are significant differences in the batch sizes, the simple unit-related measures will not suffice.

Cost

Cost is another barrier to using multiple cost drivers. In a panel discussion at the 1989 American Accounting Association meeting, noted cost accounting author Charles Horngren commented on what he called the economic infeasibility of new management accounting systems:

Cost driver is a well-chosen term that has achieved notoriety. Ideally, cost drivers should be the allocation bases for product costing. . . . However, there are major stumbling blocks to this idea. One is engineering infeasibility, and another is economic infeasibility. Despite declines in the costs of data collection, many managers believe that the resulting more-accurate data aren't worth collecting. (Robinson 1990: 22)

Horngren went on to cite an example of a large electronics firm studied by Foster and Gupta where they conducted multiple regression analyses on many potential cost drivers. After extensive study they found direct labor dollars performed as well as any of the other drivers despite the fact that direct labor comprised only 6 percent of total manufacturing cost.

At that same conference in the question-and-answer session, Kaplan rejected cost as a major consideration:

If you have to use the cost/benefit criterion to defend the use of traditional systems then basically you've given up the fight. The cost of activity-based systems is so low compared to the potential benefits that it's just not a serious concern. Robin Cooper and I are studying organizations with plants that produce 100–300 million dollars in sales. In our experiences, to design and install an activity-based system for a plant of that size costs between $100,000 and $300,000. . . . The real cost is the cost of education, of overcoming organizational resistance, of changing the way we've approached the subject the last thirty to forty years. (Robinson, 1990: 29)

Complexity

In many traditional organizations manufacturing has become so complex that neither accountants nor managers really understand the processes. In such cases it is difficult to identify cost drivers. On the other hand, these situations provide the greatest opportunity to generate significant cost management information if the mystery of cost drivers and effects can be unraveled. In more simplified processes, where just-in-time techniques have been introduced, the production is much more streamlined and visible. It is easier to identify cost drivers.

Product complexity is another facet of the problem. The more complex the product, the more difficult it is to identify all the cost drivers. Shank illustrates the complexity of the product line of American automobile manufacturers. He poses the question of how long would it take to manufacture one unit from each product line if every possible combination of regular production options were used and the automobile manufacturer could make one car per minute. In 1986 Honda could make one of each of its option combinations in 45 minutes. It would take Toyota 1 day. Among American manufacturers, it would take Chrysler 220 years, Ford 2.2 billion years, and GM 7.8 quadrillion years (Robinson 1990: 20–21). The advantage of the Japanese is consistent with the illustration of Tektronic's reduction in part numbers to reduce costs. The Japanese automobile manufacturers limit options to reduce costs.

INTEGRATING COST DRIVERS INTO
A COST MANAGEMENT SYSTEM

Once a company has identified specific cost drivers and has overcome the hurdles created by the reaggregation process and complexities due to manufacturing processes and product composition, the next step is to construct a cost management system using the drivers. The question is how the system should be structured. In today's environment there is considerable merit in providing a database system that managers can draw on and use to assemble information in any fashion they desire in order to make decisions. In other words, instead of a paper-based system in which data are assembled in one way—whether it is a variance analysis, budget report, performance evaluation, contribution income statement, cost analysis for a special order or whatever—have an on-line computer system that assembles the data according to request.

This is not futuristic, pie-in-the-sky thinking. In a recent *Management Accounting* article on Caterpillar's cost information system, Jones described the system:

It is "activated" by requests for cost information on specific parts, products, and processes. In this regard it is a "database in waiting"—a computerized cost consultant. It is used only when its services are requested. . . . A variety of product cost and descriptive data are available on-line as printed output or in user files. In each of these applications the user can select the information desired, from the cost of an individual machining operation to one part to any level up to and including a complete product. The system also includes an "estimated cost" module for use in estimating new product costs. (1991: 42)

Having different ways to assemble data for different uses is essential, particularly when a full or absorption costing system is used. The defects of an absorption costing system for making managerial decisions have been discussed at great length by many authors as have the virtues of a contribution (or variable or direct) costing system. To briefly illustrate the difficulties of using an absorption costing system, assume a decision to accept a special order to produce 1,000 units when the plant has excess capacity to produce them. The alternatives are to allow a discounted price on the special order or not to produce 1,000 units at all. The relevant cost in this case is the incremental cost of producing the units. The manufacturer who accepts the order is better off by any amount received in excess of the incremental cost. The full absorption cost contains costs that are irrelevant sunk costs since they would exist even if the additional units were not produced.

When using absorption costing, then, it is essential to have available some product cost information other than just the full product cost, which includes a variety of costs that vary as to the plant, process, or batch but are fixed or nonincremental at the product level. When using costs for decision making, it is necessary to be able to assemble costs that are relevant to that particular decision—whether it is a decision to accept a special order, discontinue a product line, or outsource a component.

Management must be able to distinguish which portions of total costs are sunk costs and are not relevant to the decisions and which are costs that will be created by the new proposal. Only the newly created costs are relevant in most cases.

The absorption cost/contribution cost debate is still very much alive with the use of activity-based costing because ABC counts all manufacturing costs as product costs (and in some cases others such as design and marketing costs). Such full product costs must be used with care in decision making. The point was made well by Sharp and Christensen in a 1991 *Management Accounting* article that earned them a certificate of merit from that periodical:

Activity-based costs are an attempt to determine the *full cost* of a cost object. As such, they suffer a deficiency common to all full cost approximations: Not all *resources consumed* by a cost object are *avoidable* in the absence of the particular object. . . . Cost measurements representing *resources consumed* are needed, but the management accounting system also must be capable of alternative cost measurements if it is to be of maximum benefit to management. (p. 32)

If the database concept of a cost management system is to be applied, what types of reports should it be capable of rendering when called on to do so? Different arrangements of the data would be helpful for different purposes. This system is especially suited to the process of evaluating the "what if" options that are typical of most managerial decisions. Along these lines the system can provide such reports as variance analyses, contribution income statements, and cost matrices.

Variance Analysis

Any cost that has a unit-based cost driver may be analyzed in the usual fashion as far as variance analysis is concerned. In other words, a spending and efficiency variance may be computed in the following format:

Actual Unit- level Expense	Actual Inputs × Actual Rate	Standard Inputs × Actual Rate
Spending Variance		Efficiency Variance

The spending variance represents the excess (deficiency) in spending considering the number of inputs used. The efficiency variance represents the excess (deficiency) in expense created by the use of excess (fewer) inputs of whatever sort.

A similar analysis can be made for batch-level expenses. The standard batch would be the number of batches usually necessary to produce the actual number of good units. The standard batch expense would be the usual expense associated with the production of a batch, such as the setup cost.

Actual Batch- level Expense	Actual Batches × Std. Batch Expense	Std. Batches × Std. Batch Expense
Spending Variance		Efficiency Variance

The spending variance represents the excess (deficiency) in spending because the average expense per batch was different than the standard batch expense, such as setup costs per batch that were too high (low). The efficiency variance represents the excess (deficiency) because there were too many (few) batches used for the amount of production.

It is doubtful that it would be useful to try variance analysis at the product or process level. However, budget comparisons can certainly be made between actual and budgeted expenditures.

Contribution Income Statements

Contribution income statements are another way to assemble the cost data in a database system. The contribution per batch, product line, or process can be computed. A format similar to that in Figure 7.1 can be used.

In this illustration unit-level as well as batch- and product-level costs are traced to product lines. Contribution margins are calculated after unit-, batch-, and product-level costs are deducted. These margins indicate the profitability of the product considering the resources it consumes at the var-

Figure 7.1
Contribution Income Statement

	Plant	Process	Product Line
Sales	$200,000	$100,000	$25,000
Less Unit Level Costs	100,000	50,000	12,500
Unit Contribution	$100,000	$50,000	$12,500
Less Batch Level Costs	10,000	5,000	1,500
Batch Contribution	$ 90,000	$45,000	$11,000
Less Product Level Costs	5,000	2,000	500
Product Line Contribution	$ 85,000	$43,000	$10,500
Less Process Level Costs	25,000	13,000	
Process Contribution	$ 60,000	$30,000	
Less Plant Level Costs	20,000		
Plant Contribution	$ 40,000		

ious levels. Provided all these costs could be eliminated if the product line were discontinued, the product line contribution would be a good indicator of whether that line should be continued. If all costs could not be eliminated, some further breakdown of costs might be necessary to make the costs useful for decision-making purposes, such as avoidable and nonavoidable costs. The process contributions give similar information on the process level while the plant contributions give information for the entire plant.

A similar reporting format could be used for performance evaluation of managers over product lines, processes, or the plant. As with all performance reporting, managers should be held responsible only for costs they control. If costs at any level are not controllable by a particular manager, a further breakdown into controllable and noncontrollable costs is necessary before performance can be evaluated. For a manager who has no control over sales, a report that shows how closely the manager's controllable costs adhere to budget would be more relevant.

Cost Matrix

A cost matrix approach is a further refinement of cost reporting. The cost matrix approach relates resources consumed (expenses) to the strategic goals of the firm. A matrix can be developed for any segment of the firm such as a work center, product line, or process. Assume a firm with strategic goals of conversion of product, quality improvement, reduction of cycle time, and reduction of inventories. These goals would form the rows of the matrix. If the firm had resources of power, setup costs, material-handling costs, depreciation, maintenance, training, and inspection, these expenses could form the columns. Analysis of cost drivers determines how many resources are devoted to a particular goal. A "Resources Devoted to Other Activities" (wasted resources) row is also necessary if row totals are to equal column totals. This row highlights the need for management action, either to eliminate the activities or to restructure the goals.

At each intersection of the matrix the cell is read as the amount spent to achieve that goal. For example, depreciation on a new machine can be shown as relating to conversion of product, reduction of cycle time, and quality improvement if the machine helped to achieve those goals. Column totals represent total expenses, and row totals represent allocation of resources to achieve goals. A matrix can be constructed on both a budgeted and actual basis and a variance determined at the end of the budget period.

Probably the biggest criticism of the matrix approach is that it requires so many estimates and assumptions. However, traditional overhead allocation also involves many estimates and assumptions, and the results are not tied to the relevant goals of the firm.

EXTENDING THE ANALYSIS TO MARKETING COSTS

If a database approach to cost management is to be effective, it must include all costs relevant to decisions made by management. Therefore the system must be thorough—it must provide data on all types of costs that will be created or that will increase as a result of deciding to undertake a new proposal. To attempt to analyze cost drivers in the manufacturing area and ignore marketing costs is to omit an important part of the analysis. In some cases marketing costs can run as much as 50 percent of product cost, particularly in situations in which physical distribution costs are high (Lewis 1991: 33).

In some ways analysis of marketing costs predated the activity-based costing concepts of the 1980s. In the 1950s the idea of functional costing was popular for marketing costs but did not carry over into manufacturing to any great degree. Functional costing advocates tried to determine the cost of a particular function such as how much it cost to process an order. If *function* equates to *activity,* the similarity to ABC is evident.

One reason functional costing did not become popular in the manufacturing area was that it is an absorption costing concept with fixed costs included as function or product costs. The resulting per-unit functional cost depended on a certain volume being achieved. If the target volume was not achieved, the per-unit cost was different. For decision-making purposes, a contribution approach using incremental costs seemed superior to functional costing. A second reason functional costing did not become popular in the manufacturing area was that the technology for analyzing a variety of cost drivers was just not available. Direct labor cost or hours as drivers were convenient and seemed to serve the purpose at the time.

Why try to identify cost drivers and use activity-based or functional costing in the 1990s? One reason is that the technology has now caught up. Another reason, as discussed earlier, is that direct labor cost or hours or other strictly volume measures are not working. A third reason is that the objections to an absorption costing approach can largely be overcome if costs are categorized according to their type of variability—with number of product units, batches, product lines, and so on. Decisions that hinge on increases in product units can then be based on the costs attached to product units, while decisions that hinge on increases in batches can be based on the incremental costs of producing and selling a batch, and so on.

Using cost drivers in an activity-based or functional costing approach for marketing costs involves a three-phase process that includes (1) identifying the activities or cost pools, (2) identifying the drivers, and (3) calculating unit costs. Reaggregation may be necessary for the first and second steps, just as it is in the manufacturing area. Additional discussion of analysis of marketing costs is provided in Chapter 11.

AVAILABILITY OF PACKAGES
FOR IMPLEMENTING THE SYSTEM

Identification of cost drivers has usually been done in association with installation of an ABC system. At least four major software packages are on the market for installing an ABC system—a package from Integrated Cost Management Systems (ICMS) of Dallas, Price Waterhouse's ACTIVA, Net-Prophet from Sapling Software Aided Planning Corporation of Oakville, Ontario, and the package that KPMG Peat Marwick developed with Kaplan and Cooper. In addition ABC Technologies of Portland, Oregon, has a relatively new, low-cost package called EasyABC.

According to software consultant Lawrence Walkin's evaluation and 1991 cost figures, the ICMS package focuses on payback and cost drivers and tests the costs. ICMS charges $25,000 for training and counseling, and the package costs $10,000 per site. Implementation takes 12 to 14 weeks. ACTIVA features a powerful database approach for product costing and cost management. Consulting fees are $150,000 to $175,000, and implementation averages about 6 months.

KPMG Peat Marwick will sell its package either with or without consulting. The package costs $12,000 plus $10,000 for the bill of materials module. NetProphet uses the 80/20 rule and concentrates project time on the 20 percent of profitable products. The software costs $5,500 and implementation takes 3 or 4 weeks. ABC Technologies is a software company rather than a consulting firm. Walkin comments that he believes this company will become a major player in the market because "the software is easy to use (it walks you through the ABC concepts), employs windows, and costs only $995" (1991: 18).

The selection of the software and consulting depends on the complexity and size of the company. Relatively small companies or segments may want to start with a package such as EasyABC, while a larger corporation may find that the software and consulting package from a major accounting firm is more cost-effective.

$$\gg \quad \ll$$

In the new manufacturing environment more sophisticated analysis of overhead is necessary because it has become a significant part of manufacturing cost. To ignore or to inaccurately assess this important category of costs is to distort product cost. In order to accurately analyze overhead, what drives costs or causes cost to occur must be determined. Identifying cost drivers may be part of an ABC installation or done merely as part of a company's efforts to control manufacturing costs. When part of an ABC installation, the cost can vary all the way from Price Waterhouse's flexible and powerful ACTIVA to ABC Technology's user-friendly PC software.

Once cost drivers are determined, the information may be used for paper-based reports or in a computerized database system that managers can draw on for a variety of decisions. Although cost driver analysis is usually done for manufacturing costs, extending the analysis to marketing costs has considerable merit, particularly when they are a significant part of product cost.

REFERENCES

Beaujon, George J., and Vinod R. Singhal. "Understanding the Activity Costs in an Activity-Based Cost System," *Journal of Cost Management*. Spring 1990, pp. 51–72.

Berliner, Callie, and James A. Brimson, eds. *Cost Management for Today's Advanced Manufacturing, The CAM-I Conceptual Design*. Boston: Harvard Business School Press, 1988.

Cooper, Robin. "The Rise of Activity-Based Costing — Part Three: How Many Cost Drivers Do You Need, and How Do You Select Them?" *Journal of Cost Management*. Winter 1989, pp. 34–46.

Cooper, Robin, and Peter B. B. Turney. "Internally Focused Activity-Based Cost Systems," *Performance Excellence in Manufacturing and Service Organizations*. Proceedings of the Third Annual Management Accounting Symposium. San Diego, March 10–11, 1989, pp. 91–101.

Dean, Joel. "Statistical Determination of Cost, with Special Reference to Marginal Cost," *University of Chicago Studies in Business Administration,* quoted by

Germain B. Boer in Michael A. Robinson, ed., "Contribution Margin Analysis: No Longer Relevant/Strategic Cost Management: The New Paradigm," *Journal of Management Accounting Research*. Fall 1990, pp. 1-32.

Garrison, Ray H. *Managerial Accounting, Concepts for Planning, Control, Decision Making*. Homewood, Ill.: Richard D. Irwin, 1991.

Haavind, Robert. "Perkin-Elmer Learns Its ABC," *CFO*. September 1991, pp. 74-77.

Hiromoto, Toshiro. "Another Hidden Edge — Japanese Management Accounting," *Harvard Business Review*. July-August 1988, pp. 22-26.

Jones, Lou F. "Product Costing at Caterpillar," *Management Accounting*. February 1991, pp. 34-39.

Lee, John Y. "Activity-Based Costing at Cal Electronic Circuits," *Management Accounting*. October 1990, pp. 36-38.

Lewis, Ronald J. "Activity-Based Costing for Marketing," *Management Accounting*. November 1991, pp. 33-38.

Raffish, Norm. "How Much Does that Product Really Co$t?" *Management Accounting*. March 1991, pp. 36-39.

Robinson, Michael A., ed. "Contribution Margin Analysis: No Longer Relevant/Strategic Cost Management: The New Paradigm," *Journal of Management Accounting Research*. Fall 1990, pp. 1-32.

Romano, Patrick L. "Where Is Cost Management Going?" *Management Accounting*. August 1990, pp. 53-56.

Sharp, Douglas, and Linda F. Christensen. "A New View of Activity-Based Costing," *Management Accounting*. September 1991, pp. 32-34.

Walkin, Lawrence. "ABC — Key Players and Their Tools," *Management Accounting*. February 1991, p. 18.

CHAPTER 8

Providing for Continuous Improvement

One of the most serious charges against standard cost systems as they exist in most firms is that they do not provide for continuous improvement. Standards, for the most part, are static. This is not to say that they are not revised from time to time, but the updates are not frequent enough to meet the requirements of continuous improvement.

The necessity of continuous improvement was brought home to American industry in the 1980s when it became apparent that foreign firms were improving in most important aspects of business while American companies were content with the status quo. As foreign manufacturers surpassed domestic firms in such areas as quality, cycle times, and cost efficiency, it became obvious that static benchmarks were not sufficient to remain competitive.

Popularization of the idea of continuous improvement came from the JIT revolution and from Goldratt and Cox's book, *The Goal: A Process of Ongoing Improvement* (1986). *The Goal* was a novel describing how a plant manager kept his failing plant open. It brought home the truth of the need for continuous improvement in a way that a manual on production or financial techniques never could.

American manufacturers who were not content with the status quo typically have tried to attain sudden, dramatic improvements. Research funds, for example, have been spent to develop breakthrough technology. In the meantime foreign manufacturers have spent their funds on less costly incremental improvements, small improvements that can quickly be brought to the market.

Goldratt refers to the striving for dramatic improvements as operating on the *green curve*. He advocates operating on the *red curve* where improvement is ongoing. He sees a danger in the green curve that "flattens out when momentum is lost. The resulting stagnation, coupled with misguided management policies, can lead to the collapse of a plant or business" (Sheridan, 1991: 44).

If manufacturers are to operate on the red curve, they need dynamic benchmarks or standards. This can be done in a variety of ways. Some of the bases for dynamic standards are:

- using last period's results as standards;
- using best performance to date as the standard;
- measuring improvement rather than absolute results;
- using industry leaders' results as standard;
- using market-driven or target costs as standard; and
- using cost-improvement curves.

LAST PERIOD'S RESULTS AS STANDARDS

Using last period's results as standards is not a particularly new idea. In fact it has been advocated as a way for small businesses to gain the benefits of a standard cost system without the expense of engineering studies to develop standards. Lawler and Livingstone discussed the approach in a December 1986 *Journal of Accountancy* article (pp. 190–194), which was amplified in another *Journal* article in July 1987 (Cheatham: 123–130).

Lawler and Livingstone point out that using last period's results as standard has an advantage over using predetermined standards in that "A predetermined standard is a theoretical performance level that may seldom (or never) be achieved in practice. However, last period performance is a concrete reality" (1986: 191).

Another advantage of using last period's results as standard is that it is familiar to most people in business. Comparative financial statements in which the current year is presented in contrast with one or more previous years is a typical way to present financial data. Budgets are usually prepared by analyzing last period's budget and last period's actual results and then adjusting for any conditions expected to change — a process referred to as *incremental budgeting*.

It is also possible and desirable to compute the percentage increase or decrease over time, if last year's results are used as standard. This provides a record of the continuous improvement (or lack of it) over time.

One objection to using last period's results as standard is that last period may have been a disaster in one area or another, or in total, and no one wants to make that the standard for the current period. If last period's results are not a valid standard of comparison, slavishly adhering to the rule makes no sense.

Last period's results can be adjusted in a number of ways. A change to the next-to-last period or some other normal period may be in order. A change to best performance to date, as discussed in the next section of this chapter, may be useful temporarily. Setting some arbitrary target may also work, particularly in the short run. The point is that just because some periods may not be good for comparison purposes, there is no reason to reject using last period's results as standard as a general rule.

A variation on the last period's results as standards is the use of a past base period. Comparisons can be made with the past base period and all periods since the base. Boer describes the system of using a base year as a "pseudo flexible budget" from which unit costs are developed. He points out that the system "encourages continuous improvement and never implies that a level of performance is adequate. Instead, it encourages managers to improve continuously" (1991: 40).

BEST PERFORMANCE TO DATE AS STANDARD

Some managers may believe that using last period's results as standard is not sufficient for motivating workers and managers to excel. If that is the case, using the best performance to date (BP) will provide a more rigorous standard. This method looks back over the actual results of the company for as many periods as seem relevant and picks the best performance—the least units rejected for quality reasons, the most efficient performance of labor, the lowest spending on overhead items, and so on. The per-unit or per-activity factor results become the standards until they are bettered.

Comparisons can be made in terms of absolute quantities—fewer dollars, hours, or units of raw materials. Comparison can also be made in terms of percentages—"We rejected 10 percent more units than we did in our BP period." Yet another comparison can be made in terms of how long it takes to break the previous BP record. A very dynamic company may operate with virtually a last period's results as standard because improvement is constant.

One objection to using BP as standard is that the record performance may have been achieved under conditions impossible to duplicate in the current environment. BP may have been achieved when there were more workers, equipment was newer, materials were of higher quality or less costly, fewer product lines were produced, and so on. If that is the case, BP results can be adjusted for the current conditions. A change to BP in the last year or two years or an arbitrary adjustment that considers current conditions may prevent the disincentive created by a BP that is too high to be reasonable.

MEASURING IMPROVEMENT RATHER
THAN ABSOLUTE RESULTS

Still another approach to achieving continuous improvement through use of standards is to measure the amount of improvement rather than absolute results. The distinction is not so much in the data gathered as in how it is analyzed and how management views the process of improvement. The amount of improvement may be in comparison to last period, best performance, or to a base period.

Analog Devices is a company that monitors improvement in its performance measurement system. It considers the improvement in terms of half lives or how long it takes to cut an undesirable rate in half. An example using half lives would be calculating how long it takes to cut the percentage of late deliveries in half (Lynch 1990).

The advantage of using an improvement measure is that psychologically, the system anticipates improvement. The variable measured is the amount of improvement or how rapidly it occurs.

INDUSTRY LEADERS' PERFORMANCES AS STANDARD

Another standard of comparison is industry leaders' performances (ILP). Use of ILP for comparison purposes is not new. The concept is frequently used with performance measures that are not tied in to the accounting system. When used with such performance measures, the process is referred to as *benchmarking*. Benchmarking became popular with many world-class companies in the 1980s, particularly as they made efforts to improve quality. Companies involved in benchmarking include DuPont, AT&T, Eastman Kodak, Digital Equipment, and Xerox.

What has been used with free-standing performance measures can also be used to develop standards for a standard cost system. The difficulties encountered are no different than the difficulties inherent in benchmarking.

Probably the worst problem in using ILP is obtaining information on the performance of other companies. One question that must be answered is "Who is the industry leader?"—that is, which company or companies will be used as a standard of comparison. In some cases the answer may be obvious. In others some investigation may be necessary. A second question is "What is the performance standard of the industry leader?" When information is a competitive weapon, data on industry leaders may be difficult to obtain.

In a discussion of benchmarking, Edward S. Finein, former vice president and chief engineer of Xerox Corporation, listed the following information sources on competitors: (1) external reports and trade publications, (2) professional associations, (3) market research and surveys, (4) industry experts, (5) consultants' studies, (6) company visits, and (7) competitive labs (1990).

Lack of information should not deter a company that really desires to be world class. What can work nearly as well as actual standards from industry leaders is what their performance is assumed to be. In other words, if company managers set standards based on what they believe to be world-class performance, the standards will provide motivation as well as information on their progress toward being an industry leader.

The real advantage to using ILP or perceived ILP as standard is that it forces the company to look outside to its competitors rather than internally to its past history. The mistake that U.S. industry made after World War II was that it had an entirely internal focus. If American companies maintained or bettered their own performances of previous years, they were content. In the meantime foreign manufacturers took American industry as their standard and set out to exceed its performance. In a few years they were able to do so. It is time, or past time, that U.S. firms evaluate their competition and consider what they must do to perform better.

Although benchmarking has typically been done by companies that are industry leaders themselves, this does not need to be a requirement for setting standards. The same results can be obtained by smaller companies or the nonleaders in an industry by using close competitors. It is not necessary to choose a world-class company for comparison if its performance would be so far out of range as to be unrealistic or discouraging.

Using the performance of industry leaders or close competitors may carry the risk of becoming a static standard if it is not updated when industry conditions change. Even if the targets are not achieved, the standards should be evaluated from time to time to ensure that the company maintains its external focus.

MARKET-DRIVEN STANDARDS OR TARGET COSTS

Probably the most exciting idea in standard setting today is the idea of market-driven standards (MDS) or target costs. With MDS the company looks at what the customer will pay for a product. Then target costs and standards are set so that the price can be achieved.

Target costs are popular in Japan. The typical targets developed with this method are quite rigorous, and the company must strive hard to drive costs down to this level. MDS or target costs are usually used with new products that are not yet even in the design stage. The cost of the design stage itself is considered, and the product is devised so that it can be manufactured at the target cost. Once in the manufacturing stage, standards are set to meet the target cost. Bringing down the actual cost to the target generally takes effort over a period of time.

The contrast with the engineering-driven standards of American companies is obvious. Engineers set standards based on the technology in place and the products as designed. The design phase probably does not include price considerations or an evaluation of manufacturing capability. The focus is internal and based on what engineers decide to design rather than external and based on what the market will accept.

Hiromoto describes the process of using target costs at the Daihatsu Motor Company. First, a product development order is issued. Then comes a cost estimation phase in which an *allowable cost* per car is calculated. The allowable cost is the difference between the target selling price and the profit margin. However, the allowable cost is far below what realistically can be achieved. Then each department calculates an *accumulated cost* based on the standard cost achievable with current technology. Finally, a *target cost* is set that is between the allowable cost and the accumulated cost.

Next comes the design stage in which engineers frequently interact with production people, and estimated costs are compared to the target cost until a product is designed that can be manufactured at the target cost. This ends the *genka kikaku* or product development stage, which typically takes about three years.

During the first year of production the target cost set during the *genka kikaku* stage is gradually tightened on a monthly basis according to a cost-reduction rate. In later years the actual cost of the previous period is used as a starting point to drive costs further down (1988: 23–24).

MDS share the externality of standards set from the performance of industry leaders. However, MDS take the process one step further in that their external focus is on the market rather than on competitors. Why is this difference important? Because an entire industry within a particular country may lose sight of what the market will bear, a condition that can prevail in the short run but will be fatal to the industry in the long run.

The disadvantage of using target costs is that the system works best for new products that have not yet gone through the design stage. The bulk of manufacturing costs is set by the design process, and improvements after that tend to be engineering- or technology-driven changes rather than market-driven changes. However, there is no reason a company cannot use MDS for new products while continuing with some other system for its current products.

CONTINUOUS IMPROVEMENT THROUGH COST IMPROVEMENT CURVES

Still another way to set standards or goals for cost reduction is by using cost improvement curves. Cost improvement curves are a new application of the old learning curve. The learning curve concept applied to reductions in labor time. With the increased emphasis on automation and the decreased emphasis on labor as a significant cost factor, the concept has seemed inappropriate for the new manufacturing environment. However, it is being revised to recognize improvement in other organizational factors.

The learning curve phenomenon was first observed in the aircraft industry in the 1930s and 1940s. T. P. Wright constructed a model called the *Cumulative Average-Time Learning Model* in 1936. While working at Lockheed in the mid-1940s, J. R. Crawford developed a similar model, which is referred to as the *Incremental Unit-Time Learning Model.* The two models differ as to variable definitions. As a practical matter Crawford's model was more often used to estimate labor costs while Wright's model was used in price negotiation (Pattison and Teplitz 1989: 38).

Basically, the learning curve model says that as cumulative quantities produced double, the cumulative average time to produce a unit will decrease by some predictable percentage—usually 5 percent to 40 percent. The learning curve percentage is usually stated as the complement to the reduction percentage. That is, if the cumulative average time decreases by 20 percent, the curve is said to be an 80 percent learning curve. Learning curves were never thought to be applicable to routine labor tasks but only to tasks that provide an opportunity for learning. They were found to apply in industries such as aircraft manufacture and electronics.

Learning curves were not used to set standards for standard cost systems but in predictive roles such as calculating a bid or estimating the number of workers needed. They were particularly useful in bidding where the objective is to bid low enough to obtain the order but high enough to make a sufficient profit. Being able to pinpoint the amount of labor needed was a significant competitive weapon in bidding.

To illustrate the learning curve idea, assume Prolific Electronics receives an order for 7,000 electronic parts from a customer. Prolific has just completed an order for 1,000 of those parts for another customer, and the company believes an 80 percent learning curve applies. The first order required 2,000 hours of labor or an average of 2 hours per unit. In this case, the learning curve could be constructed as:

Cumulative Quantity		Cumulative Average Time		Cumulative Total Time
1,000		2		2,000
2,000	(2 × .8)	1.6	(1.6 × 2,000)	3,200
4,000	(1.6 × .8)	1.28	(1.28 × 4,000)	5,120
8,000	(1.28 × .8)	1.024	(1.024 × 8,000)	8,192

All the quantities and times on the learning curve are *cumulative;* therefore, the amount of improvement on the later units produced is considerable. The last 4,000 units require only 3,072 hours (8,192 hours on the 8,000 unit increment, less 5,120 hours on the 4,000 unit increment). The average time on the later units is 3,072 divided by 4,000 hours, or only .768 hours. This is quite an improvement over the 2 hours needed for the early units.

To compute the time needed for Prolific's order for 7,000 units, the time would be the 8,192 hours needed for 8,000 units less the 2,000 hours used on the first order, which has already been sold. In other words, Prolific can project that it will take 6,192 hours to complete the order. If Prolific had projected its labor requirements based on the average time of 2 hours per unit for the first order, it would have estimated the time as 14,000 hours—a considerable difference, which could have caused rejecting of a profitable order.

The idea behind cost improvement curves is that there is the potential for reducing not only labor time and labor costs but also other costs in an automated environment. These cost reductions relate to the experience factor for the organization as a whole.

A formula for this experience factor when going to an automated environment is:

$$Rate_{new} = Rate_{old} + (1 - Rate_{old}) * L * R$$

where $Rate_{new}$ is the rate of learning for a new system, $Rate_{old}$ is the rate of learning for the old system, L is the proportion of learning attributed solely to direct labor stated as a percentage, and R is the proportion of direct labor being replaced (Pattison and Teplitz 1989: 40).

For example, if Prolific replaces 70 percent of its labor and it estimates that labor is about 25 percent of its total potential cost reductions, the new rate of learning or experience will be 83.5 percent, computed as:

$$83.5 \text{ percent} = .8 + (1 - .8)(.25)(.7)$$

The new experience rate is somewhat poorer than Prolific's old 80 percent rate because of the partial removal of labor, which reduces some potential for learning. However, researchers observe that "regardless of whether labor reduction is partial or complete, cost improvement will still occur" (Pattison and Teplitz 1989: 40).

Whether the specific formula works is not really as relevant as the fact that organizations can set a goal for some experience factor in their cost reduction efforts. This goal can be 83.5 percent, 80 percent, or 70 percent. The point is that it provides a vehicle for directing efforts to reduce output-related costs.

The Japanese stress the formula $2V = 2/3C$, or if volume is doubled, the cost should be two-thirds what it was originally. Their formula equates to a 67 percent learning curve, which is rather high. Their attitude is that learning does not just happen but should be made to happen (Pattison and Teplitz 1989: 39).

To apply the experience curve, an overall goal such as a 75 percent cost improvement curve should be set. This can be based on past experience or on market- or investment-driven goals. A 75 percent cost improvement curve means that a certain batch of output-driven costs should be reduced by 25 percent if volume is doubled. That goal may be based on the fact that the company has been experiencing an 80 percent curve it would like to improve. Alternately, it may be based on the fact that in order to price the product where it will sell, the company must drive down costs at this rate. Or in order to reach the return on investment its stockholders demand, the company may need to drive down costs in this fashion.

Once the target rate has been set, areas of cost reduction can be identified and standards set. A study of cost reduction efforts at General Dynamics found direct labor and direct supervision improvements represented 24.5 percent of cost reductions while engineering improvement represented 30 percent, tooling 25 percent, and miscellaneous factors 20.5 percent (Pattison and Teplitz 1989: 38). Obviously, these percentages are unique to General Dynamics, but the management team in any organization can identify areas where it believes there is potential for cost reduction and set goals within the overall umbrella of a 75 percent (or whatever percentage) experience curve. Standards can be derived from these goals and used in continuous improvement efforts.

PSYCHOLOGICAL EFFECTS OF CONTINUOUSLY UPDATED STANDARDS

One word of caution is in order concerning any type of continuously updated standards, whether they are derived from past performance, market prices, or cost improvement curves. The effect on workers' motivation must be considered. Shortly after the Industrial Revolution, U.S. companies began to use a piece rate system to motivate workers to work harder. The amount per piece formed a standard for the amount of labor per finished unit or component. However, as workers produced more and gained higher wages, managers lowered the piece rate. Lowering the piece rate at first produced the desired results—workers worked even harder, and production increased. But after several rounds of higher productivity and rate reductions, the workers became discouraged and ceased to try to increase output any further. Organized slowdowns, called *soldiering,* were used when demands became unreasonable.

Frederick Taylor, the father of scientific management, thought the problem was that standards were not set in a scientific manner. He believed that his scientific standards eliminated the problem. F. B. Gilbreth, on the other hand, thought that the problem was that "human engineering" was being ignored and that motion studies were the solution (Shingo 1988: 11–12).

However, it would seem that a basic psychological variable was being ignored—the attitude of the workers. The same problem may occur with continuously updated standards if not properly administered. Obviously, the effects are not as devastating to the worker as the piece rate system because the worker's basic earnings are not affected, but caution is still in order. The lesson from history is that continuously changing standards can have a demotivational effect.

Workers need to feel that they are a part of a team effort to improve performance. If this effect can be achieved, increasing standards has a positive result. The Springfield Remanufacturing Corporation (SRC) division of International Harvester provides an outstanding example of how teamwork can be fostered. The chief executive officer initiated a program in which all employees were looked upon as players on a team. Scores were based on financial results. As a result sales jumped 312 percent.

Although SRC does not use a system of continuously updated standard costs, its method of revising of standards could well be followed by others who do update continuously:

Employees learn SRC's standard cost system and how they can play a key role in developing standard costs. The initial standards are developed by the engineering department, but prior to implementation the employees who must attempt to meet the standards must approve them. Emphasis is placed on demonstrating the effect of variances from standard costs on the "bottom line" profitability. (Greer, Olson, and Callison 1992: 39–41)

» «

Some suggest that standard cost systems are no longer relevant because they use static standards. The contention here is that standard cost systems are more relevant than they have ever been as organizations strive to continuously improve. Striving to continuously improve implies some benchmark or measurement of progress. The standard cost system provides this type of metric. However, in order to provide for continuous improvement, the standard cost system must furnish dynamic standards instead of static standards.

Standards may be continuously updated in several ways. One way is to use last period's results as standard. This method is simple and easy to understand. In the past it was suggested as a way for small businesses to achieve the same results as using expensive engineering studies to set standards. Another way standards can be continuously updated is to use the best performance to date. This ensures that the organization will always be striving to do better than it has in the past. In some cases measuring the improvement rather than absolute results works well for a company, such as Analog's system of measuring how long it takes to halve an undesirable rate.

Even better ways of obtaining continuous improvement are produced by systems that focus on external markets and the competition rather than on internal results. Standards can be set to better the performance of competitors. Alternately, standards can be set to result in a market price that customers will accept.

Standards can also be dynamic by using cost improvement curves. Cost improvement curves are based on the old learning curve idea. However, learning curves apply only to direct labor while cost improvement curves apply to the organization's experience and encompass all output-related costs. Moreover, where learning curves stress prediction or estimation of costs, the cost improvement curve emphasizes using the curve as a target or objective for cost improvement.

REFERENCES

Boer, Germain B. "Making Accounting a Value-Added Activity," *Management Accounting*. August 1991, pp. 36–41.

Cheatham, Carole. "Profit and Productivity Analysis Revisited," *Journal of Accountancy*. July 1987, pp. 123–130.

Finein, Edward S. "Benchmarking for Superior Quality and Performance." Presentation at Performance Measurement for Manufacturers Seminar, Institute for International Research, Chicago, October 24–25, 1990.

Goldratt, Eliyahu M., and Jeff Cox. *The Goal: A Process of Ongoing Improvement*. New Haven, Conn.: Spectrum, 1986.

Greer, Olen L., Stevan K. Olson, and Marty Callison. "The Key to Real Teamwork: Understanding the Numbers," *Management Accounting*. May 1992, pp. 39–44.

Hiromoto, Toshiro. "Another Hidden Edge — Japanese Management Accounting," *Harvard Business Review*. July–August 1988, pp. 22–26.

Lawler, William C., and John Leslie Livingstone. "Profit and Productivity Analysis for Small Business," *Journal of Accountancy*. December 1986, pp. 190–196.

Lippa, Victor. "Measuring Performance with Synchronous Management," *Management Accounting*. February 1990, pp. 54–59.

Lynch, Richard L. "Promoting Organizational Learning through Performance Measurement." Presentation at Performance Measurement for Manufacturers Seminar, Institute for International Research, Chicago, October 24–25, 1990.

Pattison, Diane D., and Charles J. Teplitz. "Are Learning Curves Still Relevant?" *Management Accounting*. February 1989, pp. 37–40.

Sheridan, John H. "Throughput with a Capital 'T'," *Industry Week*. March 4, 1991, pp. 44–49.

Shingo, Shigeo. *Non-Stock Production*. Cambridge, Mass.: Productivity Press, 1988.

Umble, Michael, and Mokshagundam L. Srikanth. *Synchronous Manufacturing: Principles for World-Class Excellence*. Cincinnati: South-Western, 1990.

CHAPTER 9

Integrating the Organization's Information Systems

An organization typically has many information systems. A hospital, for example, has records for patients and financial records. The two databases are linked by a patient billing system.

Most businesses, including manufacturing, have three systems—a financial accounting system, a managerial accounting system (or cost management system), and an operations system. The primary link among these systems is the standard cost system (SCS). The production and inventory information, as well as the variances, provide the data that operations personnel need to make decisions about manufacturing. The product cost and responsibility accounting information provide management with the data for decisions about which products to produce and sell and which business segments should be expanded or discontinued. The output of the SCS for inventories and cost of goods sold provides data for preparing financial statements.

In the rush to update cost accounting systems for the new manufacturing environment, many organizations are discarding or deemphasizing their SCSs and are losing the one link among their separate systems. Operations people are marching off toward free-standing performance measures while financial accountants are embracing activity-based costing or even backflush costing. Activity-based costing provides information on the overhead category of expenses but typically ignores other expense categories, and backflush costing is almost a nonsystem that recognizes only that materials have been started into production and that production has been completed. It does not track production through the manufacturing operation at all. Managerial accounting is ignored, and managers are expected to get the data for their decisions by adapting information from the other systems.

The result of the loss of the link is extensive duplication and sometimes conflicting signals from the performance measures and financial indicators. Operations people and financial people tend to ignore and/or criticize each other. They seek a different set of goals and may be secretive about their actions. Rather than an organization that acts as a cohesive whole, the various segments pursue their own interests. The intracompany competition may be so great that external competition is ignored.

The purpose of this chapter is to examine the separate information needs of the financial, managerial, and operations segments of the organization and to suggest ways the systems can be integrated through the standard cost system and common databases. The objective is to provide information that can be adapted to the needs of a variety of users and that can be linked to the common goals or strategies of the organization.

PURPOSES OF THE FINANCIAL ACCOUNTING SYSTEM

The financial accounting system is geared to provide information to parties external to the business; in this sense investors are external. Other external parties are government agencies, customers, suppliers, and the general public. Financial accounting supplies this information through periodic financial statements and through government reports such as income tax returns.

Financial accounting is essentially scorekeeping for the stewardship of management. It looks into the past and reports what has occurred. It tells external parties how management is doing in using its resources to provide a profit for its investors. To the government it provides information about how well it is adhering to the laws of the land in computing taxes owed and regulations met.

Since financial accounting is oriented toward stewardship, great emphasis is placed on following accepted rules. This assures comparability among companies when investors evaluate the results. It is necessary because investors are assumed to be separate from management and have no intimate knowledge of the business. Thus the very active Financial Accounting Standards Board (with the general blessing of the Securities and Exchange Commission) provides the basis for generally accepted accounting principles (GAAP), and the Internal Revenue Service administers the tax law in a presumably equitable manner.

Because of its stewardship function and because it is historically oriented, financial accounting is geared for precision. It emphasizes exactness in accountability to investors and the government. In some cases this is more illusion than fact. A balance sheet may have cash accounted for down to the last dollar and be millions of dollars off in fixed asset valuation because of imprecise estimates of the life of plant and equipment or its salvage value.

Financial accounting is also directed toward short time periods, presumably because investors and the government are interested in short-term results. Thus quarterly financial statements and tax estimates are typically required even though much precision is lost by allocating expenses to arbitrary periods. Annual financial statements are considered the major reporting vehicle, which still emphasizes a very short period in the life of a business.

Historically, financial accounting was not the driving force in the record-keeping of a business that it is today. Most accounting was in fact managerial accounting, which was directed toward helping the owner/manager make day-to-day operating decisions. Financial accounting consisted of keeping records of transactions with suppliers and creditors so that proper payments were made. Where ownership and management were separated, it provided an accountability for profits so that a proper division could be made.

However, accountability for profits was not the short-term phenomenon it is today. Johnson and Kaplan discuss early venture accounting:

Consider a group of investors who acquired goods produced in northern Italy and chartered an expedition to sell them in India. . . . To compute overall profitability of the venture and to distribute the net proceeds (the retained earnings) among the initial investors was a worthwhile role for accounting. One has to wonder, however, whether the investors or the Venetian version of the Securities and Exchange Commission or Financial Accounting Standards Board, also asked the accountant to compute the expedition's profits during the third quarter of 1487 when the caravan was traversing the Persian desert en route to India. Probably not. Because even five hundred years ago, investors likely understood that allocating the total profits of expeditions to periods as short as three months was not a meaningful exercise. (1987: 16)

Despite the fact that short-term results are probably not very meaningful, much time and energy in financial accounting is directed toward providing this frequent accountability. Additional time and energy are required to keep up with the constantly changing rules of the Financial Accounting Standards Board and the Internal Revenue Service.

By training and inclination most accountants are more interested in the intricacies of financial accounting than in managerial accounting or the needs of operations personnel. Their preoccupation with financial results, to the exclusion of these other informational needs, has led to a schism in many companies between financial accountants and managers in the operations area.

PURPOSES OF THE MANAGERIAL ACCOUNTING SYSTEM

In contrast to financial accounting, managerial accounting is directed to the internal needs of management. A good managerial accounting system should help managers make day-to-day operating decisions as well as long-term special decisions. It also should assist management in making decisions about personnel – who should get a raise, be promoted, or receive a bonus. Managerial accounting should provide information about the various segments of the organization as well as the organization as a whole. It should indicate which branches, divisions, or stores should be expanded or shut down, and which products should be promoted.

Since management accounting is geared to decision making, it is future oriented. The past is important only in that it may indicate what will happen in the future. Precision is not as important as timeliness because all future data are an estimate to some degree. Past costs are usually considered sunk or irrelevant except as they affect future taxes. Decisions are usually made on the basis of incremental costs rather than on the total costs presented on the financial statements.

Management accounting looks at the entire period covered by the decision, which may be 10 or 20 years into the future. For periods this long it is necessary to consider the time value of money (imputed interest) as well as risk and inflation factors.

A great deal of managerial accounting is repetitive – decisions about inventory purchases, personnel, product promotion, and so on. However, a great deal is also unrepetitive and tends to deal with nonrecurring factors. These decisions are more challenging because each contains unique elements. A decision to install a flexible manufacturing system, to outsource a major component, or to shut down part of a facility because of hard economic times has factors that are difficult to evaluate. Much more ambiguity exists than in the scorekeeping function of financial accounting.

Almost all early accounting was done for the benefit of the owner/manager and was, therefore, management accounting. The Industrial Revolution brought the need for masses of capital and the demand for outside investors. However, even throughout the late 1800s and early 1900s accounting was still directed primarily at management. In the large textile mills and steel companies of the day, hierarchical organizations brought more needs for management information. It was not until the advent of the income tax law and the stock market crash, which brought about the existence of the Securities and Exchange Commission, that financial accounting gained its prominence.

In the introduction to *Relevance Lost: The Rise and Fall of Management Accounting,* Johnson and Kaplan point out that:

Unencumbered by any demands for external reporting, management accounting practices developed and flourished in a wide variety of nineteenth- and early twentieth-century corporations. Only in the past sixty to seventy years have external auditing and financial reporting systems come to perform the original function of management accounting systems. The current inadequacy of corporate management accounting systems can therefore be recognized as a relatively recent decline in relevance, not as a lag in adapting older financial accounting systems to modern managerial needs. (1987: xii)

Somewhere along the way managerial accounting became a weak stepsister to financial accounting in most organizations. Only in businesses where managers asked the right questions and accountants were willing and able to provide the answers did managerial accounting serve its intended function. In other organizations it was virtually ignored while operations managers developed their own performance measures to meet their needs.

PURPOSES OF THE OPERATIONS SYSTEM

Managers in the production area—those in charge of scheduling, inventory management, inspection, engineering, and others—have always had their own performance measures. However, during the 1980s the development of these metrics seemed to mushroom because the SCS and financial measures failed to provide meaningful information. The information they supplied tended to be in dollars whereas quantity data seemed more relevant to production. Moreover, it tended to be control or feedback information whereas production needed real time or estimated data for future use. Development of performance measures also accelerated because the 1980s brought new goals, such as minimizing inventories and increasing quality, and new ways were needed to measure progress toward these goals.

The shortcomings of financial measures were detailed in a 1990 *Management Accounting* article:

New manufacturing methods, such as just-in-time manufacturing, have exposed the informational and motivational shortcomings of traditional accounting systems. Feedback in the form of standard cost variances has been counterproductive. Other financial reports, such as profit and loss statements, budgets, and margin analyses, have been too aggregated, too late, and too one dimensional to be useful to operating managers. . . . Faced with an information gap, many companies, such as Caterpillar, Wang Laboratories, and Analog Devices, are creating new performance measurement systems that address customer satisfaction, flexibility, and productivity. (McNair, Lynch, and Cross 1990: 28)

The result of the trend toward more free-standing performance measures was a wealth of diversity and creativity. A sample of this variety was given in Chapter 6 on production performance measures. Now it seems that every day's mail brings a new brochure on a performance measurement workshop and a journal with an article on a new performance measurement system.

At some future date, it seems likely that some standardization will result. In a 1991 *Harvard Business Review* article, Eccles notes the advantages of having uniform performance measures for comparison purposes just as financial measures provide firm-to-firm uniformity. He takes the position that public accounting firms are the most likely candidates to bring about this standardization (p. 136).

Whatever the agency, it may be hoped that some degree of uniformity will be achieved and that at least partial integration with the financial and managerial accounting systems will take place. Performance measurement has generally been thought to have more in common with managerial accounting than financial accounting because it is used to assess responsibility (control or feedback function) and make decisions. However, in some respects performance measurement has more in common with financial accounting because it is a scorekeeping function that looks to the past.

Many dollar measures in financial accounting are the products of other measures that relate to quantities, time, and rates. Interest, for example, is the product of a dollar figure (principal), a rate, and a time metric. Inventory cost is found by multiplying quantity by price. If these dollar measures in financial accounting can be disaggregated, an articulated system can be built that uses the dollar figures for financial and managerial accounting purposes while retaining the quantity, time, and rate measures for performance measurement.

However, the other criticisms of financial and managerial accounting systems must also be ameliorated. If the system does not provide frequent or timely information for operations, this needs to be corrected. If the information is too aggregate, this too needs to be corrected.

BENEFITS OF INTEGRATING INFORMATION SYSTEMS

The benefits of an integrated system for performance measurement and financial and managerial accounting do not seem to be immediately apparent to everyone, particularly those who are advocating certain performance measurement systems. The questions involved include both procedural and philosophical concerns. Procedurally, the computer-integrated manufacturing systems require one type of technology while the business computers operate with a technology that uses different languages and control and data requirements. Philosophically, some would argue that multiple systems result in desirable checks and balances; others would say multiple systems only mean redundancy and potential conflicts. However, the ultimate concern should be facilitating management decision making and this seems best served by integration.

A rather pragmatic view of the lack of integration is furnished by the following tongue-in-cheek illustration:

In reviewing an operational manager's proposal for a new nonfinancial measurement system, a vice president of finance asked, "What happens when these nonfinancial measures look good but the company's financial measures disagree?" The operating manager quipped, "My resume will look great and yours won't." (McNair, Lynch, and Cross 1990: 28)

The incident may or may not have actually occurred, but it does emphasize that financial and nonfinancial measures may conflict. Customer satisfaction may be at an all-time high and inventories pared to a minimum, but the bottom line in terms of net income and return on investment may be poor. An integrated system should at least give insight into the reasons— "Customer satisfaction was high but the cost of rapid delivery and service was also high," or "Inventories were pared down but the company still has a long-term lease on the building where they were kept so the benefits have not been fully realized."

An integrated system also minimizes duplication and the accompanying cost of the extra records. Today's computerized factory environment provides a host of ways to gather information. These technologies need to be harnessed to benefit both operations and accounting personnel. Systems that use computer-integrated manufacturing (CIM), statistical process control (SPC), material requirements planning (MRP), or manufacturing resources planning (MRP II) can furnish basic data for integrated systems.

Using the information available in the factory is easier said than done. Dilts and Grabski note the various differences between the way information is gathered and used in the factory versus how it is gathered and used in the accounting system. Some major differences relate to the frequency, the flexibility, the decision focus, and the volume. In regard to volume, for example, the authors point out that "The data requirements for one completely integrated system would be more than 309 billion characters. With subsecond response time comes subsecond data collection, and the sheer volume of raw data from even the simplest plant floor could quickly overwhelm the typical accounting information system" (1990: 51–52).

Nevertheless if linkages among the financial, managerial, and operations systems are to be established, some beginnings must be made. Complete integration may be an unattainable goal at this time. However, Beischel and Smith discuss the relationship this way: "The relationship between nonfinancial measures and financial measures is not an all-or-nothing proposition but a matter of balance and emphasis. The point is that manufacturing decisions do impact financial results and should be linked" (1991: 28).

COORDINATION AND CONTROL THROUGH THE STANDARD COST SYSTEM

In most organizations the SCS is the main link for the financial accounting, managerial accounting, and operations information systems. However, disillusionment with its value has led many organizations to discard or ignore it. How should the link work and how can the SCS be restored to usefulness?

Operations Information Systems

The output of the SCS that most affects the operations area is the use of variances. Variances from standard cost were designed to signal a need for correction in the production process. However, variances such as those relating to material prices, labor efficiency, and volume are not as relevant to today's environment as they once were. In fact as companies move toward new goals such as lower inventories, higher quality, and more rapid throughput, the interim result may very well be a worsening of the traditional standard cost variances.

The problem of measuring the wrong variables needs to be corrected in the SCS. Rather than concentrating on variances that were significant in the past, new variances need to be used to measure factors now thought to be important. These include variances relating to quality, overproduction, and product mix as discussed in Chapter 5. When these factors change because of a new set of values or strategies, these variances will need to be redesigned.

A second problem in the operations area is that standards are static and not updated as they should be. Standards can be continuously updated to foster continuous improvement by looking at the previous period's internal performance or the best performance to date. Better still, standards can be updated by considering external factors such as use of the performance of industry leaders or market-driven standards. Cost improvement curves are still another way to continuously revise standards. Development of such systems was discussed in Chapter 8. Standards are goals the company strives to achieve, and setting standards for continuous improvement is one of the best ways a company can achieve constant incremental improvements.

Managerial Accounting

Managers need data from the SCS for decision-making purposes. The SCS assists them by providing cost and control data and information about responsibility. Cost data include the cost of the various products the company produces, which is useful in making decisions about production levels, sales promotions, special orders, and pricing.

The problem of static standards that has plagued the SCS in the operations area also hinders its usefulness as a tool for management decision making. If standards do not reflect target costs for an appropriate future period, prices may be set so high that the product is not competitive, potentially profitable sales orders may be rejected, and the wrong products may be promoted.

Likewise, the problem of measuring the wrong variables impedes the usefulness of the SCS as a decision tool. Emphasizing price variances for materials leads to poor decisions concerning the quality of materials purchased. Seeking low prices may also lead to the purchase of large quantities, which inflates raw materials inventories. Emphasizing volume variances leads to overproduction and excessive work in process and finished goods inventories.

Continuously updating standards and attention to the right variables will not only increase the usefulness of the SCS to the operations area but will also help in managerial decision making.

Another area of management decision making is control and responsibility accounting. Managers need information regarding personnel as well as products. Standard cost variances provide control information to operations personnel, who presumably make the necessary corrections. If the corrections are not made, it is management's function to investigate the reasons and take appropriate action. Managers also assess responsibility for overall performance and make personnel decisions regarding salary, promotions, and bonuses.

If the signals from the SCS are wrong about the performance of personnel, people may be disciplined for the wrong reasons and the wrong people rewarded. Revising the SCS to foster continuous improvement will produce recognition of creative, dynamic performance not static performance. Revising the SCS to measure today's goals will permit recognition of those who are assisting in efforts to improve quality, minimize inventories, increase throughput, and otherwise meet the needs of the current manufacturing environment.

Financial Accounting

The outputs of the SCS that directly affect financial statements are information relating to cost of goods sold, which is a major component of the income statement, and inventories, which are a major component of the balance sheet. Product cost information may influence segment-line reporting.

Also of indirect interest is transfer pricing, the price that one segment of the company charges another segment for products transferred or "sold" to it. A recent study of transfer pricing practices showed that 46 percent of the firms surveyed used a cost-based method to determine transfer prices for domestic transfers, while 41 percent used cost-based methods for international transfers. Most cost-based methods relied at least partially on standard costs (Tang 1992: 24). Transfer prices are significant because they influence the reported performance of the various segments of the company. They also are significant because international transfers have an important bearing on the amount of income taxes paid in various countries as well as on customs duties and restrictions on repatriation of profits and dividends.

Another indirect area of interest in financial accounting is how the SCS affects financial ratios. Standard costs establish the norm for the cost of goods sold and inventory amounts. Although financial statements are supposedly adjusted to actual cost, the departures from standard cost may not appear as a part of the cost of goods sold or inventories but may be treated as period costs or placed in the "other revenues and expenses" category at the bottom of the income statement. Interim statements may in fact be based on standard costs rather than being adjusted to actual costs. Financial ratios such as the cost of goods sold percentage, the gross margin percentage, and inventory turnovers are influenced by how cost of goods is computed. Other financial ratios, such as the current ratio, acid-test ratio, average sale period, and inventory turnovers, are influenced by how inventories are calculated.

Because of the direct and indirect effect on financial statements, standard costs need to be continuously updated and need to measure the correct variables. If the standards are set to foster small incremental improvements, the effect on financial statements will be positive. However, if standards reflect goals for the distant future (that is, there is considerable difference between current conditions and the standards), special care must be taken to assure that the usefulness of financial statement figures, financial ratios, and transfer prices is not adversely affected. Cost of goods sold and inventories should be adjusted to show actual results; transfer prices should be computed fairly by using adjusted standard prices, market prices, or negotiated amounts.

DEVELOPING COMMON DATABASES

Using a database to control and coordinate the operations, managerial, and financial accounting systems and to eliminate duplication has a great deal of merit. The link between the information generated in the operations area and the financial accounting database are somewhat tenuous at this time. The next generation of databases will likely have more commonality than they do now—particularly if future systems are installed with this goal in mind. However, rather than wait for some indeterminate future time, it is more logical to take the information now generated separately for financial, management, and operations uses and combine it in a common database.

The advantage of the database approach is that people from all areas of the company can draw on the database and assemble the information in ways that are useful for their particular needs. Operations personnel can draw on the database to check inventory levels, production schedules, variances, or budgets. Managers can obtain information on personnel performance or product line contributions. Financial accountants can use the data for interim and annual financial statements and to compute transfer prices and financial ratios.

Furthermore the database approach can be used to communicate and coordinate the strategies of the firms as a whole. The 1980s emerged as a time when manufacturing became an important strategic concern. Production issues once ignored by top management have become central strategic issues. These issues include quality, productivity, flexibility, and throughput time (Grant et al. 1991: 43).

Nanni, Miller, and Vollmann describe classification of data under what they call the *CAGS* (Cost Accounting by Goals and Strategies) *approach:*

The classification of data by a variety of purposes requires disaggregation of data as collected under present cost systems. . . . Rather than dividing, for example, maintenance costs between work center 1 and work center 2, we would divide them among their identifiable strategic applications such as physical production, movement of goods, quality monitoring, process improvement, etc. (1988: 45)

Such a cost matrix approach uses database information to link actions to strategies to determine progress toward organizational goals.

$$\gg \quad \ll$$

For many years financial accounting has been the driving force in the information systems of most businesses. The primary goals of managers relate to making the financial measures such as return on investment look good, and the primary goals of accountants relate to preparing financial statements that are accurate according to GAAP on a timely basis.

However, the 1980s saw a change in many businesses in that managers recognized that the information needed for financial accounting did not lead to correct decisions in the operations area. The result was a swing in the pendulum to the use of multiple free-standing performance measures rather than financial measures. Standard cost systems were frequently dismantled in favor of these performance measures or in favor of some other type of accounting system such as backflush costing or activity-based costing.

In other words, there was an overreaction to financial accounting in the direction of operations information. The key to correcting the overreaction is to restore a balance between operations and financial and managerial accounting. All three areas have information needs, and none of the systems should drive the others. A more balanced approach is to restore the lost links and look for new ones.

The SCS does provide linkage and should be updated to meet current needs. To amplify the SCS common databases should be developed. Information systems of the future should incorporate data generated in the computerized manufacturing environment.

REFERENCES

Beischel, Mark E., and K. Richard Smith. "Linking the Shop Floor to the Top Floor," *Management Accounting.* October 1991, pp. 25–29.

Dilts, David M., and Severin V. Grabski. "Advanced Manufacturing Technologies: What They Can Offer Management Accountants," *Management Accounting.* February 1990, pp. 50–53.

Eccles, Robert G. "The Performance Measurement Manifesto," *Harvard Business Review.* January–February 1991, pp. 131–136.

Grant, Robert M., R. Krishnan, Abraham B. Shani, and Ron Baer. "Appropriate Manufacturing Technology: A Strategic Approach," *Sloan Management Review.* Fall 1991, pp. 43–54.

Johnson, H. Thomas, and Robert S. Kaplan. *Relevance Lost: The Rise and Fall of Management Accounting.* Boston: Harvard Business School Press, 1987.

McNair, C. J., Richard L. Lynch, and Kelvin F. Cross. "Do Financial and Nonfinancial Performance Measures Have to Agree?" *Management Accounting.* November 1990, pp. 28–36.

Nanni, Alfred J., Jeffrey G. Miller, and Thomas E. Vollmann. "What Shall We Account for?" *Management Accounting.* January 1988, pp. 42–48.

Tang, Roger Y. "Transfer Pricing in the 1990s," *Management Accounting.* February 1992, pp. 22–26.

CHAPTER 10

Evaluating and Updating Information Systems

Most of the discussion in this book focuses on cost control systems, specifically on standard cost systems. Cost control systems assist management in controlling or managing costs. Aside from cost control systems, manufacturers must also have a method of accumulating historical costs for management information and for financial accounting purposes. The new manufacturing environment is affecting cost accumulation systems as well as cost control systems.

This chapter reviews the major types of cost accumulation systems and discusses the impact of the new manufacturing environment on these systems. Ways to update the systems are presented. Suggestions are made for revising information systems and management procedures in tandem with manufacturing changes.

The two basic types of cost accumulation systems are job order and process systems. In addition, there are hybrid operational systems, and the new manufacturing environment has bred a minimal recordkeeping system, backflush accounting.

JOB ORDER SYSTEMS

A job order system tracks each customer order that goes through the plant. This is an expensive process and is usually used in companies in which the product is tailored or customized for a particular customer. Typical types of manufacturers that would use a job order system include producers of furniture, large machinery, and aircraft, as well as printing and construction businesses.

The heart of a job order system is a job cost sheet that summarizes the material, labor, and overhead used on each order. When the job (order) is complete, the job cost sheet is totaled and the cost compared with the price charged to find the gross margin for the job.

A job order system has three inventory accounts — direct materials, work in process, and finished goods. As work is begun on materials, the materials are indicated on the job cost sheet, and an accounting entry made to transfer the materials to work in process (dr. work in process, cr. direct materials). When labor is applied to products, the cost is also entered on the job cost sheet and in work in process (dr. work in process, cr. factory payroll). As orders are completed or at the end of an accounting period, overhead is computed and shown on the job cost sheet and in the work in process account (dr. work in process, cr. overhead).

When orders are completed, their cost is obtained from the job cost sheet and an entry made to debit finished goods and credit work in process. As products (orders) are sold, their cost is transferred to cost of goods sold by a debit to cost of goods sold and a credit to finished goods. In this way the cost of products moves from direct materials inventory to work in process inventory to finished goods inventory and ultimately to cost of goods sold. If orders are customarily shipped to the customer upon completion, there may be no finished goods inventory.

When standard costs are used with a job order system, all costs go into work in process at the standard cost. Deviations from standard are shown in variance accounts. At the end of the accounting period, variances are closed and adjustments are made to cost of goods sold (or to cost of goods sold and the inventory accounts) to assure that the financial statements will reflect actual historical costs.

Several trends in the new manufacturing environment affect job order systems. The emphasis on lower inventories means fewer materials to account for in the direct materials account. More rapid throughput and use of a "pull" rather than "push" system of production means a smaller work in process and finished goods inventory. These changes affect the size of the balances in the accounts rather than the system, however.

In job order systems overhead was traditionally applied on the basis of direct labor cost, direct labor hours, or machine hours. The new manufacturing environment has brought recognition that other cost drivers can be used. Therefore, overhead may be divided into more pools than were used previously and applied with more drivers. This facilitates a more accurate costing of each job order.

In many ways the work-cell environment is like a job shop, with emphasis on producing small lots for particular customers. It would seem to follow that job order costing would gain new popularity from this trend. However, this does not seem to be the case, probably because workers are frequently transferred between job orders to keep a smooth production flow. Plants with work cells seem to be more involved in minimal inventory tracking and use of performance measures to determine their progress toward company goals.

PROCESS SYSTEMS

A second type of cost accumulation system is a process system. The process system is usually used when large masses of similar products are produced, such as chemicals, paper, cement, rubber, steel, and glass. With this type of system, the product is traced as it proceeds from one operation or process to another. The main accounting vehicle for this is a cost of production report, which is prepared each month or on the basis of some other convenient time division.

The cost of production report shows the unit cost of production, which is the actual cost in an actual system or the standard cost in a standard system. This unit cost is used to calculate the cost of units still in process and the cost of units transferred to the next process or on to finished goods. Part of the calculation of the cost of units still in process is the determination of the degree of completion of semifinished units, referred to as *equivalent units*.

The accounting entries for a process system are much like those of a job order system except that the product is tracked through the various operations, so there may be several work in process accounts through which the product passes.

The new manufacturing environment discourages production processes in which large masses of product are simultaneously processed and transferred from operation to operation. The trend is toward a work-cell environment in which small orders are produced in a relatively short time. Consequently, the process system is not as appropriate for these industries as it once was.

As with the job order system, overhead is likely to be divided into more cost pools and applied with more cost drivers. This affects a process system as well as a job order system. Minimal inventories mean fewer units to account for as work in process. The computation of equivalent units and the division of costs into those attached to units transferred out and those left in inventory is much less significant.

OPERATION COSTING

Most manufacturing processes are somewhere between the two extremes of a true job-shop operation and the true assembly line style of a process system. In other words, most manufacturing processes have some repetitive operations through which all units pass, but batches of products are customized or tailored in some way. A garment manufacturer may always go through the same operations of cutting, sewing various parts of the garments, and pressing, but different fabrics may be used. For manufacturing processes that have characteristics of both job order and process, operation costing may be appropriate.

In the operation system work orders are the major vehicle for tracing a batch of product as it goes through the various operations. Material costs are applied to a batch as materials are used. For each operation performed on the batch, a normalized (standardized) rate for labor and overhead is applied. Thus materials are accounted for in a manner similar to a job order system, except that batches are used instead of individual customer orders. Conversion costs (labor and overhead) are applied in a manner similar to a process system. Transfers from one work in process (operation) account to another as batches proceed through the plant are made in a manner similar to a process system. Standard costs may be used and variances computed just as with job order or process systems. Operation systems usually assume that fairly large batches of product will still pass sequentially through various operations rather than all operations taking place in a work-cell environment. Operation systems also assume that tracking of the product throughout the whole manufacturing process is necessary.

BACKFLUSH COSTING

Backflush costing works best in a manufacturing process that has a true JIT environment in which raw materials go from the dock to production and all products are finished in a relatively short period. Hewlett-Packard's Vancouver division, which produces printers, is one manufacturing operation that uses backflush costing (Horngren and Foster 1987: 589). Previously it used work orders for small batches.

The accounting entries are vastly more simple in a backflush system. As materials are unloaded and placed in production, they are recorded in raw and in process inventory (RIP). When products are complete, the material costs are transferred to finished goods (dr. finished goods, cr. RIP). When they are sold, the material costs are transferred to cost of goods sold (dr. cost of goods sold, cr. finished goods). All actual conversion costs are applied directly to cost of goods sold (dr. cost of goods sold, cr. conversion). At the end of the period an adjusting entry is made to remove any conversion costs from cost of goods sold that should apply to RIP and finished goods. Backflush costing has variations, but the emphasis is on minimal tracking of costs. Units are physically tracked, however.

Standard costs may be used with a backflush system and in fact may be used to determine the amount of conversion cost that should be adjusted to RIP and finished goods at the end of the accounting period. Horngren and Foster's textbook notes that:

The cost accounting literature often erroneously distinguishes among job costing, process costing, and standard costing as though they were mutually exclusive categories of product costing. Standard costing can be used in conjunction with any product-costing system (job, process, operation, JIT, or some other hybrid). Indeed, regardless of the type of production system or product-costing system, standard costing is enormously popular. The accounting for variances . . . is insignificantly different whether operation costing or JIT costing is used. (1987: 592)

Backflush costing is not without its detractors. The Calvasina brothers have likened the backflush system to the periodic inventory system frequently used by small retail businesses, in which no entries are made to the merchandise inventory account during the account period. At the end of the period merchandise is counted, and the inventory and income summary accounts are adjusted accordingly. They comment that:

Because of no reports from accounting on inventory, managers have to take a physical count. A job that contradicts one of the basic objectives of the JIT philosophy—the elimination of wasteful, nonvalue-adding functions. The physical inventory counts not only increase overhead costs directly but also disrupt production by the fact that the work force has to stop doing their work and count. (1989: 45)

CHANGING THE INFORMATION SYSTEM AS WELL AS THE MANUFACTURING PROCESS

For a company in the process of changing to new manufacturing procedures, changing the information system at the same time has great advantages. Accounting personnel should be quick to participate in companywide committees that are helping to effect change because the contribution that accounting can make is tremendous. Without measures of the usefulness of the changes, it is impossible to know whether change is in the right direction.

For example, some companies have attempted to make changes that they perceive as modeled after Japanese manufacturing systems. However, they make only partial changes and fail to take into account the cultural differences that exist between Japanese companies and U.S. companies. A typical case illustrating this problem is that of a high-level U.S. manager who visits a Japanese factory and notes the very visible fact that inventories are minimized. He returns to his company and immediately directs that inventories be reduced without regard for concurrent changes that may be necessary. The inventory system in use probably does incorrectly signal that inventory levels should be higher than necessary because carrying costs are not properly evaluated. However, an immediate reduction to minimal levels can have disastrous effects. The information system (inventory management system) and the manufacturing process (inventory levels) should both be changed.

Most companies will find that they cannot slavishly follow the model of another company in either the changes they make to their information system or to their manufacturing processes. Organizations making changes are finding themselves in the same situation as Trane Company, the manufacturer of air conditioning systems and bathroom and kitchen fixtures:

MRP II, JIT, CIM, TQC, TQM, SPC, ABC, and TCM are just a few "cures" that are supposed to bring American manufacturers to "world class" manufacturing status in the 1990s. Which "pill" or combination dose of pills is the real remedy, and how do we design a cost accounting system to support this new wave of alphabet solutions? When faced with this dilemma at the Trane Co., we blended some of the new ideas with traditional approaches to create a cost accounting system for our business. . . . Because our manufacturing system uses many of the alphabet soup philosophies, we refer to our new accounting system, developed in tandem with new manufacturing procedures, as SOUP (system of utter practicality) accounting. (Clements and Spoede 1992: 46)

Managers and accountants must work together to revise manufacturing processes, accounting systems, and management procedures in order to succeed in the new environment.

COST CONTROL AND PROCESS VALUE ANALYSIS

A great deal of benefit has come from the interest in activity-based costing (ABC). Identifying the separate activities required to produce a product and the related cost drivers has led to cost-reduction efforts by decreasing the drivers and unnecessary activities. This is one area in which many companies have updated both the information system and the manufacturing process to the good of the company as a whole.

As discussed in Chapter 7 cost drivers are literally what drives or causes costs to occur. Until the 1980s the accounting systems in most companies had the built-in assumption that the only cost driver was the volume of production. Overhead costs were applied to products on the basis of volume measures, such as number of units produced, direct labor hours, or direct labor cost. In the 1980s when ABC systems began to become popular, accountants and managers started to realize that many other factors drive costs. Although the knowledge was first applied to more accurate product costing, it was not long before managers realized that cost reduction could be accomplished by minimizing the drivers. Setup costs, for example, could be decreased by reducing the number of setups; material-handling costs could be minimized by decreasing the amount of materials moved.

As a result of installing ABC systems and the subsequent analysis of activities, managers realized that many of the activities performed did not actually add value to the product. This led to an effort to reduce product cost by eliminating nonvalue-adding activities. The examination of activities has been referred to as *process value analysis, activity-based management,* and a variety of other titles. The steps in process value analysis usually include:

1. preparing a flow chart for each manufacturing step and recording the average time the product remains at each step.

2. determining whether each step is value-added or nonvalue-added.

3. getting to root causes or the rationale for each step.

4. identifying alternative courses of action to facilitate management decisions. (Beischel 1990: 54)

ABC systems normally start with manufacturing overhead costs. However, when process value analysis is performed, it frequently becomes apparent that value is not created solely by the manufacturing operation. Research and development, marketing, and even accounting and finance do add value to the product and should be considered value-chain activities. Turney defines value-adding activities as activities that either are essential to the customer or are essential to the functioning of the organization. He places activities such as preparing financial statements in the latter category. Although financial statements may be of no concern to the customer, they must be prepared to meet the needs of stockholders, creditors, and government regulators (1992: 22).

To summarize the effects of cost driver and activity analysis, it is interesting to note Kaplan's comments in a 1991 interview:

We certainly started our work with a focus on managing product and customer mix, and that continues to be an important strategic application of ABC. In the last few years, however, we have seen the numbers coming from the activity-based cost analysis being used in conjunction with process improvements. . . . Now they are directing their improvement efforts to reducing the costs of performing many of these activities. Even better, they are attempting to understand some of the fundamental drivers of these activities and perhaps eliminate the need to perform some activities entirely. (King: 22)

Companies have benefited by instituting new systems for identifying and controlling costs (ABC and process value analysis) while they streamline the production process (reduce cost drivers and eliminate unnecessary activities).

AUTOMATION AND CAPITAL BUDGETING PROCEDURES

Some manufacturers have chosen to automate even though traditional capital budgeting procedures have indicated it will not be profitable for them to do so. Management's reasoning was that their capital budgeting models did not allow for a fair assessment of the benefits of automation. Now some are finding that automation was not the answer to all their problems and less expensive solutions such as a new factory layout would have done just as well. In some cases automation has been applied to such tasks as tracking systems and material-handling systems. Tasks such as these are nonvalue-adding activities, and management would be better off seeking ways to eliminate the activities rather than spending money to automate them.

After nearly a decade of articles in business periodicals extolling the virtues of automation at any price, a few voices are beginning to protest. Schonberger, for example, points out that managers should understand that

big machines, separated equipment, and long conveyor systems disconnect people, obscure opportunities for merging processes, and result in divided accountability. Automation has the potential to lower costs and minimize variations in quality, but it makes sense only when it solves clear-cut problems and when it costs less than simpler solutions. (1987: 95)

It is true that the capital budgeting models need to be updated or at least a better method of evaluating benefits is desirable. However, with no measurements other than subjective judgment, decision makers operate in the dark. Both the information system and the manufacturing procedures need revision.

A fuller discussion of ways to update the capital budgeting model is presented in Chapters 12 and 13. However, some critical problems with capital budgeting as it is performed in most companies has more to do with management rather than with the procedures per se. These difficulties have to do with plant and equipment reviews, the appropriation process, and audits of capital budgeting projects.

Plant and equipment should be reviewed in a systematic manner. This means that every process and every piece of equipment are reviewed in cycle for potential replacement. The length of the cycle depends on how rapidly the technology is moving. In most cases, about a five-year cycle permits fairly frequent review and yet is cost-effective.

A systematic review prevents the crisis management of equipment replacement that occurs in many companies—equipment is not replaced until it breaks down or until a manager hears about a new piece of equipment from a sales representative, a trade show, or a competitor. The increased emphasis on automation in recent years has worsened this type of decision making. Managers hear about new equipment and immediately assume it is something their company needs. A certain glamour is associated with talking about robotics or flexible manufacturing systems. Replacements may be motivated more by a desire to "keep up with the Joneses" than cost effectiveness.

Another problem with the management of the capital budgeting process is the way funds are allocated in a decentralized company. According to financial theories, all equipment replacements and other capital budgeting projects should be implemented if the returns exceed the cost of capital. However, in the short run this cannot occur because funds are limited by the financing alternatives available as well as by management policies. Therefore a company needs some procedure for authorizing the expenditure of the funds available. At the corporate level this usually involves ranking the projects by profitability and selecting the most profitable, provided they meet company objectives.

An Institute of Management Accounting-sponsored study suggests that in reality corporate management tends to focus on the total dollar amount of the projects proposed by a division rather than on specific projects. The same study also found that projects usually are classified by size when presented to management, with details for large and small projects combined in one amount (Corr 1983: 16–17, 23–25).

The ranking by size rather than profitability and the tendency to try to disburse funds to divisions somewhat evenly are crucial issues. It does not matter that individual divisions use the best capital budgeting tools available if the companywide selection is ultimately based on the size of the project. This creates an automatic bias against large-scale projects such as flexible manufacturing systems and replacement of whole technologies. Both corporate and division managers need to realize that when it is time to automate at plant A, the project may require a sizable portion of the funds available over a period of time.

Still another problem associated with the management of capital budgeting projects is the cursory nature of their postaudits. Managers who demand that the internal audit staff make sure every penny of cash is accounted for ignore the loss of millions on a capital budgeting project that has gone awry.

The expected benefits and the anticipated time frame should be outlined when the project is proposed. If those results are not achieved, there should be some accountability. Without this examination it is impossible to learn from failures or successes.

There is a tendency to think of funds as sunk once a project begins. Therefore the inclination is to ignore the results of capital budgeting decisions. The reality is that expenditures may go on for a period of years, and opportunities to make appropriate adjustments or scrap the project arise.

As company managers make decisions about automation and other capital budgeting projects, it is desirable to update the way projects are managed as well as the capital budgeting model and the manufacturing processes.

INVENTORY MANAGEMENT AND INVENTORY SYSTEMS

Automation and inventory reduction are probably the two most visible changes occurring in the new manufacturing environment. This has led some managers to think that buying the latest equipment and reducing inventories will benefit their companies, and they attempt to do so without further analysis. The hazards of buying new plant and equipment without sufficient investigation were discussed earlier in this chapter. Inventory reduction without a careful appraisal of the company's situation can likewise be dangerous.

How much inventory to carry is a function of the total inventory maintenance cost, which includes carrying costs and ordering or setup costs. Carrying costs include the costs of storage, handling, insurance, property taxes, obsolescence, breakage, and interest. Interest costs may be explicit if funds have to be borrowed to purchase or manufacture inventory. However, even if funds are internally generated, interest cost is implicit because the funds cannot be used for other purposes.

Ordering costs apply to material purchases and include clerical costs, transportation costs, and receiving costs. In the case of work in process and finished goods inventories, the comparable costs are setup costs because the product is manufactured rather than purchased. Setup costs include all the change-over costs necessary to produce a new run of product.

Most companies use a version of material requirements planning (MRP I) or materials resource planning (MRP II) to plan their inventory levels. MRP I generates a master production schedule that considers the demand levels for finished products. It plans manufacturing activities, delivery schedules, and purchasing. MRP II also considers capacity planning and labor scheduling.

In contrast the JIT system has been described as a "pull" system rather than a "push" system. Finished goods, as well as work in process at all stages, are minimized because production will not occur until just before it is needed.

JIT systems have been said to differ from MRP systems in that inventories are minimized. However, a good MRP system will also minimize inventories. The real difference between JIT and other inventory systems is in how the variables are measured or how they are regarded by management.

Critics of inventory systems as currently used say that carrying costs tend to be underestimated and that interest costs in particular are set too low. They also feel that setup costs have been taken as a given when a better approach would be to try to reduce both the time and cost of setups. They also point out that large amounts of safety stock have been carried to compensate for poor delivery performance by suppliers when a better strategy would be to work with the suppliers to achieve more dependable deliveries. A similar problem is created by carrying large amounts of buffer stock in the production area to compensate for bottlenecks and machine breakdowns. A better tactic is to tackle these problems directly.

Inventory information systems need to be revised so that the effect of the changes in the inventory itself can be evaluated. As companies work toward reducing safety stocks, setup times, and purchasing costs, these effects must be recognized. The appropriate variables in the system should be adjusted accordingly. Carrying costs should be measured as accurately as possible and should be recognized as a cost of holding excess inventories, as discussed in Chapter 5.

As production processes become more simplified, the accounting entries can also be simplified. The extreme simplification is the backflush system — costs are flushed out of the system after production is over rather than tracked throughout the process.

The backflush system works best in an environment in which there is no work in process inventory because all products are finished at the end of the day or the end of a shift. Most companies still need some inventory tracking through the production process and some control system because they have not achieved this type of production. For these companies standard cost systems can be updated as discussed in Chapter 5 to include raw materials ordering variances, raw materials inventory variances, quality variances, production (or finished goods inventory) variances, and sales completion variances.

RESEARCH AND DEVELOPMENT AND LIFE CYCLE COSTING

Another area that can benefit from revision of both procedures and accounting is the research and development (R&D) area. Many companies are taking a long look at their R&D processes and the way new products are developed.

Incremental Innovation versus Major Breakthroughs

Historically, most companies in the United States put funds into R&D activities with the hope of making a major breakthrough. Development of new products was a slow and clumsy process with activities sequenced so that full evolution took a period of years. There was little regard for how the product would eventually be manufactured, which meant that the production processes necessary to build the product were inefficient.

In the meantime foreign competitors (as well as some U.S. companies) were investing their R&D funds in what has been called *incremental innovation*. The cost was substantially less, and more changes could be brought to the market in less time. One chief executive officer commented, "A 1 per cent improvement in 1000 small items may not seem dramatic but it adds up to a significant achievement" (Humble and Jones 1989: 47).

This is not to say that there is no place for radical breakthrough thinking in R&D, but developments of this type seem more dependent on the creativity of one individual or a group of individuals than on funds invested. Nayak and Ketteringham studied sixteen companies that had major breakthroughs such as the Sony Walkman and the microwave oven (1986). In most cases they attributed the breakthrough to "technology push"—it was "a *problem* to be solved, not a fortune to be made nor a market to be exploited" (Humble and Jones 1989: 49).

Another way to obtain fundamental innovation is to purchase it. Rather than use a company's own resources to develop new products, it is possible to monitor developments in the industry and use licensing agreements to obtain access to the new products or processes. This frees up company resources to generate new markets and tailor the products for those markets.

A major study of some two hundred Japanese and American companies by Edwin Mansfield at the University of Pennsylvania's Center for Economics and Technology revealed differences in both the time and cost of product innovation in the two countries. He broke product innovation into six stages and found that Japanese firms devote a much higher percentage of their cost to tooling and to manufacturing equipment and facilities while American firms devote a much higher percentage to manufacturing start-up (training workers, debugging, and bringing quality up to acceptable levels) and to marketing start-up (pre-introduction marketing activities) (Mansfield 1988: 1157–1168).

The conclusion that can be drawn is that American firms could save a great deal of time and money in their product innovation efforts if they made more efficient use of external technology. Secondarily, it might be noted that the manufacturing and marketing start-up stages of the innovation process need reexamination.

Organization for R&D

Some problems with the R&D activities of most U.S. companies are organizational. The traditional approach to R&D is to organize by function with the activities performed sequentially. A more efficient way to organize is to perform parallel operations wherever possible. Another approach is to use interfunctional teams with personnel from marketing, design, manufacturing, and finance all working together. Some comparisons to the traditional functional factory layout and the work-cell arrangement can be made. Just as companies have tended to organize along functional lines and process sequentially in the factory, they have tended to organize along functional lines and perform operations sequentially in R&D.

Bringing manufacturing personnel into the design stage has particular advantages. More than 90 percent of a product's cost is determined in preproduction stages (Berliner and Brimson 1988: 139). In the past products have often been designed without regard for the difficulty or cost involved in manufacturing. This has resulted in expensive and time-consuming manufacturing processes with high quality very hard to achieve. Regard for such factors as setup time and interchangability of parts can greatly assist in producing a product that can be sold for a price acceptable to the market.

R&D Information Systems

As the process and organization for R&D are rethought, the information system for R&D activities needs to be revamped. The information system for R&D includes procedures for authorizing projects and expenditures, auditing projects, and financial accounting requirements.

The selection of projects is akin to the purchase of plant and equipment in that substantial periods of time are involved, expenditures may be large, and the returns are difficult to forecast. Also, as with plant and equipment expenditures, the strategic goals of the firm must be recognized. The techniques for selecting a project involve the same considerations as a capital budgeting project: investment or cash outlays, time period, cash inflows or returns, risk, and meeting strategic goals.

An interfunctional team is useful at the proposal stage as well as in the development stage because the information comes from all functions. All members of the team must appreciate the costs associated with new (as well as old) products. John Maurer, senior consultant at Westinghouse's Productivity and Quality Center at Pittsburgh, Pennsylvania, once asked so-called experts in purchasing, engineering, manufacturing, and sales to estimate the cost of products they were involved with and found that some estimates were off by a factor of 10.

Maurer's reaction was that "Many people really don't have any idea what things cost in terms of such issues as hardware, processing, and operations. . . . How then can we ask these people to make important decisions affecting the health of our business if they don't know the cost?" (Raia 1989: 63).

Auditing R&D projects is also an important consideration, and procedures for examining results should be formulated as R&D activities are revised. Auditing of R&D results should involve more than merely tracking expenditures to see that they stay within budget, although this is certainly an important consideration. Auditing should also involve a review of how well the project is meeting the company goals it was intended to meet and checking to see that cash inflows are as projected. The project should be tracked to see if results are being obtained according to the planned time frame.

Just as a host of new free-standing performance measures has been proposed for production, new measures are being proposed for R&D. One group of authors writing in *Research Management* has proposed a system that measures R&D productivity, yield, and return. Productivity is measured as technical progress divided by R&D investment. Yield is found by dividing profits by technical progress. Return is profits divided by R&D investment (or productivity times yield). Technical progress is "the difference between the current performance of the last generation product or process that the company introduced and the projected performance of the one now under development or about to be introduced." The authors believe that R&D managers should be primarily responsible for productivity while other functional managers should be responsible for yield (Foster, et al. 1985: 12–14).

Another proposed measure of overall R&D output is the percentage of sales and profits derived from technology brought into commercialization in the past ten years. Still another is patent output (Boer 1991: 13).

In many cases the financial accounting for a particular expenditure does not significantly affect the managerial accounting or decision-making function. However, in the case of R&D there is strong evidence that the way financial accounting and tax authorities view R&D expenditures does influence the amount spent.

The two basic positions on R&D expenditures are that they can either be capitalized (treated as a long-term asset) or they can be immediately expensed. Accounting theorists have argued the merits of one position over the other for fifty years or longer. Most early theorists advocated capitalization for major projects at least, and tax authorities also followed this position. However, the Revenue Act of 1954 allowed immediate write-off of R&D expenses and *Accounting Research Study No. 14,* commissioned by the Accounting Principles Board, also advocated this position. In 1974 the Financial Accounting Standards Board in its *Statement No. 2* gave its blessing to expensing R&D as it occurred (although the rule was modified in 1985 for computer software). Thus the weight of both financial and tax authorities is behind expensing rather than capitalizing.

Most authorities applaud the tax position that provides immediate tax benefits while criticizing the financial accounting treatment. They point out that financial accounting authorities in countries such as Canada, Australia, New Zealand, and Scotland permit capitalization of major development projects. They believe the position of the U.S. financial accounting authorities puts U.S. corporations in a poor competitive position in relation to these other countries.

Furthermore critics of the expense-all-R&D position also believe that this requirement creates incentive for spending on small, short-term projects with high immediate returns and short payback periods. They feel that major development projects that may take longer periods of time to bring to maturity are being rejected. The advantage of immediate expensing is, of course, that it avoids large write-offs when a project fails. A survey of U.S. R&D directors by Nix and Peters found that approximately 60 percent of the directors felt that expensing of R&D had a negative (more than "very little") effect on the amount spent on R&D. Fifty percent said that current operating profits affect the budgeting of R&D projects (1988: 39).

Until the Financial Accounting Standards Board changes its position, U.S. corporations can do very little about the way they account for R&D expenses other than lobby for a change. A few innovation methods have been proposed, such as treating R&D expenses as contra stockholder accounts (Nix and Nix 1991: 7–8), but these treatments will not affect the bottom line profit of the corporation and are not likely to affect corporate decision making concerning R&D budgets.

Some accountants propose what has been called *life cycle costing* for products. They stress that product costs should include the development stage costs as well as costs in the introduction and maturity stages. Most life cycle costing advocates emphasize an accurate accumulation of all product costs to be used in decisions about product introduction, product mix, and pricing. They generally are not clear on how the costs should be charged off for financial accounting purposes. A logical extension of life cycle costing would say that not only should start-up costs be capitalized but they should be written off according to the stage in the life cycle. However, since capitalization in any fashion is not an option, the method of writing off the costs is moot. This is probably why life cycle costing proponents have concentrated on the managerial accounting concerns.

Actual applications of life cycle costing are relatively rare (Seed 1990: 29). However, the idea has the backing of the prestigious Computer Aided Manufacturing International (CAM-I), a coalition of industrial organizations, accounting firms, government agencies, and universities formed to address the problems of cost management created by advanced manufacturing technologies. According to CAM-I:

Life-cycle costing is necessary to provide a better picture of long-term product profitability; to show the effectiveness of life-cycle planning; to quantify the cost impact of alternatives chosen during the engineering design phase; and to assign the costs of technology to products that use the technology. (Berliner and Brimson 1988: 141)

The temptation is to say that the shortened product life cycles of technologically advanced products are an argument for expensing all product development costs as they occur since writing the expenses off immediately is not that different from writing them off over a relatively short period. However, life cycle costing advocates point out that such an approach can lead to mismatches of costing between products because some require more development costs than others. Subsequent decisions concerning pricing and product mixes can also be affected.

It does seem clear that the accounting for R&D expenses needs revision along with the management of R&D departments. Managers need to rethink the idea of tying current R&D expenditures to current profits and evaluating R&D projects by short-term investment measures. Spending should be geared more toward projects that have the potential for a positive net present value as shown by projected cash inflows over the life of the products developed. Evaluation should depend on whether projects are on target for the forecasted goals. The reward structure should not penalize R&D managers whose projects are on target even though immediate results have not been achieved. It should award designers and engineers who develop quality products that can be manufactured economically.

The information system should show whether a project should be undertaken and whether it is on target as it progresses. The performance evaluation system should indicate those managers who have succeeded in terms of predetermined goals. Furthermore the accounting information system should indicate how R&D expenses should be allocated among products and facilitate decisions concerning product mix and pricing.

>> <<

As changes are made in production, corresponding changes need to be made in the information systems that report on production. The information system is, after all, just a model of the reality; when the reality changes, the model should change. Much of the discomfort with cost accounting systems in the 1980s occurred because the models had not caught up with the realities.

Accountants have numbers skills that can be put to good use in determining whether changes in production are cost-effective or beneficial. If they can move away from their traditional procedures and accept new and innovative methods of data gathering and analysis, they can be agents of change rather than barriers. Areas in which they can be of assistance include process value analysis, capital budgeting, inventory management systems, and evaluation of research and development.

REFERENCES

Beischel, Mark E. "Improving Production with Process Value Analysis," *Journal of Accountancy*. September 1990, pp. 53–57.

Berliner, Callie, and James A. Brimson, eds. *Cost Management for Today's Advanced Manufacturing: The CAM-I Conceptual Design*. Boston: Harvard Business School Press, 1988.

Boer, F. Peter. "R&D Planning Environment for the '90s—America and Japan," *Research Technology Management*. March–April 1991, pp. 12–15.

Calvasina, Richard V., Eugene J. Calvasina, and Gerald E. Calvasina. "Beware the New Accounting Myths," *Management Accounting*. December 1989, pp. 41–45.

Clements, Ronald B., and Charlene W. Spoede. "Trane's SOUP Accounting," *Management Accounting*. June 1992, pp. 46–52.

Corr, Arthur V. *The Capital Expenditure Decision*. Montvale, N.J.: National Association of Accountants (Institute of Management Accountants), 1983.

Financial Accounting Standards Board. *Statement of Financial Accounting Standards, No. 2*. Stamford, Conn.: 1974.

Foster, Richard N., Lawrence H. Linden, Roger L. Whiteley, and Alan M. Kantrow. "Improving the Return on R&D," *Research Management*. February 1985, pp. 12–17.

Gellein, Oscar S., and Maurice Newman. *Accounting for Research and Development Expenditures*, Accounting Research Study No. 14. New York: American Institute of Certified Public Accountants, 1973.

Horngren, Charles T., and George Foster. *Cost Accounting: A Managerial Emphasis*. Englewood Cliffs, N.J.: Prentice-Hall, 1987.

Humble, John, and Gareth Jones. "Creating a Climate for Innovation," *Long Range Planning*. August 1989, pp. 46–51.

King, Alfred M. "The Current Status of Activity-Based Costing: An Interview with Robin Cooper and Robert S. Kaplan," *Management Accounting*. September 1991, pp. 22–26.

Mansfield, Edwin. "The Speed and Cost of Industrial Innovation in Japan and the United States: External vs. Internal Technology," *Management Science*. October 1988, pp. 1157–1168.

Nayak, P., and John Ketteringham. *Breakthroughs*. New York: Rawson, 1986.

Nix, David E., and Paul E. Nix. "It's Time To Change the Financial Accounting Treatment of R&D Expenditures," *Research Technology Management*. March–April 1991, pp. 7–8.

Nix, Paul E., and Richard M. Peters. "Accounting for R&D Expenditures," *Research Technology Management*. January–February 1988, pp. 39–41.

Raia, Ernest. "Better Value, Bigger Profits," *Purchasing*. June 8, 1989, pp. 58–63.

Schonberger, Richard J. "Frugal Manufacturing," *Harvard Business Review*. September–October 1987, pp. 95–100.

Seed, Allen H., III. "Improving Cost Management," *Management Accounting*. February 1990, pp. 27–30.

Turney, Peter B. B. "Activity-Based Management," *Management Accounting*. January 1992, pp. 20–25.

CHAPTER 11

Effect of the New Manufacturing Environment on Marketing

The new manufacturing environment is affecting the marketing function of a firm as well as production. The efficiencies gained in production in terms of lower inventories, better factory layouts, and more automation translate into lower costs. The emphasis on value-added concepts, higher quality, and more rapid throughput translate into better customer service. Lower costs and better service mean more choice in terms of marketing strategies. If marketing managers do not capitalize on the benefits of lower costs and better service, the firm will not realize its full potential in terms of profit and market share despite more efficient production.

Techniques to upgrade the cost systems designed for production can also be used for marketing costs. Cost accounting systems in general and standard cost systems in particular have tended to concentrate on one phase of a product's life, the manufacturing phase, while other important costs are ignored. Other significant costs occur before the manufacturing stage — research and development costs (discussed in Chapter 10). Also other important costs — marketing costs — occur after the manufacturing stage.

One reason for the concentration on manufacturing is that cost accounting systems are used to determine product costs for inventory purposes. Financial accounting authorities, from the old Committee on Accounting Procedure (1938–1959) to today's Financial Accounting Standards Board, have decreed that manufacturing costs are the only inventoriable costs.

Another reason that marketing costs have been ignored as product costs is that marketing costs are less tangible and harder to attach to products than manufacturing costs. This is spurious reasoning. First, the results of analyzing marketing costs may be less accurate but can still be valuable. Second, many costs in the manufacturing category, especially certain types of overhead costs, are also difficult to analyze, but techniques have been developed to do so.

Marketing costs are product costs just as production costs are product costs and deserve the same attention. Furthermore the sales activities of the business need to be analyzed to determine whether goals are being met in terms of the revenue flowing into the company.

MARKETING ACTIVITIES AND COST DRIVERS

As noted in Chapter 7, activity-based analysis of marketing costs somewhat predated that of production costs in the form of functional costing. However, the technology of the 1950s did not support the necessary analysis, and functional costing fell by the wayside in most organizations. The concept of functional costing also was criticized because it was a full cost approach, and critics believed that better decisions could be made on the basis of variable costs (contribution approach).

These objections have been largely overcome in the new manufacturing environment. The technology has caught up in the form of computer-based analysis. The full cost/contribution approach debate has been somewhat quieted by the recognition that costs can vary with factors other than volume.

Therefore marketing costs are a fertile field for analysis in the 1990s. As much benefit probably can be obtained from a more rigid examination of these costs as from the better appraisal of overhead costs in the 1980s. After all, marketing costs can run as much as 50 percent of product cost, particularly in situations in which physical distribution costs are high (Lewis 1991: 33).

Marketing costs can be categorized in various ways. The Rayburn textbook uses the classifications of (1) warehousing and handling, (2) transportation, (3) credit and collection, (4) general marketing activities, and (5) advertising and sales promotion (1989: 1068–1075).

Each category can be subclassified into a number of activities. Warehousing and handling, for example, can be broken down into receiving, pricing and tagging, sorting, assembling stock for shipment, handling returns, packing and wrapping, taking inventory, and clerical handling of shipping orders. After the activities are identified, the associated cost drivers (units of variability) can be determined. For warehousing and handling, cost drivers might include dollar value of purchases, dollar value of shipments, number of shipments, purchase invoice lines, sales invoice lines, number of returns, physical weight of goods handled, or dollar value of average inventory (Rayburn 1989: 1069).

As in the case of overhead costs, some reaggregation of cost drivers and activities is usually necessary to arrive at a manageable and cost-effective number. Decisions about a particular function can be made from data

Figure 11.1
Marketing Cost Variances

Example:

Handling of sales returns:

Actual returns processed	1,200
Budgeted returns	1,000
Standard cost per return	$ 10
Actual cost of returns	$12,500

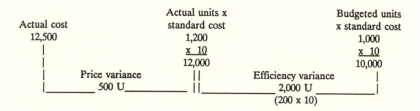

obtained about that activity. For example, a decision about whether to try to decrease the time of processing a return can use as an input the cost per return.

For some decisions it may be necessary to separate the costs into those that are variable with a particular driver and those that are fixed and to compute a unit variable cost and a unit fixed cost. The variable cost can be used for short-term decisions regarding increases or decreases in that activity while the full direct cost can be used for long-term evaluations of profitability and performance. For example, a decision to grant quantity discounts might be based on variable order-filling costs while an evaluation of the profitability of product A might be based on the full direct marketing costs plus manufacturing costs. A contribution analysis would be necessary to decide whether to discontinue a product line or territory or to refuse small orders (Lewis 1991: 34).

VARIANCES FOR MARKETING COSTS

Standard cost analysis can be applied to some marketing costs in a similar manner to its application in the factory. However, distinguishing between repetitive and nonrepetitive operations is important. Standards can be developed for repetitive operations such as packing a shipment. However, for nonrepetitive operations, such as most activities associated with direct selling, developing standards is not worthwhile. Control is better achieved by just checking for adherence to budgeted expenses.

Figure 11.1 illustrates how marketing costs may be analyzed. The example involves processing sales returns. Much the same as variable manufacturing costs are analyzed, the variable cost of processing sales returns is analyzed. The standard cost per return is $10, a figure that would be arrived at by work sampling, engineering studies, and/or examining historical data. Since 200 more returns were processed than were budgeted, the unfavorable efficiency variance is $2,000. To process the 1,200 actual returns at a rate of $10 each should have cost $12,000. However, the actual cost was $12,500, which is $500 higher than expected. The price (or spending) variance is $500.

In determining responsibility for marketing cost variances, it is important to make sure that the right department or individual is answerable for a particular variance. In the case of sales returns the $2,000 unfavorable efficiency variance is not the fault of the department handling the returns. The extra returns could be caused by higher sales than normal, lower quality, or a more generous return policy. None of these factors would be the responsibility of the returns department, with the possible exception of the return policy. The only variance for which it should be held accountable is the $500 price or spending variance. The variance analysis does assess responsibility more fairly. If the actual cost were merely compared with the budgeted cost, the returns department presumably would be charged with the total unfavorable variance of $2,500.

SALES VARIANCES FOR VOLUME, PRICE, AND MIX

The SCS of the past used the volume variance to indicate that the company was not producing and selling as many product units as it had planned. However, this indicator only showed the amount of fixed overhead that was over- or underabsorbed due to over- or underproduction. Rather than use the volume variance as a crude indicator of lack of sales orders, what is needed is the effect on contribution margins (sales minus all costs that vary with volume). The three basic types of sales variances are the sales volume variance, the sales mix variance, and sales price/cost variances. The sales volume variance may be further subdivided into a market share and market size variance. For a company using JIT techniques, the new manufacturing environment has spawned two additional sales variances—the sales order variance and the finished goods variance.

An unfavorable sales volume variance measures the contribution margin lost because sales orders were not as high as planned. The sales volume may be indicated either in number of units or in sales dollars. In companies with even a few products, using sales dollars to measure volume is more reasonable.

Unfavorable sales price and cost variances measure the contribution margins lost because sales prices were lower than planned or variable costs were higher than planned. Variable cost differences are already captured in the standard cost system in cost variances. It is duplication to also consider variable cost variances among the marketing variances. Therefore variable cost variances need not be included with sales variances. If sales and production are synchronized (the company produces just for its sales orders), there would be no difference in timing for the cost variances from the production and marketing standpoints. However, if sales and production are not synchronized, there would be some timing difference.

Unfavorable sales mix variances indicate the mix of products sold was not as planned. Arriving at the planned mix of products to be produced and sold is not a simple task. A great deal of concern in the new manufacturing environment has focused on optimal product mixes. To obtain this mix involves recognizing both market and production constraints. Where there are production constraints, linear programming models or similar logic may need to be applied to arrive at the optimal use of scarce resources. Constraints may also be of the market variety. It may be obvious which product or products are most profitable, but the market may not absorb the number of units that can be produced. Assuming management can arrive at an optimal mix or a planned mix (if different), a mix variance can be calculated. An unfavorable sales or product mix variance indicates the contribution margins lost because the mix of products sold was different than the optimal or planned mix.

To illustrate marketing variances, consider a company that produces two products, exercise bicycles and rowing machines. The sales and production budget for the month of April indicates the company will make and sell 1,500 bicycles and 1,000 rowing machines. Bicycles sell for $250 and have variable costs of $150, making the contribution margin $100. Rowing machines sell for $300 and have variable costs of $120, making the contribution margin $180. The budgeted total contribution margin for the month is $330,000, computed as follows:

Bicycles 1,500 @ $100	$150,000
Rowing Machines 1,000 @ $180	180,000
Total Contribution Margin	$330,000

Suppose, however, the company actually sold 1,800 bicycles for $270 each and 900 rowing machines for $300 each. The actual total contribution margin for the month is $378,000, computed as follows:

Bicycles 1,800 @ $120	$216,000
Rowing Machines 900 @ $180	162,000
Total Contribution Margin	$378,000

The actual contribution margin is $48,000 higher than planned. Overall, the marketing variance is $48,000 favorable. Part of the variance is because of the bicycles being sold for a price $20 higher than planned. The $20 increase in price for 1,800 bicycles accounts for $36,000 of the favorable variance.

However, other factors are at work. The planned mix of products was

Figure 11.2
Sales Price, Mix, and Volume Variances

Example:

	Product A	Product B
Budgeted sales in units	3,000	3,000
Actual sales in units	2,000	3,000
Budgeted sales price	$5.00	$6.00
Standard variable cost per unit	$2.00	$4.00
Budgeted margin per unit	$3.00	$2.00
Actual sales price	$4.00	$6.00
Actual variable cost per unit	$2.00	$4.00
Actual margin per unit	$2.00	$2.00

Price variance:

Actual sales of A @ budgeted price	(2,000 units @ $5.00)	$10,000
Actual sales of A @ actual price	(2,000 units @ $4.00)	8,000
Price variance (unfavorable)	(2,000 units @ $1.00)	$ 2,000

Mix and sales volume variances:

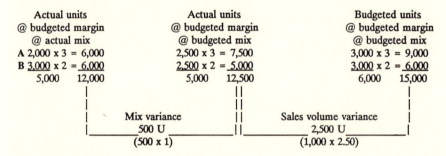

```
   Actual units              Actual units              Budgeted units
 @ budgeted margin         @ budgeted margin          @ budgeted margin
   @ actual mix            @ budgeted mix             @ budgeted mix
A 2,000 x 3 = 6,000        2,500 x 3 = 7,500          3,000 x 3 = 9,000
B 3,000 x 2 = 6,000        2,500 x 2 = 5,000          3,000 x 2 = 6,000
   5,000   12,000           5,000   12,500             6,000   15,000
          |                        ||
          |                        ||
          |        Mix variance    ||      Sales volume variance
          |_____500 U_____ ||_____2,500 U_____|
                  (500 x 1)                  (1,000 x 2.50)
```

Journal entries:

Cost of goods sold		
(2,000 x 2) + (3,000 x 4)	16,000	
Accounts receivable		
(2,000 x 4) + (3,000 x 6)	26,000	
Finished goods		16,000
Sales		26,000
Actual margin		
(26,000 - 16,000)	10,000	
Sales price variance	2,000	
Sales mix variance	500	
Sales volume variance	2,500	
Budgeted margin		15,000

1,500 bicycles and 1,000 rowing machines, a 3 to 2 ratio of bicycles to rowing machines. The actual mix turned out to be 1,800 bicycles and 900 rowing machines, a 2 to 1 ratio. The product with the highest contribution margin, rowing machines, was budgeted to be two-fifths, or 40 percent, of the mix. In fact rowing machines accounted for one-third, or 33⅓ percent, of the mix of the 2,700 products sold. If the company had sold these products in the planned mix, it would have sold 40 percent, or 1,080 rowing machines. It was 180 machines short of the planned mix.

The budgeted contribution margin is $180 for rowing machines but only $100 for bicycles. By not selling as many rowing machines, the company lost $80 in contribution margin for each one. On 180 rowing machines this amounts to an unfavorable mix variance of $14,400.

Another factor at work is volume. Some units have a contribution margin of $100 and some $180. However, the weighted average contribution margin is $132, found by taking the budgeted total contribution margin of $330,000 and dividing by the budgeted total sales of 2,500 units. Actual sales were in fact 2,700 units, or 200 units more than planned. The extra 200 units gained the company an average of $132 each, or $26,400. In other words, the volume variance was $26,400 favorable.

A summary of the marketing variances shows:

Price variance on bicycles	$36,000 favorable
Mix variance	14,400 unfavorable
Volume variance	26,400 favorable
Total marketing variance	$48,000 favorable

Obviously, most companies have product structures that are much more complex than this simple illustration. Nevertheless the principles for calculating marketing variances are the same. One modification that some firms may want to make is viewing sales volume and mix in terms of sales dollars rather than units. This will simplify the computation somewhat if there are many products.

A comprehensive illustration of marketing variances appears in Figure 11.2. This company sells two products, product A and product B. Because it sold product A for $1 less than the budgeted sales price, it had an unfavorable sales price variance. The illustration assumes that actual variable cost was the same as standard variable cost. However, even if the actual cost was different than the standard, this would be ignored in the marketing variances because the cost variances have already been captured.

This company's budgeted mix is half product A and half product B. However, the actual mix was 2 to 3 with less of the more profitable product A sold, resulting in an unfavorable mix variance. In addition, sales were budgeted at 6,000 units while only 5,000 units were actually sold, resulting in an unfavorable volume variance as well.

Figure 11.3
Market Share and Market Size Variances

Example:

Budgeted market size in units	400,000
Actual market size in units	500,000
Budgeted market share	1.5%
Actual market share	1.0%
Budgeted average contribution margin	$2.50

Variances:

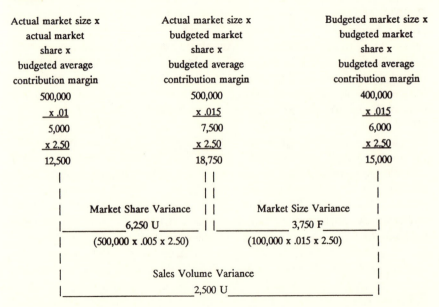

Actual market size x	Actual market size x	Budgeted market size x
actual market	budgeted market	budgeted market
share x	share x	share x
budgeted average	budgeted average	budgeted average
contribution margin	contribution margin	contribution margin
500,000	500,000	400,000
x .01	x .015	x .015
5,000	7,500	6,000
x 2.50	x 2.50	x 2.50
12,500	18,750	15,000

Market Share Variance
6,250 U
(500,000 x .005 x 2.50)

Market Size Variance
3,750 F
(100,000 x .015 x 2.50)

Sales Volume Variance
2,500 U

The journal entries show the variable cost of goods sold being transferred out of finished goods and on to the cost of goods sold account, while the sales value is recorded as a debit to accounts receivable and a credit to sales. Ignoring fixed overhead, this would be comparable to the entry made under the traditional SCS. To record the variances, the unfavorable variances are debited to an account called "Actual Margin." The offsetting credit is to "Budgeted Margin." The variances and the margin accounts would be closed out at the end of the accounting period. Of course, the benefits of the variance analysis can be achieved without actually journalizing the results.

MARKET SIZE AND MARKET SHARE VARIANCES

A further refinement of the sales volume variance that is sometimes useful is the computation of a market size and a market share variance (Horngren and Foster 1987: 805–806). Suppose the total industry market for both products in Figure 11.2 is expected to be 400,000 units and suppose that the company wishes to maintain a market share of 1.5 percent. An unfavorable sales volume variance could be caused by a shrinking market (market size variance) or by a shrinking share of that market (market share variance) or a combination of both.

The variances could be computed as in Figure 11.3. Assuming a market share of 1.5 percent of a market of 400,000 units, the company budgeted sales of 6,000 units, as in Figure 11.2. However, the actual market is 500,000 units and the company obtains only a 1 percent share, giving actual sales of 5,000 units, again as in Figure 11.2. The total unfavorable sales volume variance is 1,000 units, or $2,500. Part of this variance is caused by the company's market share being only 1 percent instead of 1.5 percent as planned. This caused a $6,250 unfavorable market share variance. However, this is somewhat offset by the fact that the market itself expanded by 100,000 units. Considering the company's budgeted share of this expanded market was 1.5 percent, the market size variance was a favorable $3,750.

Unless the company is large enough to influence the overall market itself, the only controllable part of the sales volume variance is the market share component. Subdividing the sales volume variance in this fashion helps marketing managers understand why sales were different than planned. In years when the market is expected to be poor, it gives an opportunity for increased sales efforts to increase the market share to offset an overall market decrease.

SALES ORDER VARIANCE

The section of this chapter on sales price, mix, and volume variances and the section on market size and market share variances use budgeted figures for targeted amounts. Budgets are typically prepared on an annual basis and then subdivided into shorter periods such as months. In the new manufacturing environment, the time frame may be much shorter. For companies approaching a true JIT environment, budgeted production and/or sales may have very little meaning. For a very short-run analysis of production and sales levels, the approach in Figure 11.4 may be useful.

The illustration in Figure 11.4 reproduces the production output variances from Figure 5.1. Information on sales orders placed and filled is included in addition. In the examples, scheduled production and sales orders placed are identical because they should be very close to the same in a true JIT environ-

Figure 11.4
Finished Goods and Sales Order Variances

Example:

Production (finished units):	
Scheduled production	2,000
Total production	2,500
Good units produced	2,400
Defective units	100
Sales (finished units):	
Sales orders placed	2,000
Sales orders filled	2,200
Standard cost per unit:	$2.00
Budgeted contribution margin per unit:	$1.50

Production analysis:

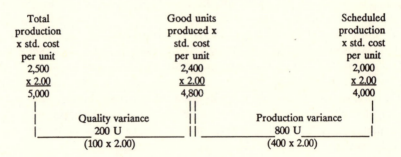

Sales analysis:

ment. If they are different, however, the analysis can still be done with no violation to the results.

As discussed in Chapter 5, the quality variance represents the investment in defective units. The production variance represents the investment in unnecessary inventory buildups. These variances are based on the manufacturer's cost.

The sales analysis is based on the contribution margin and represents lost opportunities in terms of sales. The finished goods variance represents the contribution margin on units that are completed but not shipped. The delay in shipment will cause a loss to the company because of delay in receiving payment. The effect of this loss may be determined by applying a cost of capital rate to this amount. The cause of this variance might be shipment delays or the production of units that do not match sales orders. In either case an excess of good units produced over orders filled is a negative factor. If more sales orders are filled than goods units produced, the variance is favorable because it represents a decrease in the finished goods inventory.

The sales order variance represents the difference between sales orders received and filled. In this case the company filled more orders than it received. Presumably that is because there were backorders that are now being supplied. The variance is labeled as favorable because it represents a correction of a previously negative condition—that is, that there were backorders because orders placed exceeded orders filled. When orders are placed but not filled, the variance is unfavorable because of the delay in receipt of the contribution margin from the customer. However, there is some argument for viewing any deviation of orders filled from orders placed as unfavorable because a JIT environment with rapid throughput should keep the two closely matched.

Harrell, who computes a sales completion variance based on the difference in material costs between sales orders placed and filled, comments that the variance

would be unfavorable if any deviation appeared in the analysis. If orders placed exceed orders filled, sales revenue would be lost for the period, if not permanently. Orders filled exceeding orders placed would signify the completion of back orders, again indicating the possible lost revenue from any customers who were not willing to wait for a back order. . . . Its existence would concern executive management because of the loss, or potential loss, of sales revenue. (1992: 38)

There is no duplication between the production variance, which is a cost variance, and the finished goods variance, which is based on the contribution margin. The unfavorable production variance represents the investment in excess inventory while the finished goods variance represents delayed receipt of the contribution margin. The finished goods variance may be thought of as an opportunity cost. Both are unfavorable because excess unsold inventories do hurt the manufacturer in two ways—funds are tied up in the units, and delaying the sale delays receipt of profits.

PRICING STRATEGIES IN THE NEW MANUFACTURING ENVIRONMENT

For many years after World War II, U.S. firms were essentially price makers. With the rest of the world's industries devastated, U.S. firms were the "only game in town," and they could set prices considering only their domestic competition. This happy state of affairs (for them) ended as foreign firms came onstream in the 1970s and 1980s with newer equipment and strategies for penetrating markets previously dominated by U.S. firms.

Up to this point American firms generally had a strategy of selling a low cost product at an acceptable quality level. Unfortunately, this strategy often produced neither desired effect—the cost was not as low as it might have been and the quality was not acceptable. U.S. firms frequently relied on economies of scale to maintain a low cost. Economies of scale meant producing large lots of product to lie in inventory, freezing large amounts of capital and risking obsolescence. Product costs and throughput times were taken as a given, and efficiency was measured by outdated standards. Acceptable quality levels became unacceptable to consumers as foreign firms began to produce products of higher quality while meeting or bettering U.S. prices.

Clearly the stage was set for new tactics by domestic firms, and many accepted the challenge with new manufacturing techniques throughout the 1980s. The consequence was higher quality products produced at lower costs. However, these results still may not generate profits for the firm if a proper pricing strategy is not pursued. The section that follows considers some of the pricing strategies that may be used, including cost-plus pricing, contribution pricing, value pricing, target pricing, and life cycle pricing.

COST-PLUS PRICING

Cost-plus pricing is perhaps the oldest pricing strategy; in effect it says that the selling firm will charge its cost plus a certain markup. The strategy is appropriate for a price maker because it does not consider what the competition is charging or will charge. Cost-plus pricing is also appropriate for new products without close substitutes. Cost-plus pricing may also be used to establish a floor for the price of a product while the market (competition) establishes the ceiling.

Cost-plus pricing has many variations, depending on what is taken to be the base (cost) and what is taken to be the markup (plus). The markup consists of two components—an amount to cover the costs not included in the base and a profit. It would follow then that the smaller the base, the larger the markup. Consider the following example:

Product X, per-unit costs and price:

Materials	$ 2.50
Labor	1.00
Manufacturing overhead	3.00
Research and development	2.00
Marketing costs	1.50
Profit	2.00
Price	$12.00

One base that is sometimes used is a markup on the cost of materials. This is a very small base. In order to obtain a price of $12, the markup on product X must be 380 percent ([12 − 2.5] ÷ 2.5). Prime costs (materials and labor) are sometimes used as a base, particularly when overhead rates are not very accurate. In this illustration the markup on prime costs would need to be 243 percent ([12 − 2.5 − 1] ÷ [2.5 + 1]). The markup on manufacturing cost including overhead would be 85 percent ([12 − 2.5 − 1 − 3] ÷ [2.5 + 1 + 3]). The markup on full cost, including research and development and marketing costs, would be 20 percent ([12 − 2.5 − 1 − 3 − 2 − 1.5] ÷ [2.5 + 1 + 3 + 2 + 1.5]).

This illustration is used to contrast the types and sizes of markups. Therefore the price is given. Ordinarily, the markup is set and then the price derived. The markup is set with the goal of covering other costs and making a profit. The more costs that can be accurately determined and put into the base, the greater will be the likelihood that cost-plus pricing will yield a price that makes the desired profit.

If cost systems have been updated to cope with the new manufacturing environment, costs can be more accurately determined. Overhead can be better costed to products because of the realization that more overhead cost pools and drivers are needed. Other costs that were previously unrecognized as product costs, such as research and development and market costs, can now be treated as product costs.

Sometimes *target-profit pricing* is listed as a separate pricing strategy. In this type of pricing the selling firm tries to obtain a certain desired profit for its investors. This is essentially the same thing as saying that the firm wants to recoup full cost plus a markup, which is cost-plus pricing.

Cost-plus pricing has two dangers. One danger is that it is entirely self-focused as far as the seller is concerned. It does not consider (at least in its basic form) what the customer is willing to pay or what competitors will charge. In other words, it does not consider factors that are external to the firm. The other danger in cost-plus pricing is that there is no incentive to cut costs. In fact the larger the cost base, the larger the dollar amount of the profit when the markup percentage is applied. Efficiency, economies of scale, and experience curves are all left to automatically occur, rather than management making a concerted attempt to drive down cost by these and other means.

CONTRIBUTION PRICING

Contribution pricing is a short-run strategy that says that the minimum price a firm can charge is its incremental cost. Assume that the seller of product X in the example has an offer from a large wholesaler to buy 1,000 units of product X for a reduced price. If the seller can produce the units with current capacity and the special treatment of one customer will not violate any price discrimination laws or offend other customers, what minimum price would be acceptable? A cost analysis would show:

Incremental:

Materials	$ 2,500
Manufacturing overhead	1,000
Marketing	1,000
Total incremental	$ 4,500

Nonincremental:

Labor	$ 1,000
Overhead	2,000
Research and development	2,000
Marketing	500
Total nonincremental	$ 5,500
Total costs	$10,000

The breakdown on the costs of the order includes $4,500 of incremental costs. This includes the materials and part of the overhead and marketing costs. Certain overhead would be incremental, such as the setup costs, additional supplies, and power to produce the order. Certain marketing costs also would be incremental, such as packing, transporting, and sales commissions on the order, if any.

Nonincremental costs of $5,500 include labor, research and development, and the rest of the overhead and marketing costs. Labor is often treated as an incremental cost, but a permanent work force is a committed or nonincremental cost. In a wide range of production activity the labor force is neither increased nor decreased. Research and development is a product cost; but, by the time orders are placed, it is a sunk or past cost. Some marketing costs, such as marketing salaries and the allocated portion of front-end costs to launch the product, would also be committed or sunk costs at this point.

The minimum price for the order is $4,500, which covers the incremental costs. Anything above the minimum will contribute to the nonincremental costs and profit.

The usual discussion of contribution pricing equates variable costs with incremental costs, and variable costs are taken to mean those that vary with volume. An updated cost analysis differs in several ways from the more traditional approach. In the classic approach labor is assumed to be variable even though the labor force is fixed. An updated approach recognizes that labor is not an incremental cost unless extra workers must be hired or overtime wages paid to complete the special order.

Furthermore an updated cost analysis differentiates costs that change with production volume from those that change with a batch of production or an order. Materials, power, and supplies may change with the volume, but setup costs change with the number of batches produced. Likewise, certain marketing costs may change with the order, such as packing and transporting a bulk shipment. The newer cost analysis can also differentiate product-line costs, such as research and development and advertising, which would be nonincremental as far as a particular order is concerned.

Contribution pricing is a short-run strategy. In the long run all costs must be covered. However, it is appropriate in cases such as a special order if there is excess capacity, regular business will not be affected, and price discrimination is not a factor.

VALUE PRICING

While cost-based and contribution pricing look inward to the seller's cost, value pricing looks outward to the customer and prices the product according to the economic benefit to the customer. Value pricing is usually directed at the upscale end of the market. Efforts are made to increase value and therefore increase price.

Presutti describes the premise of value pricing:

A basic tenet of value-based pricing is that some buyers are not price-sensitive and that they will pay a premium price for a product if it delivers a particular benefit that the customer values highly. Firms that use value-based pricing attempt to differentiate their products from those of competitors on the basis of some unique product-related attribute such as a high level of service. (1988: 31)

In an intriguing article called "How To Sell a Watermelon for $50," *Progressive Grocer* describes value pricing in supermarkets:

"Where else in the world can you sell a watermelon for $50?" asks one produce manager. He refers, of course, to the supermarket fruit bar, where watermelon can be transformed into a value-added item with a steep price tag. . . . Not surprisingly, value-addeds generally have the greatest sales and profit potential in middle- to upper-income areas, where there is less price sensitivity. (Linsen 1991: 101)

In the consumer market there may be little difference between value pricing and *perception* or *perceived-value pricing,* which means that the product is priced according to the value that customers perceive. For example, a scientific calculator may be priced in the $25 to $40 range because customers believe that a more expensive price means a more sophisticated tool than they need, while a lower price means it is cheap or will not fulfill their needs (Grunenwald and Vernon 1988: 69).

In the industrial market customers are presumably more sophisticated, and value pricing is based on the customer's savings from using the product. For example, Lone Star Industries developed a strong, fast-drying cement. Rather than requiring 7 to 14 days to set, it can set in 4 hours. Seven inches has the same strength as 10 inches of regular cement. The pricing question is the value of the decreased time for customers involved in construction projects such as highways and airport runways. While regular concrete sells for $60 to $80 a ton, Lone Star sets its prices at $120 to $180 a ton (MaGrath 1991: 18).

The emphasis in value pricing is to add price by adding value. Thus any extras in value in terms of quality and service are desirable and will allow the seller to increase the price. The techniques of the new manufacturing environment complement value pricing well because the emphasis is on adding value at every step and eliminating activities that are nonvalue-adding. The emphasis on quality and rapid throughput likewise adds value to the product.

Although value pricing does take into account the external element of how the customer values the product, it does not directly consider the external element of competition. Customers can still be price-conscious if a competitor offers the same value at a lower price. Caterpillar built a reputation on service with a commitment to have spare parts in the hands of a customer in 48 hours. However, Komatsu increased its volume of sales in the construction machinery market by 40 percent between 1980 and 1985 while Caterpillar's volume fell by 50 percent. Komatsu emphasized to customers that they could get 10 percent more machine for 10 percent less money (Presutti 1988: 31). Caterpillar fought back with new products, even more emphasis on quality, and cost cutting through automation, and eventually returned to its pre-1981 market share levels (MaGrath 1991: 16).

Presutti believes that:

The competitive nature of industry is changing. More aggressive international competition will make value-based pricing less attractive if the competitor can provide a valued product attribute at a lower price, thereby improving purchase value to the customer. . . . Fundamentally, buyers are price-sensitive as long as a unique product-related attribute such as service is not sacrificed. This presents a problem for higher-priced firms differentiating on the basis of an attribute (e.g., service) important to the customer when confronted with an aggressive competitor using a just-in-time strategy. The just-in-time firm uses the cost savings resulting from increased productivity to support higher levels of service. (1988: 31)

It appears that firms using JIT have a double-barreled advantage in pricing in that they can increase value to the customer and therefore seek the higher end of the market. Their increased productivity and lower cost structure mean that they can also employ a cost-based pricing scheme when faced with competitors who reduce prices. In cutting price to meet competition they must know the cost floor for their different products to keep from cutting into profits. A good product costing system is essential.

PRICES BASED ON TARGET COSTS

An extremely aggressive pricing policy is to price based on future or target costs rather than today's costs. This strategy is usually used when a firm tries to enter established markets. The idea is to set the price so low that customers will buy the product and in the meantime attack the cost structure to bring costs down enough that operations will still be profitable. This strategy considers both what customers will pay and the company cost structure. However, the cost structure is not taken as given, but rather efforts are made to bring the costs in harmony with the price.

Pricing in this fashion is a form of *penetration pricing,* in which the price is intentionally set low to gain customers in a new market. Traditional penetration pricing depended on increased volume to maintain low costs. However, firms using new manufacturing techniques can rely on other means to bring costs down to the desired levels, such as elimination of nonvalue-adding activities, more rapid throughput, and reduction of inventories.

The cost reduction side of this strategy was discussed in Chapter 8, and it was suggested that standard costs can be adjusted for this form of pricing with standards set so that they can eventually be met and a profit achieved. The strategy was Henry Ford's—he created a mass demand for his automobile by pricing it for the average consumer and then driving costs down accordingly. However, the Japanese have given it new life by using efficient product designs and JIT manufacturing techniques to bring costs down.

LIFE CYCLE PRICING

Life cycle pricing looks to the stage in the product's life to determine a pricing strategy. The idea is that a product goes through the stages of introduction, growth, maturity, and decline; each phase has an appropriate marketing strategy. For example, the introduction phase might use a market *penetration price,* a price set low to enter an existing market or it might use a market *skimming price,* which is set high to take advantage of the fact that some customers would pay a high price to obtain a new, unique product.

The product life cycle (PLC) concept of pricing is not as well accepted as it once was. One disadvantage was the difficulty in determining where the turning points were and consequently what the current phase was. Kellogg's thought the ready-to-eat cereal market might be in the mature stage with baby boomers reaching adulthood. However, a marketing strategy directed toward adults resulted in a growth in the ready-to-eat cereal market from $3.7 billion in 1983 to $5.4 billion in 1988. In 1988 the adult market of 25- to 49-year-olds consumed 26 percent more cereal than they did 5 years before (Varadarajan, Clark, and Pride 1992: 41). Clearly, the market was still in the growth stage. Also marketers found that they could control much of the life cycle by their decisions. Consequently, the PLC concept is accepted but taken as a more flexible guide.

Varadarajan, Clark, and Pride commented:

Traditional PLC wisdom suggests that sales, profit margin, competitive intensity, and the appropriate business strategy are all determined by life cycle stage; managerial action is constrained within narrow limits. But products and businesses are managerial creations, subject to human manipulation. They are not chained to the PLC "if-then" doctrine unless decision makers believe them to be so. (1992: 41)

Today's environment breeds many high-tech products that have short, compressed product life cycles. Firms need to quickly recover their research and development costs because the market for the product will not last long. Moreover both foreign and domestic competitors are likely to enter the market, forcing prices down early in the life cycle. The high-tech firm often walks a fine line between charging a price so low that costs cannot be recovered and so high that customers buy a competitor's product. Good product cost data are essential to make sure managers know the lower boundaries dictated by product cost.

» «

The challenge to the marketing function is to capitalize on the advantages of a firm whose production techniques are updated for the new manufacturing environment. New pricing strategies become a possibility. The firm should not rely on cost-based prices as U.S. firms once did when competition was not an issue. Although cost-based prices are still useful in establishing a pricing floor, firms in the new manufacturing environment can choose strategies such as value pricing, which focuses on the benefits to the customer. Another possibility is product life cycle pricing, which allows the firm to price according to whether the product is in the stage of introduction, growth, maturity, or decline.

Some firms may opt to use prices based on target costs, setting a low price for penetrating new markets and driving costs down to an acceptable level. Contribution pricing is useful in short-run situations in which a firm can take advantage of a special order. The minimum price in this situation is the incremental cost of the order.

Obviously, good cost analysis is essential to any pricing strategy because the spread between cost and price produces the profit of the firm. This cost analysis should include marketing as well as manufacturing costs. The same techniques that identify activities and cost drivers in manufacturing can be applied to marketing. Repetitive marketing activities can be subject to the same type of standard cost analysis with variances computed for efficiency and spending.

Further variance investigation can be applied to contribution margins to determine whether an organization is fulfilling its sales objectives in terms of volume, mix, and price. Contribution margins can also be examined to determine whether volume differences are due to changes in market size or in market share. For firms operating in a JIT environment, it is also useful to analyze sales orders to determine a finished goods variance, indicating orders completed but not shipped, and a sales order variance, indicating the difference between sales orders received and filled.

REFERENCES

Grunenwald, Joseph, and Thomas T. Vernon. "Pricing Decision Making for High-Technology Products and Services," *Journal of Business and Industrial Marketing*. Winter 1988, pp. 61–70.

Harrell, Horace W. "Materials Variance Analysis and JIT: A New Approach," *Management Accounting*. May 1992, pp. 33–38.

Horngren, Charles T., and George Foster. *Cost Accounting: A Managerial Emphasis*. Englewood Cliffs, N.J.: Prentice-Hall, 1987.

Lewis, Ronald J. "Activity-Based Costing for Marketing," *Management Accounting*. November 1991, pp. 33–38.

Linsen, Mary Ann. "How To Sell a Watermelon for $50," *Progressive Grocer*. February 1991, pp. 101–105.

MaGrath, Allan J. "Ten Timeless Truths about Pricing," *Journal of Business and Industrial Marketing*. Summer/Fall 1991, pp. 15–23.

Presutti, William D., Jr. "Just-in-Time Manufacturing and Marketing—Strategic Relationship for Competitive Advantage," *Journal of Business and Industrial Marketing*. Summer 1988, pp. 27–35.

Rayburn, L. Gayle. *Principles of Cost Accounting*. Homewood, Ill.: Richard D. Irwin, 1989.

Varadarajan, P. Rajan, Terry Clark, and William M. Pride. "Controlling the Uncontrollable: Managing Your Market Environment," *Sloan Management Review*. Winter 1992, pp. 39–47.

CHAPTER 12

Evaluating Automation Proposals in the New Technology Environment

One of the greatest temptations for a manufacturer today is to rush into a major capital expenditure venture to acquire the latest computer-integrated manufacturing (CIM) equipment or other state-of-the-art automation because a competitor has taken a similar action. The competitor's decision may have been based more on a desire to create an image of a firm that uses innovative technologies than on sound cost-benefit analysis. A manufacturer of kitchen appliances with a reputation for innovative product design adopted a sophisticated automated manufacturing process for that reason. Managers promoting the idea were able to get the project cleared through management by padding the estimate of cash flow projections. "Keeping up with the Joneses" can be a grave error if you do not know the logic behind the purchases made by the Joneses.

Automation and CIM projects attract interest for a number of different reasons. The fear of becoming uncompetitive with other firms that have invested in these types of projects is but one motivator for becoming more automated. Others choose this course simply because it is the fashionable thing to do. On the other hand, many successful firms have chosen this route because of a logical systematic process that evaluates the decision and resulting expenditure as a capital budgeting decision which can be justified by probable cash inflow benefits exceeding forecast cash outflow costs.

Plant and equipment expenditure to achieve a high level of CIM presents one of the highest risk scenarios of any area of capital budgeting. First, the initial cost is large, representing an investment requiring a period of years and a large number of sales units just to recover the investment. Second, projected cash flows can be cut short because of new technology that makes the CIM system obsolete before the investment is recovered. Third, demand for the product being manufactured can also decline, leaving the firm with a sophisticated CIM system designed to manufacture a product no one is willing to buy. Either of the events of obsolescence of equipment caused by more advanced technology or decline in demand for the product the equipment was designed to produce leaves the firm with a high fixed cost structure, making it necessary to maintain a larger sales volume just to break even than it would have needed had it not adopted the more sophisticated technology.

In Chapter 10 some other important reasons were given for continuing to base capital budgeting decisions on quantitative evaluation techniques, regardless of the technology level under consideration. This chapter and Chapter 13 are designed to focus on the reasons why critics of quantitative evaluation processes have lost confidence in these techniques, to illustrate the types of approaches needed to make these tools effective, to explain what is needed in terms of decision input variables, and to present some patterns that will be effective for the automation decision dilemma.

AUTOMATION – A CAPITAL BUDGETING DECISION

Any decision to automate with computer-integrated manufacturing, automate individual work tasks, or simply increase the sophistication level of existing procedures used in an automated system should be treated as a capital budgeting decision. Expenditures fall into two categories – current operating expenditures and capital budgeting expenditures. Since a decision to adopt automated manufacturing processes entails large initial expenditures for plant and equipment that typically will not be recovered for a number of years, these obviously are not current operating expenses. The only legitimate reason for making the expenditures is the incremental cash flow benefits to be produced over the useful life of the assets.

Conventional capital budget analysis techniques that rely on cash inflow projections have been criticized in the literature in recent years as not being adequate for evaluating new technology projects. Some advocates of advanced manufacturing systems are proposing to overhaul the project evaluation procedures to remove "barriers" to the adoption of new technologies. Discounted cash flow (DCF) is viewed as one of these barriers if it fails to support advanced manufacturing system projects. They are proposing alternative techniques, many of which ignore or minimize the importance of cash inflows from the expenditures (Grant et al. 1991: 44). Some of the authors are calling for a new wave of managers who are more "technically literate and aware," implying a need for more executives who will adopt new technology regardless of what the figures indicate.

Robert Grant and others point out the fallacies of this approach to what is a capital budgeting decision. The gravest error is the axiomatic assumption that benefits exceed costs and risks associated with the automation investment. Initial expenditures are usually large—in the case of computer-integrated plants, frequently exceeding $50 million—while benefits are uncertain. Returns to GM in its New United Motors Manufacturing venture with Toyota and to Caterpillar in its major shift to automation have been meager. Implementation problems and disappointing performance benefits have caused a number of firms to retreat from the frontier of technology implementation.

Capital budgeting techniques have not lost their value as project evaluation tools for new technology. The users have simply failed to compile the input variables necessary for the computation. Discounted cash flow techniques (DCF), a prime target of criticism, often produce negative net present values (NPV), indicating the anticipated expenditures for the new technology proposal cannot be justified on the basis of projected cash inflows. Critics argue the tool is not valid because the project produces non-quantifiable benefits that cannot be included in the calculations. However, any approach that becomes removed from the processes of comparing benefits in dollars with costs in dollars has a very questionable basis in both theory and application.

In proposals involving capital expenditures even before CIM, proponents of the projects were typically overly optimistic as to the expected cash inflow benefits of the proposal. For example, marketing personnel frequently develop and design new products they believe will be very profitable. Based on their reports there is no need to perform a cost-benefit analysis using capital budgeting screening techniques. However, accounting or finance must play the "devil's advocate" and scrutinize the proposal. In the process of examining all aspects affecting both costs and revenue potential, the actual figures based on careful analysis of the details of the proposal reveal that the optimism of marketing cannot be verified by sales forecasts and actual costs. Engineering costs, installation costs, and direct costs may exceed marketing's expectation. Cash inflow may be limited because of competition's ability to quickly copy the product. This is especially true today with the Japanese and others relying heavily on their ability to copy innovations quickly and then lower prices. Future demand for the new products may also be limited because of substitute products introduced after the commitment has been made to invest in plant, equipment, engineering costs, etc., necessary to produce the new product. Oversights in any of these areas quickly result in a project that appears to be very attractive on the surface becoming one that can result in catastrophic losses.

COMPREHENSIVE CASH FLOW ANALYSIS

DCF, payback period, internal rate of return, and variations of these techniques should provide the backbone of the decision process whether the project under consideration is an additional delivery truck or a futuristic new plant using the latest in computer-assisted manufacturing technology. There are several reasons to support this approach. First, these evaluation techniques provide an approach that is consistent with the method used by the owners of the firm (stockholders) when they invest in the company. They capitalize expected dividends and earnings. Finding the present value of these cash inflows provides the primary basis for the intrinsic value of the firm's stock. Therefore, to maximize the value of the company, which is the value of its outstanding common stock, capital budgeting expenditures should be based on cash flow analysis consistent with the approaches used by investors purchasing stock in the company.

Second, the input variables required for these techniques force a degree of detailed project scrutiny that will not occur otherwise. After-tax cash outflows for each year of the life of the project, after-tax cash inflows for each year of the project, and an appropriate minimum required rate of return (cost of capital) force the project evaluator to make specific estimates. In particular this forces the issue of realistic sales forecasts and projections. The process of assessing all the variables affecting sales reveals numerous limiting constraints. In the case of large expenditures for high technology processes it is critical to figure in the effects of a cash flow stream cut short by a later technological advance that makes obsolete both the equipment and processes in which the company has invested.

A third justification for using traditional analysis techniques is that they provide a consistent, objective approach lacking in any method not based on realistic cash flow estimates. For example, a firm attempting to choose between two different types of technology to produce a product faces a common dilemma. One process using the latest technology requires a multi-million dollar expenditure in year 0 (today) but is expected to produce cash flow benefits for ten years. The alternative process using a proven technology can produce the same cash flow benefits over the same period of time but has a much lower initial cost. It uses a process requiring more labor but less capital equipment. This second alternative also has a bonus benefit of providing greater flexibility because of lower fixed cost. If the cash flow stream is cut short of the anticipated period, labor can be reallocated or laid off. On the other hand, the company is stuck with the high fixed cost of the high technology plant; if it cannot be converted to another use, the company will experience a loss from this operation. The only way to compare two such diverse technology alternatives is through cash flow analysis procedures.

The scenario in which a company must decide between a new facility using leading edge technology and one using proven, time-tested methods is probably the typical dilemma rather than the exception. Critics of traditional cash flow procedures argue that technologically advanced production facilities have benefits that cannot be quantified. However, any advantages should eventually be revealed as either reduced operating costs or increased sales. Therefore, if advantages do exist they can be quantified. If they are only imaginary, they cannot be quantified.

This does not mean quantification will be easy. However, the process will not be significantly different from one used by a company when it evaluates expenditures for research and development. In pure research and development (R&D) expenditures there are many uncertainties as to future benefits. Making a commitment to use the latest technology that has not been time tested is in many ways similar. To choose to invest in R&D projects or leading edge manufacturing technology requires cash flow estimates in order to determine whether the firm would be better off investing in proven equipment producing proven products or going with the latest innovation.

Similarities and connections between R&D and capital budgeting expenditures for high technology projects were noted in Chapter 10. That chapter also noted that current accounting rules provide for a very poor matching of R&D costs to benefits from these efforts. Because of the focus on accounting for tax purposes rather than management information, R&D expenditures appear to penalize a firm rather than give it a competitive advantage. Treated as current operating expenses, they reduce before-tax income by an amount equal to the expense. Unfortunately, most financial statements do not highlight the cash flow effects of a cash savings due to the fact that R&D expenses also reduce income taxes by an amount equal to the expenses, multiplied by the marginal tax percentage, and actually increase cash inflow.

Even though cash flow statements are typically part of the financial statement package, published statements do not provide the type of comparative cash flow information decision makers need. With the exception of the cash flow statements, all financial statements are a result of the accrual system and do not reflect cash values. On the other hand, capital budgeting techniques require after-tax cash figures for both outflows and inflows.

The accrual system was never designed to provide the type of financial data needed for capital budgeting. The primary focus is to assign revenues and costs to the period of time in which they occur. The accrual system does that task well. However, with capital budgeting the crucial issue is when the cash is paid out or collected, which may or may not be when the expense is incurred or the revenue recognized. Unfortunately R&D expenses are typically not reconciled properly either because expenses must be recognized immediately, but benefit revenues are postponed indefinitely, a practice not even consistent with good accrual accounting concepts because expenses and revenues are not matched.

Financial data presented in most annual reports imply that the firm should not have spent on R&D because, in the year of expenditure, income is reduced by expensing this item. However, the very next year net income may increase to a higher level than before the R&D expenditures. These higher profits imply that R&D expenditures should not have been made because income is higher in the year when there were none. There is no provision for relating the expenditure that occurred in a previous period to the benefits that materialize in later periods.

At least expenditures for plant and equipment are capitalized and depreciated rather than expensed. However, many of the same types of allocation problems weigh heavily as negatives against accepting these projects. R&D projects and new technology projects share the same problems of under-statement of future benefits. On R&D projects accountants frequently assume zero benefits if they do not have strong evidence to support specific dollar figures. For an expenditure clearly designed to increase revenues, it is more correct theoretically and in practice to assign an educated guess to cash flow benefits than to assume zero benefits.

OVERCOMING ACCOUNTING'S LIMITATIONS ON CASH FLOW ESTIMATES

To accurately evaluate high-tech project proposals such as computer-integrated manufacturing systems, the analyst must generate comprehensive cash inflow projections as well as cash outflow projections. Cash outflow estimates typically do not create oversight problems. Most projects require large initial expenditures for plant and equipment plus other one-time start-up costs such as training expenses, hardware and software items, and facilities modifications. Parker and Lettes describe this feature as the typical economic characteristic of most flexible computer-integrated manufacturing decisions (1991: 35). Because these cash outflow expenditures occur in the initial phase, they are relatively easy to tabulate. If oversights do occur on cash outflows, they are most likely to be due to failures to allow for annual maintenance costs, technology updates, and repairs, all of which are future cost items.

On the other hand, oversights on cash inflow projections are the rule rather than the exception. Part of this problem is the result of the tendency to follow the same guidelines for preparing cash flow estimates that have been followed in the past. Bound by historical precedents, analysts are unable to prepare estimates adaptable to the flexibility needs of financial management. If a proposal is truly innovative, it is highly likely to produce types of benefits that were not provided by historical proposals. If cash flow estimators only follow historical precedents in appraisal procedures, they typically will not count what may be the most important benefit of the proposal. They often follow the same errant practice used in connection with R&D expenditures — treating benefits as zero if there is any question as to the amount.

Parker and Lettes recognize this tendency to ignore atypical benefits as a major factor preventing CIM projects from qualifying as acceptable investments. In the following statement they identify this tendency as a primary reason for losing confidence in traditional cash flow analysis techniques:

Because the new key elements of competitiveness — quality, life cycle cost, just-in-time delivery, and the ability to change a product rapidly — are considered intangibles and do not "quantify" easily they are ignored by traditional accounting practices. Thus, *justification* of investment in advanced manufacturing is often a leap of faith. (1991: 34)

While this oversight problem creates an understatement of cash inflows, current accounting practices often create overstatements or overassignments of cash outflows in several ways. Most high-tech innovations result in large start-up costs consisting primarily of items classified as plant and equipment by traditional accounting methods. These costs are then allocated through depreciation methods that typically have no relationship to the benefits received. In fact the large depreciation expenses in the early years actually lower income and provide a reason for executives concerned about this value to avoid this type of expenditure. Most benefits of the new technology are likely to be delayed past the period when the large depreciation expenses occur. Because technology-related costs typically are large, the inappropriate allocation of cost creates a significant income effect (Brimson 1989: 47).

Large depreciation expenses due to purchases of high-tech equipment provide a positive cash flow effect because they shelter income equal to the amount of the expenses from taxation. However, tax effect considerations do not override the negative connotations of declines in reported income for the stockholders and others who do not realize that cash flow can actually be increasing when income is declining if the change is due to increases in depreciation expense.

Overallocation of costs to early years of equipment is only part of the problem creating high costs for CIM projects. Standard practices require a company to record as current operating expenses any expenditures for developing program equipment, performing strategic market analysis, developing new products, training people to operate the new equipment, and any other start-up costs not classified as plant and equipment. These are real costs constituting cash outflows. As such they should be included in cash flow figures for the years in which they occur. However, cash inflow benefits received from these expenditures should be recognized as well.

The tendency to thoroughly cover all costs in the process of tabulating cash outflows and to ignore cash inflow benefits of investment in knowledge creates an immense bias against CIM projects. Start-up costs due to equipment purchases and training are very large, but operating and maintenance costs are relatively low. On the cash flow benefits side (operating cost savings) flexible computer-integrated manufacturing systems produce increasing returns over time because the systems assimilate knowledge and improve efficiency. Production costs decline over time because the system benefits from a learning curve effect (Parker and Lettes 1991: 35–56).

AN EXAMPLE OF AUGMENTED ACCOUNTING DATA

Because of the tendency to understate and even ignore major cash inflow benefits of technology-oriented projects, the decision maker cannot rely exclusively on data of this type. Cash inflow projections must include those real, but difficult to quantify, benefits that are typically ignored. Lee relates how cash inflow adjustments were made by United Architects, Inc. (UAI), a medium-size architectural firm located in Los Angeles (1991: 45–58).

Top management relied heavily on DCF techniques and net present value computations as the basis for capital expenditures. A project manager had repeatedly attempted to convince top management of the need for computer-aided design and drafting (CADD) equipment with technology capabilities equivalent to that used by competitors. UAI had installed a limited version of CADD a few years before at a cost of $42,000. A modern sophisticated system like the ones used by competitors would cost an additional $572,000 but would result in significant reductions in operating costs and labor costs while simultaneously increasing productivity and cash inflows. Computations of net present value (NPV) with UAI's 20 percent cost of capital and a tax rate of 33 percent resulted in a negative NPV of $237,186. The proposal was rejected on the basis of this figure.

The project manager knew the cash benefits were understated and began to search for ways to quantify a type of benefit that had not been counted. Within the last quarter UAI had lost bids on three large jobs. In each case the loss had not been due to incompetence, higher bid price, or quality of the proposal. The primary reason for the rejections was the more impressive presentations made by the competition using leading edge CADD equipment with the innovative feature of 3-D perspectives. The sophistication level of these presentations was conveying the message that the companies using this equipment would also be more sophisticated and reliable when in fact UAI was equally qualified to perform contract tasks.

With the help of the company comptroller, the project manager began to search for a way to include the effects of incremental revenues the company would receive with the more impressive sales presentations. If sales could be increased due to capital expenditures, these after-tax revenues should also be included in cash inflows. Since 3 contracts had been lost in one quarter, there was a basis for assuming the company would forfeit an average of 12 contracts per year. With an average cash flow contribution of $25,000 per contract, the capital expenditure could be expected to produce an additional $300,000 cash flow annually over the 10-year life of the project. NPV increased to more than $605,000 by including this incremental cash flow, making the project very attractive (Lee 1991: 45–48).

Capital expenditure analysts must be innovative like the project managers at UAI. This example illustrates the steps necessary to produce credible cash inflow projections:

1. Be aware that cash inflow oversights may exist. Innovative thinking is necessary to look for types of benefits not typical of routine capital budgeting decisions. After all, if innovative technology projects are not providing new types of benefits that are unlike previous capital budgeting projects, they do not represent technological advancements. In the UAI example the oversight of increased revenue

from capturing sales being lost was more than $300,000 per year, which was larger than any other single inflow item. Project analysts must thoroughly review any analysis for omissions.

2. Identify the source of the oversight. Quantification of cash flow benefits first requires identifying the cause of a potential cash flow benefit before data can be collected to determine its magnitude. UAI was losing business to competitors because the competitors were using more sophisticated CADD equipment, resulting in more effective sales presentations. UAI was making sales but could have been making considerably more. Losing bids on large jobs was resulting in unproductive labor costs because of the time and effort required to make presentations on behalf of the company only to have bids rejected because competitors were armed with better sales artillery.

3. Compile evidence to verify cause-and-effect relationships. Documentation is necessary to support cash flow estimates. UAI's project directors had collected correspondence in the form of bid rejections clearly pointing to the sales presentations as the reason for losing the contracts. This correspondence complimented UAI on performance and competence and found no fault with any other phase of its operations. The only remaining hurdle was the sales presentation advantage of the competition which was due to the use of the higher technology CADD equipment.

4. Prepare estimation formulas for cash inflows. Making estimates is the most difficult step because quantification must begin at this stage. It is also a step in which the analyst must generate numbers based on logical justification. This is also a step in which accountants and managers or engineers can work together to gather the data needed. For example, in the UAI case the contribution from each of the bids lost was a type of information already available from the accounting department. However, the analyst needed to use this information along with an estimate of the number of bids lost per year to obtain an evaluation of the total loss. The term *formula* as used in this step does not necessarily mean a long mathematical equation. Instead, it is a logical reasoning process tailored to the specific variables of the project and capable of producing cash flow estimates which can be justified, especially to top management.

Accountants have come under fire from a number of sources because they have been reluctant to quantify the "unquantifiable benefits" from automation projects. However, Tatikonda observes that it is not necessarily the responsibility of the accountant to provide the data inputs:

What critics fail to realize is that any cost justification technique is only as good as the data presented and used in formulating it. Data plays an important role in investment selection. The person who is requesting the project has an obligation to provide adequate, reliable, and objective data. . . . They (engineers and production managers) should not expect the accounting department to fully understand new engineering designs, machine performance, and intangible benefits such as flexibility. (1987: 28)

It should go without saying that when such information is not forthcoming from engineering, production managers, or project managers, the accountant or

Figure 12.1
Calculation of Weighted Average Incremental Cash Inflows

Number of Contracts	Cash Inflow per Contract	Total Cash Inflow	Probability of Occurrence	Weighted Average Cash Inflow
6	$18,000	$108,000	10%	$ 10,800
8	20,000	160,000	10%	16,000
12	25,000	300,000	70%	210,000
15	30,000	450,000	10%	45,000

Expected annual cash inflow = $281,800

other capital budgeting analyst should persistently seek such data until there is a valid basis for analysis.

5. Calculate cash flow estimates. Once the outline of the procedure for quantifying the cash benefits has been determined, the analyst can then plug in the values and generate the cash flow numbers. After the procedure has been established, the analyst is in a position to also perform sensitivity analysis to allow for elements of uncertainty and to produce sets of values under a variety of assumptions. If a higher level of rigor is deemed necessary, a weighted average projected cash flow estimate can be calculated.

In UAI's computation of incremental cash benefits from the purchase of the high tech version of the CADD, the value most likely to be questioned is the estimate of 12 additional contracts per year gained as a direct result of the asset investment. This is the "most likely" estimate based on opportunity loss experience. The actual number of additional contracts per year could be above or below this figure. If the UAI project manager believes there is at least a 70 percent probability that 12 contracts is the correct figure to use, he can then begin to estimate the probabilities that comprise the other 30 percent.

Suppose the "worst case" scenario is an incremental benefit of only 6 contracts resulting in annual cash contributions of only $18,000 instead of $25,000. This event has a 10 percent probability of occurring because the economy could turn sour, and there could be a general reduction in new contracts and new contract amounts. There is also a 10 percent probability of 8 annual contracts with annual contributions of $20,000 each. In addition, there is a 10 percent probability that annual contracts could total 15 because of improvements in economic conditions. Under these circumstances contributions of cash inflows per project might average $30,000 per year instead of $25,000. All these variables can be incorporated in one weighted average annual cash flow figure by the process illustrated in Figure 12.1.

The expected annual cash inflow of $281,800 includes the composite effects of all possibilities included in the forecast benefits. An analysis such as that shown in Figure 12.1 is especially useful in squelching arguments of critics who doubt the accuracy of cash flow benefits based on only the most likely estimates. Top management personnel who have the final word of approval or disapproval for capital expenditures usually play "devil's advocate" and ask what happens if the project does not produce the estimated amount of new business. Weighted average computations combine the effects of pessimistic, most likely, and optimistic projections to produce one statistically calculated "expected value" estimate.

The initial procedure used at UAI in its evaluation of expenditures for the CADD system necessary to be competitive in the industry illustrates why the literature is full of arguments to abandon DCF methods for high-technology products. At the same time this case also clearly reveals that these methods have not lost their credibility. Traditional accounting practices have been inadequate to produce viable cash inflow estimates, thereby typically understating cash benefits. The solution is not to abandon the traditional methods but to fully utilize them because of their distinct benefits mentioned earlier. Procedures used at UAI illustrate how non-traditional benefits can be quantified to reflect a more realistic picture of innovative technology expenditures. An added level of rigor is provided if a weighted average cash flow figure is prepared rather than a single figure based on the "most likely" scenario only.

REASONS FOR NOT INVESTING IN HIGH TECHNOLOGY

Just because firms tend to understate cash flow benefits from high-technology projects does not imply that they always produce acceptable cash flow benefits. Numerous factors can reduce forecasted cash inflow amounts and an even longer list of factors can cut short a projected stream long before the forecast date. The key to accurate estimates of both cash inflows as well as outflows is an accurate evaluation of the impacts of all variables likely to affect the outcome of the project and to arrive at dollar values that consider the composite effects of all the variables combined. To achieve this objective first requires an assessment of constraints that may limit the project's life and in turn total cash inflows. This must be followed by a similar procedure for making an assessment of the positive features of the proposal. The purpose of these two tasks is to identify all variables, or at least as many as possible, that will have an impact on the future performance of the investment in high-tech plant and/or equipment. This step should take place before attempting to generate actual cash flow estimates.

Constraints with the potential to reduce cash flows from normal projection levels or cut cash inflow streams short of projected periods should be used as moderating elements to temper cash projections. On the other hand, strong positive factors associated with the proposal should be used to boost the size of normal projections. This process produces cash flow projection adjustment factors to be used to justify modification of cash flows projected for average circumstances.

This section examines a list of items that might be referred to as the *risks of automation*. This is a generic list applying to all automation proposals requiring large expenditures in plant and equipment and/or other types of start-up costs.

Risk of Higher Fixed Costs

Any expenditure for plant and equipment increases a firm's fixed costs. Automation expenditures are typically quite large and therefore make fixed costs a matter of greater concern than when most of the firm's costs are variable. Automation is basically a process of substituting machinery for labor. Labor is either replaced with computers, robots, or other machinery, or existing labor is retained and production from that labor is increased in lieu of hiring more labor to achieve the higher level of production. In either case high-tech equipment is a labor substitute. Wages represent a variable cost that can be adjusted by changing the number of workers to meet production needs. Wages also are paid as production occurs. A switch to CIM requires a large initial investment that can only be recovered through future sales of products; it commits the firm to a course of action with much less flexibility than manufacturing processes relying heavily on labor.

The most visible, and probably the impact of greatest concern regarding increased fixed cost is an increase in the firm's break-even sales quantity (BEQ). The most important implication of higher fixed cost is that the company must maintain a higher sales volume just to break even. A hypothetical firm, XYZ Corporation, manufacturing flange gaskets for aircraft fuel cells, is faced with the opportunity to purchase a robotic machine that will lower its labor cost per unit by $1 on a gasket it sells for $5. Current variable costs per unit total $4. The new equipment will cost $1 million and have a useful life of 10 years. Straight line depreciation is used for management purposes even though accelerated depreciation is used for tax purposes. Fixed costs per year will increase from the current level of $40,000 per year to $140,000 due to the additional $100,000 of incremental depreciation expenses. This will change the break-even value as follows:

With existing facilities: $\text{BEQ} = \dfrac{\$40,000}{\$5 - \$4} = 40,000 \text{ units}$

With robotic facilities: $\text{BEQ} = \dfrac{\$140,000}{\$5 - \$3} = 70,000 \text{ units}$

Assuming price and variable costs per unit do not change over the life of the new asset, management's decision hinges primarily on the level of sales anticipated. If current sales volume is 50,000 units, the robotic operation is a moot question. Even allowing for potential increases in sales, starting with any existing level below 70,000 units is an unacceptable risk.

At production and sales levels slightly above 70,000 units, existing facilities will still produce higher profits. By the time production is up to the level to break even with the robotic operation, the old method will have already produced $30,000 of profit before taxes since the contribution margin is $1 per unit; at a production level of 70,000 units it is 30,000 units above the level needed to break even. A point of sales volume indifference at which the two alternatives produce equal profit is computed as follows:

Indifference Point Computation

$$\text{Existing facilities revenue} = \text{Robotic facilities revenue}$$
$$\$30,000 + \$1 \text{ (additional units above 70,000)} = \$2 \text{ (additional units above 70,000)}$$
$$\text{Additional units above 70,000} = 30,000$$
$$\text{Total production required for equal profits} = 70,000 + 30,000 = 100,000 \text{ units}$$

Verification of Computation

Existing facilities
  $1 contribution margin (100,000 units − 40,000 BEQ) = $60,000

Robotic facilities
  $2 contribution margin (100,000 units − 70,000 BEQ) = $60,000

Either alternative generates $60,000 profit if sales total 100,000 units per year. If the sales volume is lower, existing facilities produce higher profits. If sales are above 100,000 units, the new robotic facilities produce higher profits than existing facilities.

XYZ Corporation's decision depends on its sales forecast. Obviously, if sales are averaging 200,000 units per year it should purchase the new equipment. With a $2 contribution margin compared to only a $1 contribution margin on sales, profits before taxes would total $260,000 instead of $160,000. On the other hand, if sales levels are not expected to exceed 70,000 units annually the robotic option is not a viable alternative. Even if sales forecasts approach the 100,000 unit level, the firm is taking a major risk with the high fixed cost structure.

An additional risk element not reflected in the preceding illustration is the effects of higher volume on products sensitive to price competition and the effects of variable costs being influenced by the relevant efficient output range of a particular combination of fixed assets and labor. An article by Dunn, Cheatham, and Cheatham (1991) shows the real world implications of price and variable costs changing, rather than remaining linear as implied in the preceding computation.

BEQ is a result of the two variables of total fixed costs and contribution margin, which is the difference between the price per unit and variable cost per unit. Because of the relationship between contribution margin and fixed costs, any reduction in price or increase in variable cost per unit raises the BEQ above the level anticipated when these two variables are assumed to be constant. Attempts to increase sales volume may necessitate price reductions, causing the BEQ to increase. At the same time the variable cost per unit may be higher than anticipated because production is not occurring in the efficient range for which fixed assets were designed. This higher than anticipated variable cost per unit is likely to be a problem for a firm that is only producing slightly above the break-even point calculated by using the constant variable cost assumption. For example, XYZ Corporation may not actually realize a $1 reduction in variable cost when it is only producing slightly more than 70,000 units. As a consequence, it may not have even reached break even at that level because the contribution margin is less than anticipated (1991: 7-10).

The first and one of the most important steps when considering a major automation proposal is assessing the feasibility of living with the fixed costs created by the capital outlay. This requires sales forecasts, and no capital budgeting expenditures should be initiated without this prerequisite step. This process can screen out some high dollar projects without further investigation when it reveals sales volume requirements that are totally unrealistic for the firm.

Risk of Change in Economic Conditions

Fixed costs create risk because of the possibility that sales will not generate an adequate amount of revenue to cover fixed costs plus total variable costs which are a direct result of production levels necessary to produce the products. Consequently, any variable affecting sales volume and selling price is a factor that must be considered in the decision to go with sophisticated manufacturing technology.

Sales forecasts are a mandatory prerequisite for any automation proposal requiring large initial expenditures. As the preceding example of the robotic replacement decision illustrates, the choice depends primarily on expected sales volume. Therefore to even consider a high-tech manufacturing process that requires a significantly higher break-even sales volume than current production, mandates detailed, objective sales projections to determine whether the firm will realistically be able to produce and sell products in sufficient quantity to make a profit with the new manufacturing process.

Sales volume often depends on many variables over which the firm has little or no control. Because of this lack of control, forecasts should be moderated to allow for risk elements. Probably the greatest element of risk is that the demand for products the equipment is designed to produce will drastically decline or disappear. If this happens and the firm has invested in equipment that has no alternative uses, it becomes an immediate albatross.

To avoid this problem the project analyst must thoroughly assess economic factors that can affect future sales of the product and prepare sales forecasts reflecting the risk of unfavorable economic events.

The place to start is an analysis of product sales behavior under varying economic conditions in the past. To do this requires historical sales data. Even when new products are to be produced, typically historical economic condition response data on substitute products are available that are relevant to the decision. If a new product is a substitute for an existing product, whether the old product is manufactured by this firm or another, similar economic conditions in the future will probably have the same type of effect on sales volume of the new products as they did on the old product being replaced.

Firms often make projections from the peak of the mountain top of the business cycle, assuming sales will remain at that level or even increase. This is a critical mistake on high-tech expenditures because of the high fixed cost structure and the problems of maintaining volume necessary to produce profits or even reach break even. To avoid this pitfall, the firm must determine where it is currently located in the business cycle and forecast sales to allow for the effects of the cycle. If a firm is currently producing in the "trough" of a cycle, it has more reason to project sales increases. On the other hand, if it is operating on a "peak," it has every reason to anticipate a decline in sales in the near future. Sales forecasts provide the base from which cash flows are calculated. Since timing of flows is a crucial value for DCF evaluation techniques and even payback period computations, it is vital to allow for business cycle effects.

These effects can be incorporated into sales forecasting by a four-step process. First, analyze the sensitivity of the product to be produced or a product it is designed to replace to changing economic conditions by analyzing past behavior responses to changes. Second, determine where the firm is operating on the business cycle. Third, generate a business cycle forecast, either by using one provided by government groups or one produced for the firm. Finally, adjust annual sales forecasts for the future periods in which the proposed project will produce benefits, according to the declines and increases that have occurred historically when similar phases of the cycle existed.

Risk of Price Competition

The key to recapturing the high initial cost of innovative manufacturing equipment is the total dollar contribution that results from both sales volume and contribution margin per unit sold. Failure to achieve payback and profit goals can result from a shortfall in either of these two variables. Maintaining an adequate sales volume is not sufficient. Contribution margin, which is the spread between selling price per unit and variable cost per unit, must be maintained at projected levels to produce anticipated results. Price competition forces a firm to reduce its price to prevent loss of sales volume. When this occurs, contribution margin declines.

Some distinct pricing implications are associated with the varying stages of a product's life cycle; they must be considered when estimating contribution margins from product sales. According to McCarthy and Perreault, product life cycles are divided into four stages: (1) market introduction, (2) market growth, (3) market maturity, and (4) sales decline. The marketing mix must change over a product's life because customers' attitudes and needs change. A more significant effect from a cash flow perspective is that competition tends to move progressively toward pure competition or oligopoly. Oligopoly often results when many firms succumb to the effects of price competition and are unable to survive, leaving only a few remaining firms in the industry (1990: 250).

Price competition begins to become a factor during the market maturity phase due to aggressive competitors entering the race for profits. Contribution margins are not only reduced due to price cuts to meet competition, but variable costs also increase due to promotion costs necessary to maintain market share. Price competition becomes even stronger in the final phase due to declining sales and firms struggling to survive.

Because the stage of product life cycle produces predictable effects on product prices, a firm considering purchasing high-tech equipment to manufacture specific products should determine the life cycle stages of those products. Firms often make a mistake of being attracted to a product during the market growth stage when customers are increasing in number and other firms are making large profits. Many of these same firms discover that by the time they have the necessary facilities to begin producing, the product has reached market maturity and they are faced with the accompanying problems created by mandatory price reductions due to increased competition. In the final stage of the life cycle, firms must contend not only with the problem of lower pricing but also with declining sales volume.

Product life cycle assessment is even more important in today's business environment because cycles are tending to become shorter. McCarthy and Perreault say this is due to a large extent to rapidly changing technology: "One new invention may make possible many new products that replace old ones. Plastics changed many products—and created new ones. Tiny electronic 'microchips' led to hundreds of new products—from Texas Instruments' calculators and Pulsar digital watches to electronic fuel controls on cars" (1990: 253).

If there are fast "copiers," the cycle is shortened at an even faster pace. "In the highly competitive grocery products industry, cycles are down to 12 to 18 months for new ideas" (1990: 253).

Japanese manufacturing is currently producing the greatest wave of fast copiers ever faced by American industry and is tending to significantly shorten life cycles of new products in the market introduction and market growth stages. A study conducted by Edwin Mansfield in 1988 revealed evidence indicating Japanese manufacturers have great advantages in carrying out innovations based on *external technology,* which is technology developed by other firms. There was overwhelming evidence of their ability to adopt borrowed technology and produce at a lower cost than American firms attempting to do the same thing. At the same time the Japanese appear to better understand the effects of the product life cycle because when a decision has been made to copy a product or process, they emphasize speed in getting the products on the market as quickly as possible. Therefore they are able to compete more rapidly than American companies (1988: 1157–1162).

The Mansfield survey provides evidence indicating reasons why "copiers" will continue to thrive on the process of using external technology rather than internal technology as a pattern for economic growth and development. In Japan firms take about 25 percent less time and spend about 50 percent less money to carry out an innovation based on external technology than one based on internal technology they have developed themselves. This pattern was evident in all industries in the survey, including chemicals, rubber, machinery, metals, electrical, and instruments.

Theoretically, this is the type of pattern one would expect if a firm does not have to incur the cost and time required to produce a totally new product. However, the study also revealed that for American manufacturers, the commercialization process beginning with product development and ending when the product is introduced to the market, resulting in time and cost figures that are just as large when utilizing external technology as when the firms employ internal technology. Because of cost and time advantages, Japanese manufacturers have a greater incentive to be copiers. American manufacturers have not learned how to utilize external technology as efficiently. Utilization of external technology is likely to continue to shorten product life cycles. The Japanese most assuredly can be expected to depend more heavily on it than internal technology because of cost and time advantages. If American manufacturers learn to become more efficient users of external technology, they will create an impetus for additional reductions in the cycle.

Patents and copyrights provide only minimal protection for new products or innovations resulting from internal technology. Theoretically, a mechanical patent is good for 17 years and a design patent is good for 14 years. However, these are only as good as the language of their specifications. Even something as simple as substituting a material in the product can bypass the coverage of the patent. It is far easier for a user of external technology to find a loophole in a patent than it is for the inventor to devise language that covers all the varying ways a product might be copied. This is especially true today when large corporations in other countries have staffs of experts to find loopholes in patent coverage on products they wish to copy.

Risk of Technological Obsolescence

While rapid changes in technology have been a major factor contributing to shorter product life cycles, they pose an even greater threat to cash inflows from investment in high-tech manufacturing equipment if they cause a product to become obsolete prematurely. If millions of dollars have been spent on specialty equipment that can be used to manufacture only one product, the equipment becomes immediate scrap if the life cycle of the product produced by that equipment is abruptly cut short because a competitor has a process that produces a substitute product of better quality and/or lower cost.

Manufacturing processes that employ leading edge technology often create the greatest obsolescence risk. Once a firm has selected a particular type of technology, it may have committed itself to a path that has no exits or detours. As was emphasized previously in this chapter, high-tech production processes are characterized by the substitution of machinery for labor. Machinery creates fixed costs; labor creates variable costs. Therefore characteristically the more sophisticated the technology used in a process, the less flexibility the firm will have in making changes if its products become obsolete because of technology changes in the industry.

In a sense the best way to avoid technology obsolescence risk is to not adopt any high-tech manufacturing procedures so the firm is always in a position to adopt whatever technology happens to be the most efficient. This, however, is obviously not the solution. On the other hand, firms that adopt leading edge technology have the greatest exposure to this type of risk. There is less obsolescence risk if a firm allows others to blaze trails in leading edge areas. Some of the trails do turn out to be dead end paths that do not even include the option of salvaging funds invested in the project.

The wisdom of Japanese manufacturers' practice of utilizing external technology more extensively than internal technology becomes even more apparent when technological obsolescence is considered. They may have found the optimum compromise. By copying technology that has proved successful, they avoid much of the risk faced by trail blazers. At the same time they are reaping the benefits of recent technology. Their emphasis on speed in converting once a decision has been made to adopt a technology also greatly reduces the risk of obsolescence because they become players while the technology is thriving. Time delays greatly reduce the probability of success for high-tech projects because obsolescence eventually will occur due to new innovations replacing existing ones, thereby reducing the period over which cash flows can be expected from a particular product produced using a dated technology.

Technology obsolescence risk should be evaluated thoroughly and critically and adjustments made to forecasted cash inflows to reflect it. A firm's ability to commercialize technology, to move a product from concept to market quickly and efficiently, is crucial in light of changes in the business environment. Trends of increasing proliferation of new technologies and the speed with which they render previous technologies obsolete make quick action a necessity, not an option.

WAYS TO REDUCE RISKS

Fortunately, exposure to risks of economic conditions, price competition, and technological obsolescence can be reduced. In 1990 Nevens, Summe, and Uttal conducted a study to identify features of firms in the United States, Japan, and Europe that have been most successful at commercializing technology. "Success" can basically be described as investing in high-tech equipment and start-up costs that ultimately are recaptured along with sufficient additional cash inflows to generate profit margins significantly higher than industry averages. It was determined that leading companies:

1. commercialize two or three times the number of new products and processes as their competitors of comparable size;
2. incorporate two to three times as many technologies in their products;
3. bring their products to market in less than half the time; and
4. compete in twice as many product and geographic markets. (1990: 154)

Each trait reflects an understanding of today's product markets, which are significantly different from historical markets and are changing rapidly. Customers are technology conscious. Consequently, product life cycles are shortened by new technology. Time is of the essence for the commercialization process. Rapid commercialization reduces exposure to risk from changing economic conditions, price competition, and technological obsolescence. Rapid commercialization should not be confused with early entry. Development of new technology is early entry. Commercialization encompasses the entire process of making money from the technology. Rapid commercialization is a forte of Japanese manufacturers in their adoption of external technology.

The net effect of all types of risk associated with capital budgeting expenditures is the probability that cash inflows will not be adequate to produce anticipated rates of return or may not even be adequate to reach payback. This unfavorable prospect can occur in two forms. Either annual cash inflows are smaller than expected, or the cash inflow stream is cut short of the period of time for which inflows were anticipated. Changing economic conditions and their effects on sales, increasing price competition, and the possibility of technology obsolescence are factors that can result in these undesirable outcomes. However, the likelihood of any of these forces creating a negative impact increases with time. In the case of commercialization of a technology, time is referenced to product life cycles. A firm that can get its new products to market during the first phase of the product life cycle (market introduction) can often command premium prices because of few competitors. Witness the prices on early personal computers and compare them to prices today when the market is approaching the maturity stage.

Prices continue to hold well during the market growth stages as more customers learn of the product and enter the market. Early firms receive much larger cash inflows than firms entering during the market maturity phase. Not only do they sell products at higher prices but increasing demand with a limited number of suppliers ensures high volume sales. Large cash inflows result in rapid payback and early profits.

Unfortunately, managers in many U.S. firms are failing to realize the opportunity cost of delaying new product introductions. They frequently postpone an introduction date to keep expenses within a budget or to hit target costs. Nevens, Summe, and Uttal explain the problem as follows:

What they don't know is the overall economics: assuming that the market grows 20 percent a year, that prices drop 12 percent a year, and that the product life cycle is five years, launching a laser printer six months behind schedule can reduce the product's cumulative profits by one-third. In contrast, under the same set of assumptions, a development cost overrun of 30 percent will trim profits by only 2.3 percent. (1990: 157)

Budget-conscious managers are concerned about a cost that is minute in comparison to lost revenues resulting from product introduction delays. Cost-benefit analysis clearly shows the need for expediency despite a significant cost overrun. This example illustrates the necessity of quantifying both costs and benefits in all types of decisions. Just because costs increase due to a particular choice does not mean that the best course of action is to avoid the costs. Both benefits and costs must be quantified; otherwise, there is no valid basis for the decision and choices represent mere speculation. Quantification of all benefits and all costs is even more important when considering a capital expenditure like CIM because of the size of the investment.

The two traits of successful innovation firms—commercializing a larger number of new products than competitors and competing in twice as many product and geographic markets—represent insurance actions to maintain sales volume and improve the chances of reaching break-even payback and earning a profit on high-tech investments. Leveraging core technology across a broad base of many different products and numerous geographic markets provides a broader range of revenue resources. This results in more rapid payback, thereby reducing risk due to changing economic conditions, price competition caused by product life cycle maturity, and technological obsolescence since the risk level of each of these increases with time.

Proliferation of new products from a technology enables a firm to continue to operate in the first two stages of the product life cycle where price competition is not a factor. New products are continually coming on line to replace older ones reaching the market maturity stage where they are beginning to encounter price competition. Technology obsolescence in products becomes less of a problem for a firm that is already introducing many new products. A broad range of products also hedges sales volume changes due to deteriorating economic conditions since not all products are affected equally by this factor. Geographic diversification of product markets is especially useful in hedging the effects of unfavorable economic conditions if a firm sells products in different countries with different economies. Recessions and depressions are often confined to the economy of a single country. Therefore firms that do not have all their "eggs in one basket" in a single economy, like the United States, are not as vulnerable to the effects of economic conditions.

The risk reduction benefit of internationalization is verified by the presence of lower beta coefficients for stocks of companies selling products in several foreign countries. Beta coefficients are basically measures of the relative changes in stock prices for a firm compared to changes in stock prices in general, which typically decline in response to new market information indicating deteriorating economic conditions. Lower beta coefficients of multinational firms reflect less impact on these firms from changing economic conditions in the United States because they are not totally dependent on markets in one geographic location (Weston and Brigham 1990: 144–145).

Breadth of technologies gives the successful firm an edge in remaining ahead of the competition so it can continually introduce new products in the first two stages of the product life cycle where contribution margins are high due to strong product demand and few competitors. Firms that are able to milk their products well during these stages do not have to worry about price competition and the increasing costs associated with the market maturity stage because they have achieved the required return before products reach that stage. Often they choose not to compete in the mature market, but instead, shift to other new products in the early stages of their life cycles. Companies employing large numbers of technologies in their products have at their disposal more combinations from which to generate new products. Since most new products represent only minor modifications of existing products, firms combining a large number of technologies are in a better position to generate a continuous stream of new products. A minor innovation in any one of the employed technologies can result in a new product. Consequently, this characteristic is complementary to the product proliferation ability of successful innovator firms.

In today's highly competitive manufacturing environment, in which product life cycles are getting shorter, ability to generate a continuous stream of new products may no longer be merely a way to make higher profits; it may rapidly become the only way to survive. Adizes explains the pitfalls if a company becomes too committed to the products responsible for its initial success. Such a commitment results in a rise and fall of the firm synonymous with the product life cycle (1989). Survival is difficult if a firm never manufactures products selling in the first two stages of the cycle. Contribution margins are so low in the market maturity stage that significant profits require an extremely large sales volume. Earnings prospects only get worse during the fourth stage of the cycle when total industry sales volume declines.

CORE TECHNOLOGY CONSIDERATIONS TO MINIMIZE RISK

Technology flexibility and adaptability appear to be primary qualities of a core technology characteristic of successful firms. When Honda developed multivalve cylinder heads with self-adjusting valves, it did not use this innovation in just one application — it applied the technology to motorcycles, cars, lawn mowers, and power-generating equipment. Core technologies that cannot be applied to a broad range of products and markets should be viewed skeptically. Cash flow benefit estimates should be moderated to allow for the stronger influences of the major types of risk — plant and equipment that cannot be placed in alternative uses. On the other hand, technologies providing standby alternative product opportunities do not entail the same level of risk. If comparing two alternative technologies, the more flexible one is often the better choice even though it may be less sophisticated. Using weighted average expected cash inflows based on risk probabilities is an effective way of evaluating cash flows from technologies characterized by different degrees of flexibility.

Firms should strive to avoid dead-end core technologies. CIM and the accompanying high-tech equipment commit a firm to a path that cannot easily be changed. This path must have connecting channels for technological advances that are bound to occur. A system must be compatible with later technology, not one that has to be scrapped only to start over again. Unfortunately, firms operating on leading edge technologies may be unable to distinguish temporary dead-end technologies from those that will survive. Strong evidence supports the wisdom of letting others be trail blazers for core technology. The Japanese have been very successful in using external technology. However, when it comes to producing innovative products employing the core technology, they are proliferators. The rule appears to be the more proliferation the better, as evidenced by the fact that over a ten-year period, Casio, the industry leader in the Japanese market for hand-held calculators, introduced 2.5 times as many products as Sharp, the follower (Nevens, Summe, and Uttal 1990: 158).

RISK FACTORS ASSOCIATED WITH LABOR AND CAPITAL RESOURCES

American manufacturers should be cautious in trying to emulate Japanese manufacturing technologies too closely because of differences in capital availability and labor supply. Japan's highly automated production processes make extensive use of the country's abundant capital and advanced engineering skills. Intensive use of capital, sophisticated engineering skills, and flexibly trained production workers with problem-solving and communication skills are all prerequisites of flexible automation and CIM.

Unfortunately, the United States is generally inferior to the Japanese in each of these categories. An ever increasing federal deficit and an accompanying low savings ratio have reduced the availability of funds for business investment. The education credentials of the U.S. labor force are headed in the wrong direction. Doctoral degrees in science and technology have declined in some fields by as much as 50 percent below the level of the early 1970s. Engineering skills are much scarcer than in Japan and Germany where the ratio is more than twice the number per 1,000 employees. The future does not look any brighter because studies show 13-year-olds in the United States lagging behind Japan and Germany by a significant margin. One source summarizes the situation as follows:

In general, manual workers in the United States are less educated, less literate, more culturally and ethnically diverse, and less likely to share a common mother tongue than their Japanese counterparts. (Grant et al. 1991: 48)

The trend of encouraging minorities in the United States to perpetuate their customs and languages will create even greater communications barriers in the workplace than the traditional attitude of a single "melting pot" for all citizens. Profiles of the U.S. labor supply imply that highly automated, computer-based manufacturing technologies are better suited to Japan, while more traditional, mass-production manufacturing techniques are better suited to the general labor supply of the United States.

Because of the scarcity of qualified personnel in the U.S. labor market, a firm considering CIM must not underestimate the labor costs associated with converting to automated processes. Seldom does a conversion take place without the need to hire new workers with the necessary training instead of being able to retrain existing workers to cover all positions. Incremental labor costs include not only those of the new hires but also costs associated with displaced workers such as severance pay and continued fringe benefits.

A successful transition to advanced manufacturing technology requires a work force that is both willing to accommodate the change and has the ability to be trained in skills necessary to perform required tasks. One company operating leisure, entertainment, and catering outlets decided to computerize data collection of its food production without considering the conversion impact on its existing employees. Because of labor resistance the company continued to incur high overhead, and the project was eventually abandoned (Bromwich and Bhimani 1991: 45).

The problems of employee acceptance and ability to cope with automation changes are lessened if technological innovations are adopted in increments that do not exceed the firm's learning capacity. A firm taking giant steps in implementation may defeat its objective of cost reduction due to disproportionate implementation and learning costs, which also limit future technological improvements. Evidence indicates that modest but frequent increments in technology maximize the rate of performance improvements from the cumulative learning curve effect (Grant et al. 1991: 52).

Failure to adequately allow for labor conversion costs understates a project's cash outflow. If a proposal will result in layoffs among the existing work force, estimates must be made of that effect both in terms of the predictable costs, such as direct compensation and fringe benefits, plus the unpredictable effects on attitude and morale of remaining workers. While this aspect may be difficult to quantify, it translates into higher variable costs because of worker inefficiencies.

>> <<

Although critics of the capital budgeting process have said that the techniques have no place in automation decisions, DCF is the best way to evaluate both automation proposals and major R&D projects. Accountants, as well as engineers and project managers, need to quantify cash inflows in order to justify these expenditures. Risk needs to be evaluated using probabilities and sensitivity analysis.

If DCF techniques are ignored, the danger is that the benefits will be overestimated and the risks ignored. Risk elements associated with automation projects include higher break-even sales volumes due to increased fixed costs, changing economic conditions, price competition, and technological obsolescence. However, these risks can be lessened by timely entry into the market with new products, competing in international markets, and leveraging core technology.

Although the Japanese have been successful in reducing their risk by all three of these methods, U.S. firms should not try to emulate Japanese firms without a full assessment of their own capabilities. Japanese firms have the luxury of abundant capital resources and a highly trained work force, making adaptation of their techniques more questionable for U.S. industry.

REFERENCES

Adizes, I. *Corporate Lifecycles: How and Why Corporations Grow and Die and What To Do about It.* Englewood Cliffs, N.J.: Prentice-Hall, 1989.

Brimson, James A. "Technology Accounting," *Management Accounting.* March 1989, pp. 47–53.

Bromwich, Michael, and Al Bhimani. "Strategic Investment Appraisal," *Management Accounting.* March 1991, pp. 45–48.

Dunn, Paul, Leo Cheatham, and Carole Cheatham. "A Practical Approach To Determining When To Expand and When To Stabilize Sales," *Journal of Small Business Strategy*. November 1991, pp. 1–15.

Grant, Robert M., R. Krishnan, Abraham B. Shani, and Ron Baer. "Appropriate Manufacturing Technology: A Strategic Approach," *Sloan Management Review*. Fall 1991, pp. 43–54.

Lee, John Y. "Investing in New Technology to Stay Competitive," *Management Accounting*. June 1991, pp. 45–48.

Mansfield, Edwin. "The Speed and Cost of Industrial Innovation in Japan and the United States: External vs. Internal Technology," *Management Science*. October 1988, pp. 1157–1168.

McCarthy, E. Jerome, and William D. Perreault. *Basic Marketing, A Managerial Approach*. Homewood, Ill.: Richard D. Irwin, 1990.

Nevens, T. Michael, Gregory L. Summe, and Bro Uttal. "Commercializing Technology: What the Best Companies Do," *Harvard Business Review*. May–June 1990, pp. 154–163.

Parker, Thornton, and Theodore Lettes. "Is Accounting Standing in the Way of Flexible Computer-Integrated Manufacturing?" *Management Accounting*. January 1991, pp. 34–38.

Tatikonda, Lakshmi U. "Production Managers Need a Course in Cost Accounting," *Management Accounting*. June 1987, pp. 26–29.

Weston, J. Fred, and Eugene F. Brigham. *Essentials of Managerial Finance*. Chicago: Dryden Press, 1990.

CHAPTER 13

Justifying Automation Proposals

Before any cash inflow benefits are computed for comparison with cash outflow costs, the project analyst should make a comprehensive list of all variables he or she can think of that will affect the outcome. The latter part of Chapter 12 focused on the types of risks associated with projects requiring large initial investment and start-up costs. A type of worksheet should be prepared for each category, and through a brainstorming process a list should be compiled of everything that could go wrong. At this point the analyst should not worry that some events are more likely to occur than others but concentrate on just compiling a complete list. Others in the firm should be brought in for discussions to determine if any factors have been overlooked.

Once the analyst is satisfied that a comprehensive list of all negative aspects of the project has been compiled, the next step is to determine the relative significance of each item on the list. The analyst eventually needs to determine two items of information—the magnitude of impact and the probability the event will occur. Both pieces of information are necessary inputs to identify and separate key variables representing high risk for a particular project from those that are insignificant. Allowances for negative cash flow impacts of key risk elements should be incorporated in actual cash flow projections, whereas items that either have a very low probability of occurring or that would have a minimal impact if they did occur can be omitted from cash flow adjustment factors.

Probabilities, sensitivity analysis, and Monte Carlo simulation applied to projected cash inflows provide appropriate alternatives for treating project risk. Risk should be reflected as reduced cash inflow values from a project. It is incorrect to inflate the hurdle rate, which is supposed to reflect the firm's actual cost of capital, to compensate for risk in the investment. Risk is not in the financing, as inflating the hurdle rate implies. It is in the assets in which the funds are invested (Cheatham and Cheatham 1989: 31). However, according to a study conducted in 1988 by the National Association of Accountants, 30 percent of surveyed firms were using hurdle rates greater than 19 percent when the prime rate was 8 percent, and the cost of capital for most firms was in the 10 percent to 12 percent range (Howell and Soucy 1988). It appears that inflating the hurdle rate is a popular, if not recommended, way to compensate for risk.

Positive forces affecting the automation decision should be given attention equally thorough to that given to negative elements. As was emphasized in Chapter 12, one of the most common reasons for loss of confidence in cash flow analysis techniques as tools for evaluating high-tech projects has been failure of analysts to include and count all benefits. The example presented in the previous chapter of a major oversight in cash flow benefits of the CADD equipment purchase decision by the architectural firm illustrates a common problem. Once incremental new revenue benefits for the CADD equipment were included, net present value computations clearly showed the proposal to be favorable. The next section of this chapter contains a discussion of some important elements that may not typically be considered in cash flow benefit computations but which, because of their long-run implications, should be incorporated in the quantitative decision process. They might also be called *the risks of not automating*.

REASONS FOR AUTOMATING

CIM and other automated production techniques produce types of benefits that enable firms to become and remain more competitive both in terms of quality of products and prices at which they are sold to customers. These benefits result from substituting computers, robots, and other machinery for labor and lowering variable cost per unit in the process.

Rising Labor Costs

Labor cost is a major cost driver and will probably increase more rapidly in the future than any other variable cost driver. Furthermore cost control of this factor of production is increasingly becoming an exogenous variable, more under the control of government than business. Gone are the days when workers were paid on the basis of marginal revenue product. Today minimum wage laws, occupational safety regulations, unemployment compensation laws, social security taxes, and numerous other types of government controls are setting prices on labor. Recent history reflects a pattern in which federal, state, and local governments are totally oblivious to labor cost impacts on industry when enacting legislation in these areas. Minimum wage laws probably have the least negative impact of any government-imposed labor costs. Costs disguised as taxes have the greatest impact.

Current trends are for governments to expand coverage of programs like workmen's compensation to encompass situations they were not intended to cover. Recently, the state of California opened a Pandora's box by allowing compensation payments to employees claiming mental stress from the job. This type of legislation or judicial interpretation is extremely dangerous because there are very few jobs that do not create some degree of mental stress. Because of the vague nature of proof that the job is causing severe mental problems, the door has been opened to an unprecedented volume of compensation claims.

A whole new arena for unanticipated labor cost has opened up because of liability lawsuits. Governmental agencies are a major culprit in this trend. Every time the Environmental Protection Agency identifies a hazardous chemical or other material in the workplace, it opens the door for a new wave of lawsuits from current and former employees claiming damages. With the passage of time this agency will continue to add to its list, giving lawyers additional ammunition with which to bring suits against employers.

Liability for health hazard exposure is rapidly becoming a major problem because employers are victims of circumstances over which they have no control. For example, many firms concerned about fire danger to employees years ago installed asbestos to protect their workers. This material was installed in good faith and was recommended by many governmental advisory personnel. Today some of those same employees and former employees the company was attempting to protect are being allowed to sue the firms because they were exposed to asbestos in the workplace.

Labor unions have assisted government in making labor costly. Wage increases with no consideration for productivity levels have caused major industries to encounter problems. It is no coincidence that some industries, such as steel and automobiles, which are having the greatest difficulty competing in world markets, are also those over which unions exercise the greatest control. High wages are only part of the cost effect. Union restrictions preventing flexibility of labor within factories create gross inefficiencies. The Japanese train employees in all tasks and readily move workers around as needed.

Labor union control appears to be lessening somewhat, but there is no indication that governmental intervention affecting labor costs will lessen. If anything, it will become greater. If labor, as a group, was more efficient, the higher costs could be acceptable. However, its productivity has not improved to offset the combined cost effects of high wages and other indirect costs such as health insurance, employers' taxes, and lawsuit settlements. While labor costs are increasing, computers and robotic technology are decreasing in price because of many competing producers. Trends are such that even though a CIM system does not produce the lowest cost production alternative, it may do so in the near future.

Analysts should base cash flow savings projections on incremental benefits for CIM proposals on calculations using forecast labor costs. CIM benefits will be much larger than if labor costs used in the calculation are based only on current direct wages. Current direct wages are actually only a portion of current costs. Fringe benefits plus employee taxes must be included. Also, the cost of anticipated lawsuit settlements should be factored in. After all these variables are considered, the average total per-unit cost of labor should be computed. Next, the analyst should project levels of per-worker cost for each year of cash inflow savings that result from reducing units of labor. These projections should allow for the effects of trends of continuing increases in all labor costs. The average annual increases in total labor costs over the past ten years provide a useful rate for estimating annual increases because the forces responsible for increases in recent years are unlikely to change.

Checking Other Options

When projections of rising future labor costs signal the time to automate is approaching, other types of options, which do not create a high fixed cost structure for the firm and allow the company to operate at lower break-even levels, should be investigated. The objective is to reduce labor costs by hiring fewer employees since all types of direct and indirect costs for this factor are a function of the number of workers hired. If fewer workers are employed, labor costs will decline. There are other ways of acquiring labor than hiring employees. Three possibilities include renting labor from personnel services, contracting for "south of the border" assembly, and purchasing previously assembled components. Each produces an employee reduction benefit.

Renting Labor. An increasing number of firms are supplying work forces with broad ranges of skills to business customers under personnel leasing contracts. This option does not eliminate labor costs, but all costs do become explicit. There are no hidden costs, and uncertainties such as lawsuits are less likely. A bonus is that labor is only paid for the time it is actually used. During slack periods the number of workers is reduced to adjust for work loads. Total labor costs can easily be lower for a firm with a variable work load even when the temporary workers are paid higher rates. This type of plan allows management to view labor as a production factor and compare output with cost without the commitment to keep an employee on the job when not needed.

"South of the Border" Assembly. The northern border of Mexico is booming due to firms contracting with U.S. manufacturers to perform labor-intensive assembly tasks. Wage rates are very low (in the $.50 to $1 per hour

range) for tasks requiring little or no skills. Skilled tasks are paid slightly more. These operations, which started by catering to U.S. manufacturers, are now serving customer firms in countries around the world, including Japan and Germany.

These industrial assembly contract operations have the full blessing and support of the Mexican government. Unlike the U.S. government, which seems to be antibusiness, the Mexican government views these industries as a major factor contributing to employment in that country. The only tax associated with the operation is a value-added tax charged to the firm for which the assembly operation is being performed. This tax is very low since it is based on actual labor costs for work performed by the contractor.

"South of the border" is just one option for utilizing low-cost labor outside the United States. There are others. However, if this package deal located next door to the United States is good enough to attract cost-conscious manufacturers from Japan who may have to ship materials half way around the world and back, there are bound to be some features deserving consideration by U.S. manufacturers dealing with labor cost problems.

Outsourcing. Manufacturers can reduce the number of employees required by reducing the number of tasks performed in the manufacturing process. *Outsourcing* refers to the purchase of pre-assembled components or subassemblies of products a firm is manufacturing instead of manufacturing these components "in-house." A firm manufacturing products from purchased components does not need as many workers as it does if it also makes the components.

Cash flow benefits of outsourcing are not limited to cost savings due to fewer employees but encompass some other important cash flow considerations. Most of the outsourcing today utilizes inexpensive foreign labor and/or more efficient foreign production techniques as in the case of Japanese components. For example, a manufacturer of vacuum cleaners can purchase electric motors made in Brazil, where labor is cheap, or Japan, where technology is efficient, at a significantly lower cost than these can be manufactured in-house. The savings is typically greater than most firms realize because the cost of purchasing the motors is all-inclusive. There are no delayed costs like compensation payments and lawsuit settlements that may materialize later because of the workers employed to produce in-house.

Reaping the benefits of comparative advantage of foreign-produced components encompasses more than just labor cost savings. A firm is able to reduce its investment in inventory because it reduces the time required to produce the products. Inventory levels are partly a function of this time period. Outsourcing reduces work in process inventory because the component is ready to install as soon as it arrives. Instead of a holding a collection of raw materials in the form of copper wire, bearings, metal shafts, graphite brushes, and a host of other components, the firm delays the purchase of these components, which are embodied in a complete electric motor, until it is ready to install that motor in a vacuum cleaner. Cash savings due to lower cash requirements to maintain adequate inventories should also be added to cash flow benefits when considering this option (Cheatham, Dunn, and Cheatham 1989: 1–9).

Outsourcing provides an opportunity to benefit from high-tech manufacturing without having to contend with the negatives associated with that option. A firm can buy components from other manufacturers that use high-tech processes in component production. This way a firm such as the vacuum cleaner manufacturer has all the benefits of high technology in purchased electric motors but has not exposed itself to the risks of higher break even due to high fixed costs, commitment to an inflexible manufacturing process, or the risks of technological obsolescence of the processes used to make the motor. The extreme of outsourcing is to cease manufacturing a product and purchase completely assembled units. This means the firm is no longer a manufacturer but has become a retailer or wholesaler, an alternative that should not be ignored. Employee costs will most assuredly be lower for a firm that only sells products if an equal volume is assured. A decision of this type rests on analysis of cash flows.

These three options are alternatives to automation as ways to reduce labor costs. Others are available, as these represent only sample illustrations. The point to remember is that automation is not the only solution to uncontrollable labor costs. Choices among the options require cash flow computations for each to be compared with projected cash flows from a "status quo" operation and high-tech automation proposals. Any of the substitute options offer a higher degree of flexibility because they do not create the high fixed cost structure associated with conversion to automated production facilities.

Contending with Price Competition

When the inevitable price competition for a product becomes a reality in the market maturity stage of the product life cycle, firms with the more automated production processes will usually be the survivors. Inventors and innovators can thrive in the market introduction and in the market growth stages of a new product's life cycle because the contribution margin (selling price less variable cost per unit) is adequate to provide profits for both low cost producers as well as those that are less efficient.

A product in the market growth stage will attract a large number of producers. When hand-held calculators were increasing in popularity, there were hundreds of manufacturers. Most were successful as long as demand for the product was increasing. Today, prices for hand-held calculators, which are far more elaborate and sophisticated, sell at a fraction of the price of the early units. At the same time only a small portion of the original manufacturers are producing the majority of calculators being sold. The survivors are the low cost producers. That status was achieved through automated processes and labor-reducing techniques.

Chapter 12 presented two scenarios for XYZ Corporation, which was considering the purchase of robotic facilities to reduce labor costs. At that point in the discussion the negative aspect of higher fixed costs and resultant higher break-even sales quantity requirements were emphasized. However, there is also a positive implication for this switch to a higher fixed cost structure.

Suppose a competitor, ROB Corporation, employs the latest robotic technology while XYZ continues with labor-intensive manufacturing techniques. XYZ continues to enjoy the benefits of a low break-even point of 40,000 units and earns profits on sales levels above that figure. ROB must sell 70,000 units to break even. In the long run XYZ must be concerned over what happens after payback has been reached and price competition in the market begins, if the firm expects to continue to produce profits during the market maturity stage. ROB has replaced labor, a variable cost driver, with machinery, a fixed cost driver. As a consequence, when both firms are pricing gaskets at $5, ROB receives a contribution of $2 per unit because variable cost per unit is only $3, while XYZ generates a contribution margin of only $1 because of the higher variable cost of $4 per unit due to larger labor costs. Once the fixed costs are covered, ROB earns a higher profit on each unit sold.

When a large number of firms has entered the market, firms must begin to compete for market share. ROB has a greater incentive to cut price to maintain sales volume than XYZ if it has not recovered total fixed costs because of its higher break-even point. Moreover once price cutting begins, there is an additional incentive for even more cuts because lower prices cause the break-even point to rise even higher. However, even if payback has already been achieved, ROB has an incentive to cut price to the point of eliminating less efficient competitors. Working with a variable cost of $3 per unit, ROB can cut price to $3.75 and still realize a $.75 per-unit profit before taxes. XYZ cannot match a price of $3.75 because its variable cost per unit is $4. In the battle of price competition, the automated firm will win because it has lower variable costs.

The operating leverage provided by a high fixed/low variable cost structure has special significance for capital budgeting decisions in today's environment. Because of rapidly escalating labor costs, XYZ's contribution margin is likely to be squeezed from both sides. Not only will it decline when price reductions are forced by competitors' actions but variable costs will likely rise above $4 because a large portion of this variable cost is due to labor.

Total labor cost projections are vital to the process of cash flow estimates. These figures should encompass the effects of any costs that are a function of the number of employees and should include estimates of all fringe benefits and even exogenous values such as anticipated lawsuits from employees and former employees. Cost-saving cash flows of high-tech equipment are typically understated because project analysts do not compile comprehensive labor costs when computing the incremental cost reductions projected for the new equipment. As a result, incremental cash inflow benefits for high-tech proposals are understated, making the projects less likely to pass tests of quantitative screening techniques.

COPING WITH THE FLOOD OF CASH FLOW VARIABLES

Because of the variety and magnitude of required input information necessary to prepare comprehensive cash inflow figures as well as cash outflow figures, accounting must have input assistance from all departments and divisions of the firm. There is a greater information requirement from non-accounting sources than from the records of the accounting department. After all, accounting records represent reporting of historical performance. Most aspects of any capital budgeting decision are focused on future events. The only financial accounting information that is applicable is data associated with past events, which provide patterns in costs and revenues having predictive value for the future.

Accountants are an easy target for a firm having difficulty competing in today's new manufacturing environment. Cost accountants have been blamed for low labor productivity, less than expected performance, lack of capital investments, increased inventories, and just about everything that can go wrong with the organization. They are an easy target because they are the only ones supplying any data to criticize. Tatikonda expresses their role and limitations in the following statement: "Accountants only collect and process data. They do not create data. If production managers do not know how to define and measure quality, how do they expect cost accountants to measure and incorporate its impact in financial statements?" (Tatikonda 1987: 26–27).

People working with a particular benefit or cost driver are in the best position to quantify the effect of that element. Production managers note quality effects of using new equipment. They should ask such questions as what the improvement in quality will do for the firm. Does this mean there will be fewer rejects at the end of the production line? If so, how many per day or week? The manager can then go to the accountant with this information, and the accountant can supply a dollar figure reflecting labor and materials lost as a result of the defects. Between the input from the production manager and the cost information supplied by accounting, a cash flow benefit for the quality feature of the high-tech equipment can be computed.

Improved quality may also lead to higher sales volume. That feature represents another incremental cash flow benefit. Marketing analysts and researchers should be responsible for determining how much of an incremental increase in sales can be anticipated from such factors as quality improvement, decreased lead times, or a broader product mix. This information can then be supplied to the accountant. The accountant can then compute the cash flow effect based on revenue and contribution margins.

Compiling realistic cash inflows depends more heavily on marketing analysts and other individuals in the firm performing sales forecasts than any other data source. No after-tax cash inflows can be calculated until sales have been estimated. When scenarios are numerous, sales forecasts must be anticipated for each. Unfortunately, much of the market information needed by accountants for preparing cash flows is never supplied, and the accountant has to make educated guesses. Other than forecasters and market analysts, many marketing personnel are not trained or skilled in measuring either costs or benefits.

In theory engineers should be good sources of quantified data for cash flow estimates. However, in practice they typically do not adequately estimate cash flow benefits of high-tech proposals. For example, on one occasion company engineers recommended a $250,000 project for which they had estimated a $50,000 annual direct labor cost savings over the five-year life of the assets. Because of the length of the five-year payback period, the project was rejected. Engineers criticized the accounting department for rejecting the project. After further investigation it was discovered that the robot would also result in a reduction in rework costs and warranty work of $40,000 per year. It would also improve sales because of better product quality, producing another $35,000 cash benefit, bringing the total cash inflow per year to $125,000 instead of $50,000 (Tatikonda 1987: 28). If the engineers would focus on placing values on these types of benefits, many projects that are being incorrectly rejected would be accepted. Engineers working on a project are in a much better position to estimate this information than accountants. If product quality improvement is a forte of a high-tech robot or an entire CIM system, it makes little sense to completely ignore that element in the cash inflow computation.

The cost accountant's role in the team approach necessary to compile cash inflow data, assuming the accountant is the chief project analyst, is that of a team captain. However, a team captain must have input from all players — production managers, marketing analysts, sales personnel, engineers, etc. The cost accountant should serve as a consultant to whom these individuals can turn but cannot do their job for them. Because of their knowledge of the tasks they perform in the business, the players should be responsible for identifying ways a proposed automation or other high-tech project will affect activities in which they are engaged. It is also up to them to estimate the magnitude of impact. However, before assigning an actual dollar figure to costs and benefits, they can check with the cost accountant, who can help provide pricing for the identified cost and benefit effects.

Since omissions and oversights are the most important problem limiting the application of cash flow analysis methods to the high-tech project decision, it is imperative that lists of both negative and positive benefits be comprehensive. The best way to guarantee that the list is complete is to have input from large numbers of people. Even if a salesperson does not know how to quantify a project effect, that person still has a feel for the impact it will have on his or her job and can go to the project analyst for quantification help. The project analyst may in turn call on a market analyst or an engineer to assist. This way the person who performs the cash flow calculations utilizes all the input information resources of the firm more efficiently. Instead of doing their job for them, the analyst becomes an assimilation point for cash flow information supplied by all departments and divisions.

Some types of costs and benefits on a comprehensive list always will be difficult to quantify, and some will be impossible to quantify. Bromwich suggests using a matrix system applied to checklist items with a weighting scale for non-quantifiable effects. The process is initiated by first classifying each cost or benefit in one of the following categories:

1. items expressed directly in monetary units, which can be computed now,
2. items having monetary effects but uncertain magnitude, and
3. items not easily converted to monetary terms (1991, 45–48).

Costs and benefits that are most obvious and for which the firm has a good estimate of the dollar effect would be entered in the first category. The second category includes items for which dollar effects are expected, but for which dollar values are unknown because of high risk or contingencies of certain events. The third category contains items that may seem impossible to quantify.

Bromwich's plan consists of using actual dollar cash flows or discounted cash flows for the first category and assigning scores from 1 to 10 for each of the items in categories 2 and 3. The concept of the scoring system requires a comparative basis. For example, if a project is assigned a value of 7 on quality improvement, it represents a higher rating than an alternative project assigned a value of 4. A basic feature of the procedure, even though actual dollar figures are not compiled for all items, is the critical examination of individual cost and benefit impacts. Totals of the actual dollars for category 1 and weighted values for categories 2 and 3 are compiled separately. These totals for a proposal can be compared with totals for alternatives prepared through a similar process. One alternative could be the status quo option of no change (1991: 47–48).

This approach can provide a complementary step to the cash flow computation process. With the initial classification steps some items will be listed in categories 2 and 3 that the firm can quantify if it searches for an innovative measurement technique. The project analyst's objective should be to find ways to convert as many of the items listed in categories 2 and 3 to dollar values like the more obvious cash flows in category 1. This framework provides an organizational tool for computing actual cash flows as well as a weighting evaluation scheme for effects that cannot be quantified. Computed cash flows should still provide the backbone of the decision process.

CHOOSING A CASH FLOW ANALYSIS TECHNIQUE

Once comprehensive cash outflows and inflows have been prepared, the project analyst must determine whether a high-tech proposal meets the firm's standards for capital budgeting expenditures. The choice of screening tools is important because different methods can lead to conflicting rankings when several proposals are considered. Methods such as the payback period consider only the recapture of investment and do not reveal profits. Techniques employed should be those that incorporate assumptions consistent with the circumstances under which the firm is operating.

Several studies have been conducted over the years to determine which cash flow analysis methods managers prefer, as evidenced by the ones they actually use. Internal rate of return and payback period are the most widely used tools. Internal rate of return (IRR) is more commonly used than net present value (NPV) (Horngren and Foster 1991: 686). This preference is probably due to the fact that managers not well versed in discounted cash flow (DCF) techniques have more difficulty understanding NPV than they do IRR. It is sometimes difficult to explain to people without adequate knowledge of the procedures why a project with an NPV of zero dollars is acceptable. Since 1970 the percentage of firms using DCF techniques steadily increased for all types of capital budgeting decisions (Klammer, Koch, and Witner 1989).

Findings of a study conducted by Kim, Crick, and Kim in 1986 concur with the conclusions of the Klammer study about corporate executives' choices. A sample of Fortune 1000 top financial executives showed 90 percent of respondents employing at least one DCF method in major capital expenditure decisions. More than twice as many preferred IRR to NPV. Reasons given for this preference in order of frequency of response were:

1. Executives are more comfortable with IRR;
2. IRR is easier to visualize and interpret; and
3. IRR does not require the prior computation of cost of capital. (Kim, Crick, and Kim 1986: 52)

This study also revealed a common practice among the large firms of using more than one project evaluation technique. While DCF methods of either IRR or NPV were the most common choice as the primary method, payback period was the most common choice as a companion secondary evaluation technique (Kim, Crick, and Kim 1986: 50).

The combination of IRR and payback period actually provides a viable approach to effective analysis of cash flows. IRR considers the time value of money, rates of return, and overall profitability impacts. However, in theory NPV may do a better job at these tasks. Payback period provides additional information. Calculating the period of time required to recover the investment is especially important today with the limited amount of financing from external sources. Firms with liquidity problems are finding cash management to be of equal importance to the goal of long-run profits. If cash cannot be generated to pay current debt obligations, the firm may not be around to enjoy long-run profits. Payback period also provides a type of liquidity measure. Almost all the risk elements associated with the high-tech capital budgeting expenditures discussed in Chapter 12 are affected either directly or indirectly by time. As a result the longer it takes a firm to recover its investment, the greater the likelihood that it will not be recovered.

For many firms the payback period is the only quantitative value calculated that embodies risk considerations. Some of the suggested treatments in the literature include standard deviation of returns, variance analysis, decision trees, computer simulation, and sensitivity analysis. These tools can be used to calculate expected annual cash flows reflecting risks associated with project inflows. More than 70 percent of the firms surveyed in the Kim study were not utilizing any of these tools. Only 27 percent used sensitivity analysis exclusively or in combination with other risk assessment methods.

Earlier in this chapter the concept of the weighted average expected cash flows was presented as the "best" way to allow for risk effects. Sensitivity analysis and the other risk tools provide a way to do this. However, most academicians presenting these concepts and attempting to explain how to use them become so concerned about the detailed mechanics of the process that they tend to overcomplicate the issue. They are usually working in a vacuum as far as their presentations and assume information practitioners do not have available. Constructing weighted average cash inflow estimates requires probability of occurrence of such events as type of economic conditions. Academicians explain a detailed process with a host of rules for compiling just the probability estimates. That is fine for firms with a staff to do it, but many do not have the personnel. Through consultation with others in the firm, the project analyst can usually assign subjective probabilities to the events in lieu of the elaborate processes presented by academicians. It is better to make subjective risk estimates as input into the process of calculating expected cash flows than to not include these risk effects at all.

This section of the chapter presents two suggested cash flow evaluation methods that should prove especially useful in today's new manufacturing environment characterized by shortened product life cycles. Input data for these methods are projected cash outflows and projected cash inflows that have been calculated to reflect risk elements having an impact on these variables. Payback and internal rate of return are the basis for the suggested combination of tools. These already have the advantage of management acceptance. With only slight modifications they can produce information that is even more useful than that produced by their traditional form.

Discounted Payback Period

Despite its strengths of focusing on promptness of cash inflow, ease of calculation and understanding, and indirect reflection of exposure to risk, the unadjusted payback period method is still confined by its traditional limitations. First, it does not reflect profitability because it only reveals the period of time required to break even as far as cash inflows and outflows are concerned. Second, it does not consider the time value of money since a cash inflow received in the third year is taken at face value, as is that received in the first. The order in which cash inflows occur, as long as they are within the payback period, has no impact on the calculated values, even though flows for individual years may vary significantly in size.

The discounted payback period, as a modified method, is not saddled with these two limitations, which provide the most common source of criticism for the payback period method. It also provides additional information content. Payback period reveals the period of time required to recover cash outflows. Discounted payback period reveals the amount of time required to recover the cash outflows and earn the required rate of return as reflected by the cost of capital percentage used to compute the DCF.

To illustrate the differences between the two payback techniques, suppose XYZ Manufacturing Company is attempting to choose between two types of assembly line equipment; one consists of high-tech automated operations while the other consists of less sophisticated equipment requiring more labor to operate. Project A, the high-tech proposal, will require a large initial expenditure but will have low maintenance costs. On the other hand, Project L using less sophisticated technology will have lower initial costs but will require significant cash outflows every three years for overhauls and upgrades. Both proposals will result in equal production output and will have equal lives of ten years. The firm has a cost of capital of 12 percent. Annual weighted average expected cash flows for the two mutually exclusive proposals have been estimated as follows:

NET AFTER-TAX CASH FLOWS

Year	Project A	Project L
0	− $400,000	− $100,000
1	92,000	48,000
2	105,000	52,000
3	107,000	− 10,000
4	100,000	50,000
5	97,000	46,000
6	95,000	− 15,000
7	92,000	44,000
8	90,000	43,000
9	89,000	− 15,000
10	87,000	41,000

Even though either machine is capable of producing the same level of production, cash outflows and cash inflows vary significantly. This is typical of many decisions requiring comparison of high-tech alternatives with cash flows of more traditional equipment for which replacement is being consid-

ered. Cash inflows from Project A are higher because of two types of benefits. The primary benefits are reduced labor cost, technological competitive
advantages, increased sales effects of better products, etc. A secondary positive cash flow impact is also created by the large depreciation expense that
will shelter some income from taxes and generate an annual tax savings of
an amount equal to the marginal tax rate multiplied by the depreciation expense for each year in which the expenses are allocated. At the same time
cash inflow benefits of Project L are smaller in dollar amounts because this
project does not offer the unique advantages of the high-tech option. Negative cash flows (cash outflows) in years 3, 6, and 9 result from major expenditures for overhauls and upgrades in those years. There are also positive
cash inflows in those years. However, since cash outflows exceed inflows,
only the net difference is used in the calculation. Before applying evaluation
techniques, both inflows and outflows should be netted out to only one figure
for each interval of time. In this illustration the interval is one year. However,
it could be more frequent—every six months or every quarter if the analyst
feels the additional detail would be beneficial.

Figure 13.1 illustrates the difference in the computations for the traditional
payback period and the discounted payback period for these two proposals.
Payback is reached in 3.96 years for Project A and in 2 years for Project L.
Discounted payback is reached in 5.82 years for Project A and 3.72 years
for Project L. These two sets of calculations used together not only tell the
analyst how long it takes to reach a cash break-even point but also how
much longer it will be before the required rate of return is earned. On Project
A cash investment is recovered in 3.96 years, but it will require an additional
1.86 years to earn the required rate of return of 12 percent (cost of capital).
On the other hand, Project L will reach payback in 2 years but will require
1.72 additional years to earn the required rate of return.

Since the primary objective in investing in projects is to make a profit, the
discounted payback period is a logical extension of the concept of the payback period. Payback calculations have become even more popular with the
short product life cycles and other risks associated with today's manufacturing environment. By simply discounting cash flow estimates used to compute
the payback period, a tool is employed that overcomes two of the most
common criticisms of the payback period—failure to consider the time value
of money and failure to consider profitability.

This method also offers many other possibilities as a management tool.
In Figure 13.1 a discount rate of 12 percent is used because this is the firm's
cost of capital. By merely inserting any desired discount percentage, the
analyst can quickly determine the period of time required by the project to
achieve different rates of return. Typically the figure used for cost of capital
should represent the minimum acceptable hurdle rate. Therefore its use
should result in a payback period calculation that reflects the period of time
required for the project to produce the minimum acceptable return.

Computations in Figure 13.1 could have ended when the process reached the point at which the project began to generate positive net present value inflows if the only objective was to find the discounted payback period. However, there is significant additional information if the calculation process is carried out to the end of the project life. "Ending Balances" shown for each year represent the NPV of the project at that point in time. Therefore the last NPVs calculated for Projects A and L at the conclusion of the cash flow stream are the NPVs for the projects that would have been computed if straightforward NPV techniques were used instead of the discounted payback period.

Net present value by definition is a value calculated by subtracting the present value of cash outflows from the present value of inflows. Therefore the ending balances shown in Figure 13.1 for each year show the net present value of the project for the respective years. Using NPVs for each year of the life of the project, the analyst has data to use in simulated "what if" situations. Suppose new competing products introduced 5 years into the life of the proposed project suddenly make obsolete both Projects A and L and cash inflows are abruptly stopped at the end of 5 years. Project A has a NPV of −$39,396, meaning it has not reached discounted payback, nor produced the required rate of return of 12 percent. However, at the end of 5 years Project L has a positive NPV of $35,070, indicating it has not only reached payback and earned the required rate of return, which would be true if NPV were equal to zero, but it has an NPV higher than zero indicating a rate of return higher than the required 12 percent. This information is even more appropriate for today's manufacturing where unexpected and unpredictable events can shorten the projected cash inflow stream.

Assuming the cash flow estimates for Projects A and L are correct and there are no cash inflow oversights for Project A, the evidence provided by the discounted payback computation process should probably lead the analyst to recommend Project L. It clearly has the advantage on risk avoidance with the significantly earlier payback period and discounted payback period plus the fact that NPV has become positive by the end of the fourth year. On the other hand, proponents of NPV methods would argue that Project A is best because of an end-of-stream NPV of $146,801, compared to an NPV of $72,533 for the same point in time for Project L. The recommendation to accept the project with the higher NPV is based on the logic that the project will contribute more to stockholders' wealth than the one with the lower NPV because both calculations have considered the stockholders' required rate of return, which is a component of the cost of capital used in the discounting process (Weston and Brigham 1990: 576).

Discounted payback period provides the project analyst with a way to incorporate NPV techniques in the project decision process that is likely to be more readily acceptable by top executives than the traditional NPV approach. Since payback period is already a commonly accepted technique, the added

Figure 13.1
Payback Period Compared to Discounted Payback Period

Machine A:

Traditional Payback Period Calculation:

Year	Beginning balance	+	Annual cash flow	=	Ending balance	Number of years
1	-$400,000		$ 92,000		-$308,000	1
2	- 308,000		105,000		- 203,000	1
3	- 203,000		107,000		- 96,000	1
4	- 96,000		100,000		4,000	.96*

Payback period = 3.96 years

Discounted Payback Period:

Year	Beginning balance	+	Discounted annual cash flow at 12% cost of capital	=	Ending balance	Number of years
1	-$400,000		($92,000 x .8929) $82,147		-$317,853	1
2	- 317,853		(105,000 x .7972) 83,706		- 234,147	1
3	- 234,147		(107,000 x .7118) 76,163		- 157,984	1
4	- 157,984		(100,000 x .6355) 63,550		- 94,434	1
5	- 94,434		(97,000 x .5674) 55,038		- 39,396	1
6	- 39,396		(95,000 x .5066) 48,127		8,731	.82*

Discounted payback period = 5.82 years

Continue process to find NPVs for remaining years

Year	Beginning balance	Discounted cash flow	Ending balance
7	8,731	(92,000 x .4523) 41,612	50,343
8	50,343	(90,000 x .4039) 36,351	86,694
9	86,694	(89,000 x .3606) 32,093	118,787
10	118,787	(87,000 x .3220) 28,014	146,801

206

Figure 13.1 (continued)

Machine L:

Traditional Payback Period Calculation:

Year	Beginning balance	+	Annual cash flow	=	Ending balance	Number of years
1	-$100,000		$ 48,000		-$52,000	1
2	- 52,000		52,000		0	_1_

Payback period = _2 years_

Discounted Payback Period:

Year	Beginning balance	+	Discounted annual cash flow at 12% cost of capital	=	Ending balance	Number of years
1	-$100,000		($48,000 x .8929) $42,859		-$57,141	1
2	- 57,141		(52,000 x .7972) 41,454		- 15,687	1
3	- 15,687		(-10,000 x .7118) - 7,118		- 22,805	1
4	- 22,805		(50,000 x .6355) 31,775		8,970	_.72*_

Discounted payback period = 3.72 years

Continue the process to find NPVs for remaining years

5	8,970	(46,000 x .5674) 26,100	35,070
6	35,070	(-15,000 x .5066) - 7,599	27,471
7	27,471	(44,000 x .4523) 19,901	47,372
8	47,372	(43,000 x .4039) 17,368	64,740
9	64,740	(-15,000 x .3606) - 5,409	59,331
10	59,331	(41,000 x .3220) 13,202	72,533

*Assumes cash inflow for the year is evenly distributed throughout the year.
 (Example: 96,000 / 100,000 = .96 years.)

benefit of showing the period of time required to earn the required rate of return is a natural augmentation of an accepted process. Then NPVs shown for each successive year can be explained as excess cash flows, expressed as present values representing additional returns above the required minimum.

Once a project has been chosen, the discounted cash flow schedule produced by the process and illustrated in Figure 13.1 becomes a benchmark for measuring project performance. Each year actual cash flows can be discounted and compared with the original projections. When variables do cause a change in patterns, the rest of the schedule is revised to reflect that change. For example, product price may have to be reduced more rapidly than planned in the initial projection. This results in more rapid reductions in contribution margins, causing cash inflows from the project to decline at a more rapid pace than anticipated. With recalculated NPV figures for each year of the project's remaining life, the analyst has values that can be used for comparison with alternative uses of the facilities if they were converted to producing other products.

Modified Internal Rate of Return

When two mutually exclusive projects are evaluated to determine which should be chosen, the NPV and the IRR techniques sometimes produce conflicting results. Two conditions can create this conflict situation: projects can differ in scope and total investment, and cash flow patterns from one project may be concentrated in early years while those of the other project are concentrated in later years. The proposals under consideration by XYZ Corporation are characterized by the first condition since Project A requires an initial cash outflow of $400,000 while Project L only requires $100,000.

Internal rate of return for Project A is 20.6 percent while the rate for Project L is 31.7 percent. A conflict exists because NPV for Project A, as shown in Figure 13.1, is $146,801 while NPV for Project L is $72,533. The IRR rule says to choose Project L while the NPV rule says choose Project A. Most of the literature tells the analyst to go with NPV for two reasons: (1) a larger NPV results in a greater contribution to stockholders' wealth, and (2) reinvestment rate assumptions of NPV are more appropriate. However, both of these reasons are correct only under certain assumed conditions.

Choosing a mutually exclusive project with a higher NPV when its IRR is lower than an alternative maximizes stockholder wealth only under the condition of unlimited capital resources. If capital must be rationed due to limits in availability, IRR criteria may be more appropriate. In today's financial markets it is safe to say that capital is rationed. Firms are finding financing is becoming increasingly scarce and more expensive. Therefore most executives preferring IRR over NPV may be more theoretically correct than the critics realize.

The reinvestment rate assumption of IRR is its greatest weakness. Both IRR and NPV methods are bound by constraints of the discounting process:

1. Discounting is the reverse of compounding;

2. Compounding implies reinvestment; and

3. The NPV method discounts cash flows at the cost of capital, whereas the IRR method discounts cash flow at whatever rate of return happens to be the IRR of the project. (Brigham and Weston 1990: 576)

As a result NPV is using a constant reinvestment rate assumption for every proposal, while the reinvestment rate for IRR computations is changing every time a project is evaluated that has a different IRR.

For XYZ's interpretation of the IRR of 20.6 percent for Project A compared to the IRR of 31.7 percent for Project L, the implicit assumption is that if it chooses Project L it will be able to reinvest early inflows from that project in other projects at a higher rate of return than if those inflows had come from Project A. To actually achieve a 31.7 percent rate of return on Project L over the 10-year period, the cash inflow of $48,000 in year 1 must be reinvested at 31.7 percent for the remaining 9 years, the $52,000 reinvested in year 2 must be reinvested at 31.7 percent for the remaining 8 years, etc. By the same token, reinvestment of year 1 cash inflow of $92,000 on Project A must be reinvested at 20.6 percent for 9 years, with each successive inflow reinvested at the same rate for the duration of the project to produce a 20.6 percent average return for the 10-year period.

The reinvestment rate assumption of NPV is more appropriate because it is the cost of capital rate, which remains constant regardless of the rate earned on the specific project being considered. Reinvestment rate does not depend on the rate earned by the project producing the cash inflow. In XYZ's case, funds received from year 1 cash inflows would likely be reinvested in the same new project or use whether they were generated by either A or L. The initial screening criterion used on the new project would be cost of capital. Since it is a constant screening value for all projects, it is more likely that it would be a relevant factor affecting reinvestment of funds than the rate of returns earned on either Project A or L.

Since IRR is already the accepted choice among practitioners and since firms must be more concerned today with capital rationing, a logical solution is to modify the internal rate of return procedure so that it incorporates the same reinvestment rate assumption as NPV.

Figure 13.2 illustrates the computation procedure for modified internal rate of return (MIRR). The objective is to find the weighted average return over the life of the project if cash flows are reinvested at the firm's cost of capital. The analyst needs to compute the rate of return on a lump sum cash outflow investment today, which is represented by the cumulative lump sum cash inflow at the end of the project. Achieving this objective requires three steps:

1. Compute the present value of all net cash outflows combined;

2. Compute the future value (compound value) of all net cash inflows combined; and

Figure 13.2
Modified Internal Rate of Return (MIRR)

Machine A:

Internal Rate of Return: 20.6%

Modified Internal Rate of Return:

Step a: Present Value of Cash Outflows = $400,000
(Since outflows only occur in Year 0, the total outflow value needs no discounting.)

Step b: Future Value of Cash Inflows

Year	Cash inflows	Number of years at rein- vestment rate	12% interest factor (FVIF)	Cumulative value of cash inflows
1	$ 92,000	9	2.7731	$ 255,125
2	105,000	8	2.4760	259,980
3	107,000	7	2.2107	236,545
4	100,000	6	1.9738	197,380
5	97,000	5	1.7623	170,943
6	95,000	4	1.5735	149,483
7	92,000	3	1.4049	129,251
8	90,000	2	1.2544	112,896
9	89,000	1	1.1200	99,680
10	87,000	0	1.0000	87,000

Cumulative cash inflow balance at end of 10 years = $1,698,283

Step c: Average Rate of Return for Period   (MIRR)

Future value of cash inflows	=	Present value of cash outflows	x	Future value interest factor for 10 years
$1,698,283	=	$400,000	x	FVIF
FVIF	=	4.2457		
4.2457	=	FVIF for 10 years and 15.5%		
MIRR	=	15.5%		

210

Figure 13.2 (continued)

Machine L:

Internal Rate of Return: 31.7%

Modified Internal Rate of Return:

Step a: Present Value of Cash Outflows

Year	Cash outflows	12% interest factor (PVIF)	Present value of cash outflows
0	$100,000	1.0000	$100,000
3	10,000	.7118	7,118
6	15,000	.5066	7,599
9	15,000	.3606	5,409

Amount of cash required at Year 0 = $120,126

Step b: Future Value of Cash Inflows

Year	Cash inflows	Number of years at rein-vestment rate	12% interest factor (FVIF)	Cumulative value of cash inflows
1	$48,000	9	2.7731	$133,109
2	52,000	8	2.4760	128,752
4	50,000	6	1.9738	98,690
5	46,000	5	1.7623	81,066
7	44,000	3	1.4049	61,816
8	43,000	2	1.2544	53,939
10	41,000	0	1.0000	41,000

Cumulative cash inflow balance at end of 10 years = $598,372

Step c: Average Rate of Return for Period   (MIRR)

Future value of cash inflows	=	Present value of cash outflows	x	Future value interest factor for 10 years
$598,372	=	$120,126	x	FVIF
FVIF	=	4.9812		
4.9812	=	FVIF for 10 years and 17.4%		
MIRR	=	17.4%		

211

3. Find the MIRR as the unknown variable in the compound value equation for which present value, future value, and number of years are known.

Step 1 is necessary to allow for time value effects of cash outflows delayed until later in the flow stream. Cash outflows at year 0 are already present values. However, as the illustration shows for Machine L, with a net cash outflow in year 3 of $10,000, this value should be discounted for three years and 12 percent (cost of capital). This is because the amount of cash allocated for the project today does not have to be $10,000 but only $7,118 because these funds will be invested in other uses earning the 12 percent return during the interim period. Therefore all cash outflows are discounted to allow for this time value effect. They are discounted at the firm's cost of capital.

Step 2 is where the reinvestment rate assumption of the traditional IRR is replaced by the assumption of reinvestment at the cost of capital. Cash inflows received at the end of the first year are assumed to be reinvested to earn a rate at least equal to the cost of capital for 9 more years if the project life is 10 years. Cash flow received the next year earns this rate of return for 8 years with flows for other years reinvested by this same pattern.

After the first two steps are completed, the analyst has figures for (1) the present value, representing the beginning principal for the project, (2) the future value of a cumulative lump sum of cash inflows at the end of the period, and (3) a figure for the number of years of the project. All that is necessary then is to simply calculate the percentage rate of return as the fourth variable in the compound interest equation for which the first three have already been calculated.

Results of the MIRR computation process applied to Projects A and L in Figure 13.2 show a significant difference between these values and IRRs for the two projects. Project A has an IRR of 20.6 percent but MIRR is only 15.5 percent while Project L has an IRR of 31.7 percent but MIRR is only 17.4 percent. The difference is entirely due to the reinvestment rate assumption. Both Project A and Project L are generating the IRR only up to the point of cash inflow generation. The actual rate of return over the life of the project also depends on the return produced by the reinvested funds.

Computed MIRR percentages for Projects A and L still show Project L as the preferred choice. However, the margin by which the MIRR exceeds that of Project A is much less than the IRRs suggest. The percentage point differential is now only 1.9 percent with MIRR at 17.4 percent for L, compared to 15.5 percent for A. With a spread this narrow it may be advisable to go back and reevaluate cash inflow estimates from the high-tech proposal, Project A, for oversights since this is a frequent problem. Only slight boosts in that project's benefits can swing the decision to Project A.

Differences in the spread between the two IRR amounts of 31.7 percent vs. 20.6 percent and the spread between the MIRR amounts of 17.4 percent vs. 15.5 percent are due to a distortion effect caused by using two different reinvestment rate assumptions. The greater the difference in IRRs, the greater this distortion. It is more realistic to assume that reinvested cash flows from either project would be invested in the most attractive projects, judged by screening processes using cost of capital, than to assume they would be invested in projects for which the IRR of the previous project was used as the screening criterion.

While the firm's cost of capital provides a viable reinvestment rate assumption for the MIRR, the procedure illustrated in Figure 13.2 presents some other useful opportunities. Suppose XYZ Manufacturing has already identified a project to which the cash flows from either Project A or L, whichever is chosen, will be channeled. Starting with year 1 cash inflows from A or L, all inflows will be allocated to Project R. Instead of using the 12 percent cost of capital as the reinvestment rate for Projects A and L, the analyst could find the MIRR for Project R and use it instead. The point is to use the actual return on the specific project in which the funds are to be reinvested if that information is available. Otherwise the cost of capital provides a legitimate reinvestment assumption rate.

As a project audit tool the MIRR procedure can easily accommodate changes in cash flows and even cost of capital. Effects of changes in any variables can be revealed by recalculations. If the cost of capital increases after the project begins, the increases can be inserted for only those years to which the changes apply.

The Logic of Discounted Payback and MIRR

Both the discounted payback period and the modified internal rate of return methods of screening high-tech proposals offer benefits especially suited to today's new manufacturing environment. The chance of management acceptance is probably their greatest advantage. Since executives are already familiar with and have a preference for IRR and payback as capital budgeting decision tools, augmentation of these is a natural. If it can be shown that additional useful decision information can be added by making only minor changes in tools that management already understands and has confidence in, the discount payback period and the MIRR are likely to be welcome additions or even replacements.

Modifications suggested for both the payback period and IRR techniques are designed to eliminate basic flaws in the commonly used versions. Discounted payback period actually complements the payback period calculation by enabling the analyst to determine how long it takes to make an acceptable profit from the project. It also provides a time map of cash flows, showing where the company will be in regard to NPV at any point during the anticipated project life. At the same time this entire procedure is built on the original payback period principle but incorporates informational content of the NPV method.

MIRR computations are designed as an improvement modification to eliminate the most viable criticism of IRR. By changing the reinvestment assumption rate to that of cost of capital, the user not only calculates a more theoretically correct percentage but also produces percentages that more accurately reflect the rates of return that can be expected over the life of the project. While the steps used to compute MIRR may not look like those used to calculate IRR, the concept is the same, with the exception of the change in the reinvestment assumption rate. Executives can use MIRRs in decisions the same way they have been using IRRs. With MIRR they have rates of return values providing a more accurate representation than has been provided by IRR.

Modifying the payback period and IRR cash flow analysis tool is a recommendation consistent with the theme of other topics covered in this book. The suggested approach is to modify existing practices, procedures, and methods that have proven to be effective in the past as a means of coping with a rapidly changing manufacturing environment. It is typically less disruptive and more efficient to begin with existing accounting procedures and capital budgeting decision techniques familiar to personnel than to scrap everything and seek something totally new that may not work as well. Because of the learning curve effect, building on previous experience with familiar tools allows personnel to avoid the loss of efficiency and competence often accompanying a sudden shift to a system or procedure that is radically different from the one currently in use. Evidence presented in this book clearly indicates some of the most successful manufacturing innovators rely on proven technology for success. However, they are continually coming out with a steady stream of innovative products developed from a proven core technology. This same technique can be applied by accountants and other suppliers of information for management decision makers who must contend with the complexities of the new manufacturing environment. The best strategy for accountants and other project analysts is to use the core technologies of capital budgeting that have worked in the past but continually look for ways to improve them when they appear to be inadequate. Discounted payback period and MIRR are two tools consistent with that objective.

REFERENCES

Bromwich, Michael, and Al Bhimiani. "Strategic Investment Appraisal," *Management Accounting*. March 1991, pp. 45–48.

Cheatham, Carole, and Leo R. Cheatham. "Investing in the '90s: Making the Best Decision for Plant and Equipment," *Business and Tax Planning Quarterly*. Vol. 5, No. 4, 1989, pp. 30–32.

Cheatham, Leo, J. Paul Dunn, and Carole B. Cheatham, "Working Capital Financing and Cash Flow in the Small Business," *Journal of Business and Entrepreneurship*. October 1989, pp. 1–12.

Horngren, Charles T., and George Foster. *Cost Accounting: A Managerial Emphasis.* Englewood Cliffs, N.J.: Prentice-Hall, 1991.

Howell, Robert A., and Stephen R. Soucy. "Capital Investment in the New Manufacturing Environment," *Factory 2000 +*. Montvale, N.J.: National Association of Accountants, 1988.

Kim, Suk H., Trevor Crick, and Seung H. Kim. "Do Executives Practice What Academics Preach?" *Management Accounting.* November 1986, pp. 49–52.

Klammer, T., B. Koch, and N. Witner. "Capital Budgeting Practices — A Survey of Corporate Use," Working paper, University of North Texas, 1989.

Tatikonda, Lakshmi U. "Production Managers Need a Course in Cost Accounting," *Management Accounting.* June 1987, pp. 26–29.

Weston, J. Fred, and Eugene F. Brigham. *Essentials of Managerial Finance.* Chicago, Ill.: Dryden Press, 1990.

Selected Readings

Berliner, Callie, and James A. Brimson, eds. *Cost Management for Today's Advanced Manufacturing.* Boston: Harvard Business School Press, 1988. Presents the ideas of the prestigious CAM-I consortium concerning changes needed in cost management systems.

Deal, Terrance E., and Allan A. Kennedy. *Corporate Cultures.* Reading, Mass.: Addison-Wesley, 1982. Classic reading in the area of corporate culture and how to effect cultural change.

Fox, Robert E. "Coping with Today's Technology: Is Cost Accounting Keeping Up?" *Proceedings, Cost Accounting for the 90s: The Challenge of Technological Change,* National Association of Accountants, Boston, April 28-29, 1986. One of several valuable presentations at a groundbreaking NAA seminar on the need for change in cost management systems.

Garrison, Ray H. *Managerial Accounting, Concepts for Planning, Control, Decision Making.* Homewood, Ill.: Richard D. Irwin, 1991. Good basic managerial accounting text updated to include activity-based costing, backflush costing, and a number of the newer cost management techniques.

Goldratt, Eliyahu M., and Jeff Cox. *The Goal: A Process of Ongoing Improvement.* New Haven, Conn.: Spectrum, 1986. The novel that presented Goldratt's idea of continuous improvement and theory of constraints.

Harrell, Horace W. "Materials Variance Analysis and JIT: A New Approach," *Management Accounting.* May 1992, pp. 33-38. An article that contains valuable ideas on how to revise material variances in a standard cost system. For the past five years or so *Management Accounting* has printed many articles on the effect of the new manufacturing environment on accounting systems. Almost every issue has several excellent articles.

Horngren, Charles T., and George Foster. *Cost Accounting: A Managerial Emphasis.* Englewood Cliffs, N.J.: Prentice-Hall, 1991. Probably the most respected text in the cost accounting area. This edition is updated to include most of the newer techniques that relate to automated factory environments.

Howell, Robert A., and Stephen R. Soucy. "Capital Investment in the New Manufacturing Environment," *Factory 2000+*. Montvale, N.J.: National Association of Accountants, 1988. One in a series of five significant articles originally published in *Management Accounting* and accumulated in this paperback book.

Johnson, H. Thomas, and Robert S. Kaplan. *Relevance Lost: The Rise and Fall of Management Accounting*. Boston: Harvard Business School Press, 1987. The book that catalogued the history of management accounting and its deficiencies.

McNair, C. J., William Mosconi, and Thomas Norris. *Meeting the Technology Challenge: Cost Accounting in a JIT Environment*. Montvale, N.J.: National Association of Accountants, 1988. Research study sponsored by NAA and Coopers & Lybrand containing case studies of companies working to change their cost accounting systems.

Rayburn, L. Gayle. *Principles of Cost Accounting*. Homewood, Ill.: Richard D. Irwin, 1989. Excellent basic text in the cost accounting area.

Umble, Michael, and Mokshagundam L. Srikanth. *Synchronous Manufacturing: Principles for World-Class Excellence*. Cincinnati: South-Western, 1990. Good source on theory of constraints (synchronous manufacturing).

Walkin, Lawrence. "ABC—Key Players and Their Tools," *Management Accounting*. February 1991, p. 18. An informative short article on ABC software packages and their cost.

Weston, J. Fred, and Eugene F. Brigham. *Essentials of Managerial Finance*. Chicago: Dryden Press, 1990. Basic finance text with discussion of capital budgeting techniques such as the modified internal rate of return recommended in Chapter 13.

Index

About the Authors

CAROLE B. CHEATHAM is Professor of Accounting at Northeast Louisiana University. She is the author of *Cost Management for Profit Centers* and more than sixty articles which have appeared in journals such as *Journal of Accountancy* and *Management Accounting*. Dr. Cheatham serves on the editorial boards of *Journal of Business and Entrepreneurship* and *Delta Business Review* and is a Certified Public Accountant and Certified Management Accountant.

LEO R. CHEATHAM is Associate Professor of Finance at Northeast Louisiana University. He was a research economist for the Division of Business and Economic Research at Mississippi State University for ten years and, as a project manager, investigated business and industry problems for the U.S. Department of Commerce and various private firms. His articles in recent years have focused on working capital management and cash flow problems for business.